191P

PETER H. LIDDLE

THE AIRMAN'S WAR 1914~18

BLANDFORD PRESS
POOLE · NEW YORK · SYDNEY

First published in the UK 1987 by Blandford Press
Link House, West Street, Poole, Dorset BH15 1LL

Distributed in the United States by
Sterling Publishing Co, Inc,
2 Park Avenue, New York, NY 10016

Distributed in Australia by
Capricorn Link (Australia) Pty Ltd
PO Box 665, Lane Cove, NSW 2066

British Library Cataloguing in Publication Data

Liddle, Peter, *1934-*
    The airman's war 1914-1918. — (Personal
    experience 1914-18 trilogy)
    1. World War, 1914-1918 — Aerial
    operations, British   2. World War, 1914-
    1918 — Personal narratives, British
    I. Title   II. Series
    940.4'4941'0924   D602

ISBN 0 7137 1592 8

Typeset by Graphicraft Hong Kong
Printed in Great Britain by R.J. Acford, Chichester

Contents

Foreword

The author of this book, Peter Liddle, has earned the admiration and appreciation of all three Services and many others for his dedication to the work of collecting together in one place, the Sunderland Polytechnic, as many records as possible of the personal experiences of individuals who served in the 1914–1918 war. His labours over many years have resulted in a vast collection of records which are of great value because they help to bring the histories of that war to life.

The Airman's War 1914–18 is of unique interest because these are the accounts of those who flew, fought and served in what was the first war in the air. When it started, the aeroplane was but ten years old but such were the strivings of both sides to use this new element and dimension in warfare in every way possible to gain advantage in the main struggle that by November 1918 the aeroplane had developed into an aircraft which had become an important factor in the fight for victory.

The personal records in this book help the reader to imagine what these airmen felt and experienced. Common to all of them was pride in belonging to something new; a flying service.

But the pilots had stronger reasons to spur them on, and I speak as one of them. We could not help knowing that we were regarded with special respect by our sailor and soldier friends and by the public and this was added to the thrill of flying itself and the opportunity it constantly offered of doing something that had never been done before.

These records also remind me how proud we were of our flying Services, the Royal Naval Air Service and the Royal Flying Corps, and how in March 1918 with what concern we viewed the prospect of our amalgamation. But the remarkable fact is that by November 1918 such was our enthusiasm for our new venture that we had forgotten that concern and had become proud members of the Royal Air Force.

I am therefore privileged to be able to commend *The Airman's War 1914–18*. I am sure it will be read with much interest and that its readers will get a good idea of what those particular airmen felt and experienced.

Marshal of the RAF Sir William Dickson
GCB KCB KBE CBE OBE DSO AFC

Preface and Acknowledgements

Having attempted to convey something of the essence of personal experience of life in the Senior Service during World War One, I have delved into the air Services section of my 1914–18 archives in search of letters, diaries, photographs, log books and other official papers which would document at a personal level the range of experience of those serving in the Royal Naval Air Service, the Royal Flying Corps and the Royal Air Force during the Great War. The perspective illustrated in the book which grew out of this research is that of the young officer, the non-commissioned officer and the man in the ranks. The most senior viewpoint depicted is that of the Officer in Command of a squadron and then each level of work and responsibility is represented from that of the Flight Commander and other flying personnel to that of the non-commissioned ranks of the ground support staff.

Quite apart from rank and responsibility, further elements of differentiation required consideration like the impact of geography, climate and the strength of enemy opposition in fronts far from Flanders like Palestine, Macedonia or Mesopotamia. There were additional demands for specific exemplification in the differing nature of the work being undertaken on active service, for example, reconnaissance, artillery spotting or offensive patrol.

It has to be stated that substantial technical information on machines does not come within the terms of reference of this book, furthermore the book is neither a potted history of the three flying Services nor of the top level policy debates and decisions which laid down the framework within which they operated.* The

*See Bibliography for some essential sources for serious study in these areas.

book aims to inform and raise the reader's sense of identification with the airman in the Great War but in a way which properly relates individual experiences to its appropriate setting in the air war and even to some extent in the complete panorama of the war itself.

The Western Front must dominate – a very reasonable literary consequence of its actual dominance of the British war effort on land-fighting fronts. Furthermore, it is British and Commonwealth experience which is under review, not German or French, for such a comprehensive analysis using archive materials would have been beyond the source materials readily available to me. Finally, in laying out terms of reference, the material selected to illustrate personal experience will, in the vast majority of cases, be from unpublished documentation within my 1914–18 archives presently based at Sunderland Polytechnic.

From a careful examination of this large body of personal papers, what can legitimately be distilled to reveal the essence of involvement with the air Services during World War One? Never having been wholly at ease in the tempting but perilous task of making generalisations from personal accounts, I would like to suggest possibilities for what I believe encapsulates the true spirit of the airman, rather than putting forward conclusions. There was indeed something stimulatingly new about war in the air; there was the fascination with something experimental, revolutionary, something akin to the contemporaneous fascination with polar exploration, about joining the new flying Services. For the outsider looking in, the RFC may have been epitomised by the distinctive uniform, but for those wearing the uniform or perhaps the pilot's wings or observer's brevet on an army service jacket, there was a feeling akin to regimental pride or identification with one's ship, or perhaps even the donning of an exclusive school or club sport's team blazer: membership of a rather special association had been achieved.

Motivation for enlistment or for transfer to this special association was naturally a part of the very essence of membership of the flying Services. A schoolboy's fascination with flight combined with an accumulation of knowledge of engines and the appetite for still more understanding of them, mechanical capability too, such starting points were likely to be basic for many. For officers in the Army, joining the RFC was also a means of opening new fields to them in their Army career and bringing the newly gained expertise into the Army text book.[1] For other ranks, recognition of technical skills brought additional pay in the RFC and a change from the confines of 'Depot soldiering' or even from the routine of 'Regimental soldiering'. There was also, once the war had begun, a psychologically based impulse in some to do one's bit in a different way from that chosen by the huge flood of volunteers. Then, transfer from the Army on the Western Front could be not only for the readily understood reasoning of getting away from the trenches but also because acquired expertise in various ways, for example in map reading, photographic interpretation or aspects of artillery work, with its obvious relevance to aerial reconnaissance and spotting for registration on targets, fulfilled a pressing need created within the expanding air Services. All these reasons would explain why men transferred to or were seconded to the Royal Flying Corps. As for the Royal Naval Air Service, again increased need created new excitingly different opportunities for those who with certain skills and a sense of adventure, grasped at the chance of work in almost uncharted areas of service experience. Of this the RNAS airships provide the clearest example.

In a certain way the technology of the air war preserved an individuality which was so swamped by sheer numbers and the nature of the work of the Army. Even in the tightly knit community of the ship's company of a destroyer where the sense of fellowship and interdependence in the fulfilment of specific duties must have been tangibly evident, that freedom, conferred by the aeroplane, to escape earthly bounds but with the ever present constraints of duty to perform and perhaps danger to face, gave pilots and observers in an active service squadron in every sense extended horizons. It was shared in a real sense by their ground staff but by no others in the war. Had Rupert Brooke been a pilot rising above the brown desolation of the forward areas in Belgium or France, he would surely have found an ethereal equivalent to his memorable image of the nation's youth in its response to the 1914 crisis as 'swimmers into cleanness leaping' for, in casting off the limitations of the groundling, there certainly lay the very heart of that distinctive factor which was in the spirit of many a man who could never have been able to express it with the facility of C.S. Lewis but who felt it nonetheless.

If then the marriage of man and machine allowed for a liberation of the spirit distinctive in the air war, then on the ground in the exercise of military discipline and formality was there something less rigid and structured than in the other Services? Almost certainly the answer to this would be a qualified affirmative, for the rigid channels of communication for contact between officers and men could not be maintained in a technical service, but it is not a point which should be over laboured. On less contentious grounds it can be stated that airmen enjoyed better living conditions. It is going too far to suggest that in contrast to the soldier, the airman lived at peace and went daily to war, that he slept and ate under civilised conditions undisturbed by the war and then during the day visited the war, became a part of it but even then detached from it. Those men whose airfield was bombed and in certain cases shelled, those men who, in 1918, had swiftly to vacate one airfield after another in the changing tide of war, would not be satisfied by such a picture but they would almost certainly recognise it as having a fundamental basis of truth. Legends are frequently well founded and binges in the RFC mess, parties of officers in a Crossley tender returning rather riotously from celebrations in the nearest town to their airfield, while not being weekly occurrences, were not as rare as some astral phenomena. Unrestricted relaxation may have occasioned temporarily sore heads and a fair amount of debris for someone to clear up but it also proved a great sustenant to morale.

I think a further point might be made and that is the considerable degree to which the airman shouldered responsibility for his own salvation coupled with the freedom I have outlined to exercise his stimulating, cherished but dangerous independence from the entrenched imprisonment of those below him. Not for a moment would I suggest that men rationalised their experience in this way: of course not; but those interested in the war in the air are almost inevitably drawn towards a consideration in general terms of what special feelings about his Service distinguished the airman from his soldier and sailor counterpart.

As in *The Sailor's War* I have tried briefly to outline an aspect of the war in the air and then to select extracts from original diaries, logs and official papers, to choose photographs and sketches and occasionally to use well-substantiated recollections to illustrate that aspect at a personal level. In the preparation of this book I have been indebted to a number of published sources which are listed in the bibliography but mention must be made here of the splendid volumes of the *Official History of the War in the Air*, of articles in the Journal *Cross and Cockade Great Britain*, and of course the book which for graphic detail and for the felicitously evocative recreation of a wholly convincing atmosphere of the times, is somehow at one and the same time both inspiring and inhibiting because it is so good – C.S. Lewis's *Sagittarius Rising*. I would also like to express my appreciation for being able to quote from documents held at the Public Record Office, then in two particular cases from documents held at the Imperial War Museum and in one such case at the Royal Air Force Museum.

The Airman's War is respectfully dedicated to men of the squadrons of the air Services in World War One and in particular to those men

and their families whose support has generously been given by the placement of papers and souvenirs in my archives. I thank especially those men whose material has been selected for use in the text or for illustrations; their names are noted appropriately throughout the text as well as being listed separately among the sources.

Every placement of papers, every endeavour to supply recollections has been appreciated. I hope it will not be thought invidious to mention quite specifically the following men and women who have done all that was possible to further my work: A.N. Barlow, Group Captain R. Barton, Wing Commander J. Bentham, R.D. Best, Air Vice Marshal C.N.H. Bilney, the son of the late A.H. Bird, Lord Braybrooke, Air Vice Marshal Sir Geoffrey Bromet, Squadron Leader H.A. Buss, Miss Rose Heaword for J.S. Castle, Mrs Tindall Collins for her brother-in-law the late R.F. Collins, Brigadier B.U.S. Cripps, Squadron Leader A.B. Fanstone, Sir Norman Frome, Air Commodore P.F. Fullard, the Rev. Dr T.C. Gordon, Air Chief Marshal Sir Donald Hardman, Colonel T. Hawker for his brother Major L.G. Hawker VC, W.E. Hedley, Stephen Horscroft, Hugo Ibbotson, Air Chief Marshal Sir Ronald Ivelaw Chapman, Miss Storm Jameson for her brother H. Jameson, Major Maurice Le Blanc Smith, Group Captain C.N. Lowe, Wing Commander Lywood for his father Air Vice Marshal O.G.W.G. Lywood, Mrs V.L. Jones for her brother B.S. Marshall, Lady Medhurst for her husband the late Air Chief Marshal Sir Charles Medhurst, Mrs Betty Morton for her father-in-law Brigadier Alan Morton, Bernard Oliver, Air Marshal Sir Lawrence Pendred, Air Vice Marshal A.L.A. Perry-Keene, E. Pryce and his family, Air Vice Marshal H.J. Roach, Mrs Alice Dobson for her father C.L. Roberts (Robert Sielle), Sir Frederick Russell, Air Chief Marshal Sir Hugh Saunders, Marshal of the RAF Sir John Slessor, Captain T.L.W. Stallibrass and his family, Squadron Leader C.T. Stoneham, F. Thorp, Edgar P. Thorne, Air Vice Marshal T.C. Traill, Air Vice Marshal F.N. Trinder, the family of the late Air Vice Marshal S.F. Vincent, the sons of the late H.R.H. Ward, Mrs Watt for her husband the late W.P. Watt, G.I. White, Mrs H.D. Williams for her brother W.E. Gray, Air Chief Marshal Sir John Whitworth Jones, Lady Peggy Hamilton and Mrs Ursula Birnstingl for the late O.B.W. Wills.

While the book was being prepared, Mrs Joyce Henshaw, whose death so shocked her friends in the archives, Charlie Ward and Maureen Hine were stalwart in supporting me in Sunderland in the general 1914–18 work, the late Eric Hawden helping in this too. Further afield, Stuart Stott in Hythe, Miss Frances Williams in Malvern, Barrie Herbert in Great Missenden, Bill Lawson in Ponteland, Brenda and Norman Paulding in Chelmsford, Colin and Morag Bailey in Middlesbrough and the Rev. John Croft in South Devon have generously given of their time and talents in cataloguing accessions of material. For any merits the book may have, and certainly not for its defects, I owe an unfathomable debt to two friends of the archives whose knowledge is profound, judgement shrewd, capacity to take pains infinite and helpfulness limitless. The labours of Squadron Leader 'Nobby' Clark and of Kevin Kelly on the air section of the archives have enormously developed the knowledge to be gained from a closer examination of the papers of over 200 men and the recollections of still more. A career summary was prepared for every man for whom we have papers and this enabled a cross-reference system to be built up which facilitated the swift location of men in certain squadrons, in certain types of machines, engaged in certain kinds of work or who had certain significant experiences. Nobby prepared the cross-referencing of this body of detailed information and he and Kevin have been wise counsellors in every single aspect covered by the book. In a very

real sense the book is the fruit of seeds planted in the archive by 1914–18 men then nurtured and studied comparatively by Nobby and Kevin. I have been quite exceptionally fortunate.

Guarding me still further from solecism have been Air Marshal Sir Victor Groom and Major Maurice Le Blanc Smith who have read and valuably commented upon the text as it developed. It has been a great privilege for me, though one requiring a degree of courage in its exercise, to submit my work to the overseeing eye of 'men who were there.'

Kathleen Barnes, having worked before the mast to type The Sailor's War, has now typed the airmen and their machines out of their billets and hangars ready for their ordained flight; to this end valuable help also came from Birgitta Scott, Morag Bailey and Barbara Peebles. The documents and photographs have been skilfully copied by Albert Snell, Head of Heworth Grange Comprehensive School, and it remains for me affectionately and gratefully to associate my wife Louise in every stage of the development of this book from the collecting of papers and tape-recording of men to discussing the text and then finally in checking the completed versions with their supporting material. That all this has been done while Louise successfully completed her own academic course and kept contentment within us and on the faces of our little children, Felicity in her fourth year and Alexander in his second, is one of those remarkable facts not diminished at all by our awareness that it is of course paralleled in so many families.

Peter H. Liddle, FR Hist. S.
DIPITY COTTAGE,
LIME STREET,
WALDRIDGE FELL,
COUNTY DURHAM.

Introduction: A War in the Air

OPPORTUNITY AND CONSTRAINT AS
PARENTS OF INVENTION

In looking at the airman and his work in World War One, there should be no misunderstanding whatsoever about the role envisaged in 1914 for the Air Arm and there must be an awareness that while the naval authorities directing the use of the RNAS had certain proper terms of reference which allowed for a wider role for the RNAS and indeed a role which was with remarkable speed extended well beyond what might be termed the Navy's needs, the RFC was and had to be at the service of the Army, its role dictated by policy formulated in the War Office in the Directorate of Military Aeronautics. Reconnaissance was what was expected of this supportive arm. The short history of flight by heavier-than-air machines, the sheer technological limitations of the machines developed by the date of the formation of the Royal Flying Corps in 1912, determined all thinking on the use of the air in warfare.

Balloons and man-lifting kites had of course an infinitely longer pedigree well documented in both volume one of the *Official History of the War in the Air* and in Brigadier Peter Mead's recent volume, *The Eye in the Air*, but clearly they too could only be of 'supportive' utility in war. Airships had their own birth and precocious pre-war infancy and they more obviously held an offensive capacity in the potential carrying of some form of explosive device for dropping on a military target, but the principal machine used by the RFC in 1914, the BE2a two-seater biplane, with which two of the four squadrons of the BEF were equipped, had a maximum speed of 70 mph, could not operate above 10,000 feet and had a three-hour endurance. The Avros and the Henri Farmans could offer similar performances. These statistics were the basis for the planners' exclusive concern with an intended role for these and other flying machines as an instrument for reconnaissance. However, it is unhistoric to leave a picture of fixed permanence until major technical developments rendered these parti-

January 1913: An aircraft line up at the Central Flying School, Upavon. From left to right are shown two Avro Type Es, two BE4s, a Henri Farman, a Short School Biplane and two Maurice Farman Longhorns. Army and Naval personnel in the photograph appropriately indicate that this Training Establishment was common to the Military and Naval Wings of the RFC. (Group Captain R.F. Barton)

An air to air photograph, as the obtrusive flying wire indicates, of an RNAS BE2c flying over Yorkshire in the autumn of 1915. The observer in the front cockpit seems to be standing, perhaps to look at something which would otherwise have been hidden by the lower right wing or the fuselage. In so doing he demonstrates one of the weaknesses of the BE2c in combat. The Union Jack marking on the rudder was standard on RFC machines for a period before the introduction of roundels and rudder stripes. (Major C. Draper)

cular aircraft obsolete because the same BE2a could be armed by giving the observer a rifle or a carbine or pistols and it could take 'one or two fiery Grapnel weapons or three 20 lb bombs'.[1]

In a machine airborne for the specific purpose of observation of the ground, obviously a second man without the responsibilities of piloting the aircraft could search the ground,

Standing in front of a Caudron G IV of No. 1 Wing, RNAS, both the RNAS observer and pilot in this 1915 photograph are wearing inflatable life jackets. Note the binoculars and map cases. Sadly, all three men shown here – from left to right, Casey, Allen and Mackenzie – were killed during the war. (Lord Braybrooke)

use his map and make his notes more freely. As tasks for aircraft had scarcely been defined in any detail, the duties of aircrew were equally unstated. Reconnaissance on manoeuvres had generally meant the carrying of two pilots, but the exigencies of active service had proved this impractical. Many pilots were officers of the Regular Army with inherent knowledge of what detail would be required but RFC pilots without such background needed appropriate training or an observer fitted to his task. It is not quite straightforward to claim that the observer's role was superior to that of the pilot even though the pilot flew his machine in order that the observer could do his work but some idea of the significance of the observer's work may be gauged from the German practice of making the observer the Captain of the aircraft.

The training required for observation work was so akin to that already being given to artillery subalterns that in the need for extended numbers the obvious solution of re-cruitment from these ranks was quickly taken.

The second man introduced the problem of power-to-weight ratio. Flights of long duration could not be undertaken with the increased weight of the second man: sufficient fuel could not then be carried for the completion of the task. This problem reared its head further with the carrying of bombs, wireless transmission equipment, cameras and armament, for the whole complex of interlinked factors had a relation to the development of machines to fulfil different types of work. As a result, the aircraft designer was faced with the task of devising a means to overcome the inhibiting problem of power-to-weight ratio if the offen-sive capacities of the machines were to be increased.

Upon the aircraft designer there were also external pressures for development. Some were simple and almost self-evident, like the hard lessons of the effect of active service under stress-inducing conditions on machines hith-erto proved only under more ideal circum-stances. Others were far-reaching. As each antagonist learned that he could not without penalty permit a mobile eye in the sky to oversee his position and evidence of prepara-tions to extend or defend it, he had at one and the same time to prevent this, and secure from the air information of his enemy's activities. Accordingly an aerial as well as a ground defence capacity had to be created and an aerial protection developed for his 'eye in the sky'.

The original reconnaissance role, which was developed without serious complications to a degree of sophistication and utility by photo-graphic work, was now being defended by the reconnaissance aircraft themselves being armed. A logical development from this was the protection of the reconnaissance machines by faster armed aircraft which could also be used to deny the sky to the enemy. The chal-lenge to designer and to factory production was clear. Specialist machines for reconnaissance and others for offensive or defensive action had to be conceived and brought into production.

RECONNAISSANCE

The next stage of development was also deter-mined by the logic of the original concept of the Royal Flying Corps Military Wing properly serving the needs of the Army: this was practi-cal assistance in the planning and carrying out of military operations of an offensive nature. In 1914, the reconnaissance role had been carried out efficiently – perhaps even decisively in early September, when we consider that for Ger-many to have won the war, the war had to be short and that the Schlieffen Plan gave what-ever hope there was for a swift German victory. Whatever inherent flaws there were in the plan, it was aerial reconnaissance which gave early warning of the eccentric change of direction of the German 1st Army which exposed its flank to counter-attack. It was, however, in 1915 that the first British planned offensives were launched and here there lay the opportunity for the RFC in its supportive role to do far more than had hitherto been considered. This exten-sion had been earned by the September achievement and its significance.

The sheer novelty of the Air Arm is always deserving of re-emphasis. Despite the striking success of aerial reconnaissance in the 1912 manoeuvres, there really was no tested area of performance under combat conditions, as opposed to pure performance in the air, by which potentiality could be assessed. Only the enthusiasts were well-informed and to a large extent only from them could come flights of imagination which had the necessary founda-tion of scientific knowledge. Even this had to be related to conditions of warfare which few professionals in the forces of any country had forecast. If the War Office and GHQ of the BEF had been well staffed with men closely familiar with aircraft capability and potential it would have been truly remarkable: such an unnatural phenomenon did not obtain.

In March 1915, aerial photo reconnaissance led to the bombing by aircraft of a supposed German Divisional HQ behind Neuve Cha-

An Aviator's 'ticket'. In the pre and early war years the tuition fees necessary to reach the standard to qualify for this prized document were £75. Prospective candidates for the RFC had to possess such a certificate to be considered for pilot training. Those accepted had their fees refunded. Later, the Certificate possession requirement was waived and Royal Aero Club Aviator's Certificates were granted to applicants who had graduated from service flying training establishments. (J.M. Allen)

pelle. Railway lines seen to be essential for supply to this sector also received attention. Two months later, attempts were made to gather information from the air both to locate hostile batteries, reporting their position to the ground by wireless transmission and also to attempt 'contact patrolling' which was noting and reporting infantry positions reached in the Aubers Ridge offensive. White strips were laid on the ground for identification purposes and a message could then be dropped by weighted streamer to HQ positions behind the Allied attack. For the major offensive at Loos in September, aerial photography, tactical bombing and the aerial assisted registration of the shelling of specifically identified targets were used on a larger scale than in the spring of that year but the contact patrol work planned was not successful.

THE FIGHTING SCOUT AND AIR SUPERIORITY

It had become clear that information gathered from the air and, to a lesser extent, attack launched from the air were of vital importance to the ground forces. Even with warfare in the air in its infancy it is reasonable to speak of the beginnings of a struggle for air superiority. This could be tackled in three ways: by anti-aircraft shell fire; by arming aircraft for attack and defence; and by design improvements to give aircraft greater offensive capability. The latter approach in fact led not merely to better aerodynamic performance but also to an awareness that differently designed machines could be produced for the fulfilment of different roles. For the steady platform required for artillery observation and photo reconnaissance, the slower, stable RE8 and the Armstrong Whitworth FK8 were to be developed, for an armed faster fighting aircraft, the DH2, the Sopwith Camel and the SE5. The effect of carrying armament on the power-to-weight ratio had to be overcome by development of more powerful engines like the Clerget rotary, and the Hispano-Suiza and Wolseley inline engines. This too was a factor if machines were to carry a bomb load of anything more than negligible proportions.

The mounting of a machine-gun for a pilot in a single-seat aircraft and its field of fire presented a special problem. In two-seat aircraft, providing a machine-gun for the observer was less of a problem because the observer had greater freedom of movement, unhindered by the need to pilot the aircraft, and a wider field of fire over the tail and on the beam, and various pivot mountings were designed in an attempt to give the observer/gunner, in for example a BE2, an improved degree of elevation, depression and traverse. Obviously, for pilots to be able to pilot and aim a gun in the same direction drew together the dual problems of flying and fighting into one simple element. Pusher aircraft presented no problem as the propeller was placed behind the nacelle or cockpit compartment and this design for a fighter aircraft had pre-war origins. A tractor aircraft, that is one with the propeller at the front of the fuselage, clearly had no field of fire immediately ahead and along the line of the fuselage as the propeller would have its blades shot off.

For the tractor, interim measures were developed to minimise the problems, for instance, mounting the gun on the top plane of a biplane firing over the propeller arc, with the gun activated by a cable linked to a trigger on the control column. Experiments were conducted with firing through the propeller arc but with bullet deflector plates made of steel to protect the propeller. Some success was gained by this means but it was clearly no complete solution to the problem. What is more surprising is that the answer had been pioneered in France and Germany before the war but not fully developed. Perhaps this is an indication of

Senior NCOs of No. 56 Squadron at London Colney in 1916: Left to right, Sergeants Leach, Moody, Quick, Ryder, Bastable and Nevill. Only the last two survived the war. R.J. Moody (bare-headed) became an NCO pilot and was shot down in France 4 March 1917, his fall usually being credited to von Richthofen, the top German Ace. (E. Vousden, Flight Sergeant)

Seasonal celebrations for No. 60 Squadron, RFC. The commander of 'A' Flight, Roderic Hill, No. 60 Squadron designed this Christmas card. In the coloured original, the nearest Nieuport scout has a red spinner fitted to the propeller, a personalised adornment which identifies it as Albert Ball's machine. (Air Vice Marshal S.F. Vincent)

tional use first, in July 1915, and for many months British pilots and observers paid a dreadful price for the technical deficiency of their armament. The price was made still higher in later periods of inferiority by the British policy implemented from early 1916 of aggressive patrolling over the enemy lines in numbers in an attempt to deny the Germans the use of the sky, while the Germans concentrated their resources to achieve maximum effectiveness in the sectors they judged to be most vital from day to day.

It is somewhat ironic that German superior-

the lack of vision displayed in the consideration of aircraft potential. A mechanical means of protection of the propeller from the stream of bullets flying through it could in fact be achieved by two methods: the gun could be prevented from releasing a bullet when the propeller was in line of fire by geared linkages operated by the propeller itself – this was the 'interrupter' gear – or by the prevention of the gun being activated through an engine-driven gear until the propeller was out of range – this was the 'synchronized' gear. Through the Dutchman, Anthony Fokker, the Germans were to get an interrupter-geared gun in opera-

'Contact!' While Air Mechanic Ward takes hold of the propeller, 2nd Lt J. Sellers is in the cockpit of this No. 3 Squadron Sopwith Camel in the field in 1918. Note the twin Vickers guns and the empty bomb rack between the undercarriage struts. (J. Sellers)

An Australian airman with a noteworthy record: Flight Sub-Lieutenant R.S. Dallas with his Nieuport Scout at No. 1 Wing RNAS, Dunkirk in early 1916. Dallas was an infantry officer in the Australian Imperial Force but he had paid his own fare to England to join the British Flying Services. He was commissioned into the RNAS in 1915, serving with No. 1 Squadron, No. 1 Wing from December 1915 until March 1918. For almost the whole of that period he was on active service in France. He was awarded the DSC and Bar, the Croix de Guerre and several Mentions in Despatches, being promoted to Squadron Commander in June 1917. In March 1918, he was appointed to command No. 40 Squadron RFC, his award of a DSO being gazetted in April. He was killed in action on 1 June of that year, having been credited with a total of victories – (39) – almost certainly lower than than which he had achieved. (Lord Braybrooke)

ity in the air was first successfully challenged by pusher aircraft, the DH2 and the FE2b, but it was the single-seater fighter biplanes with forward-firing guns like the French Nieuport and then later the two-seater British Sopwith 1½-Strutter which for some time reversed the balance until they themselves were out-classed by the German Albatros D.1 fighter, whose twin Spandau machine-guns fired over 1,000 rounds a minute, over three times the British rate of fire allowed by their interrupter guns.

The further development of British fighter aircraft and their armament will be mentioned later in the book, but the principles for advancement can be quite simply stated: the need for better armament, greater speed, better manoeuvrability and longer endurance. Atten-

Major J.B. McCudden VC, DSO, MC, MM, Croix de Guerre. The original photograph is inscribed 'To Galley' and signed 'Mac', 21 April 1918, the date being several weeks after McCudden had left No. 56 Squadron in which he had been E.D.G. Galley's Flight Commander. (Colonel E.D.G. Galley)

tion must now be turned to that other extension of the role of aerial reconnaissance, bombing, though with regard to the root of British 'strategic' bombing, we must be mindful of the German airship and then aeroplane raids rather than purely insular considerations.

THE BOMBER AIRCRAFT

There may seem to be a straightforward, even if precipitated, line of development from the 1914 days of the dropping by hand of little bombs from reconnaissance aircraft speculatively upon targets in forward enemy positions to the deliberate employment of specially designed bomb-carrying aeroplanes to attack industrial targets in Germany. The evolution of strategic bombing in the industrial sense is in fact rather more complex and attention will be paid to this in Chapter Nine. This whole question of attempting by bombing to cripple

St Pol. A very effective near miss! A German bomb concludes the flying service of a BE2c. (Lord Braybrooke)

Germany's war effort was a matter of contention at the time and has been a subject of vigorous debate since. All that need be noted here is that technological factors quite as much as policy divergence determined that any attempt during the war decisively to destroy German industrial capacity quite simply had to fall derisively short of the hopes of the most enthusiastic theorists or policy makers then and of any armchair literary protagonists today. Furthermore it seems evident to the

author of this book that the Air Arm on the Western Front by the very nature of World War One had to be principally at the immediate call of the Army authorities. Blood let or ink spilled on the question of whether the RFC were to have allowed by default the great opportunity of an earlier winning of the war through long range bombing of industrial targets does not seem to have been conspicuously well employed.[2]

Certainly deserving of admiration were the remarkably early efforts by the RNAS to attack distant targets, their incapacity to do so effectively by no means diminishing the credit attached to such pioneering endeavour. Later in the war, in the summer of 1916 from an airfield at Luxeuil, the RNAS began long-distance bombing of industrial targets in the Saar, but this enterprise was viewed with disfavour by military authorities as it had not been endorsed by the War Office or BEF HQ. The related controversy highlights an unfortunate period of Admiralty War Office discord over matters as wide-ranging as overall policy and the procurement of aircraft and engines.

The contribution of the RFC towards long-range bombing was associated with the establishment of the 41st Wing, set up as a direct consequence of a German aeroplane night-bombing raid on London in September 1917. The Wing, in which RNAS and RFC squadrons had DH4s, FE2bs and Handley Page O/100s carrying in the case of the single-engined machines two 112 lb bombs and for the Handley Pages sixteen 112 lb bombs, flew from near Nancy to bomb industrial targets at Saarbrücken, Volklingen and Thionville.

The final stage in the development during the Great War of strategic bombing dated from the establishment in June 1918 of the Independent Force, perhaps ironically under the command of Major-General Sir Hugh Trenchard, first and foremost a believer in supporting the immediate needs of the Army. Trench-

An FE2d probably of No. 25 Squadron, RFC, at 6,000 ft over Loos in the early summer of 1917. Flight Commander's streamers can be seen behind the wing roundels and from the tailplane elevators. (Captain F.B. Ransford)

ard himself states that the object of this force was the breakdown of the German Army in Germany, its Government and the crippling of its source of supply. He attempted to do this by striking at as many large industrial centres as he could reach in order to achieve the moral effect of bombing which he judged to be twenty times greater than the effects of the material damage caused. An attempt was made to knock out of action German airfields, railways and blast furnaces but the war ended before the inability of his force to do its set task had been clearly demonstrated. Strategic bombing had indeed made an appearance in the evolution of modern warfare, even though as a creation it was in its earliest stage of development.

In the pages of this book an attempt will be made to deal with the general principles of many facets of the air war, illuminating this by personal experience. In this introductory section it has been judged inappropriate to do more than cover in the merest outline the basic development of flying and fighting from an aircraft as the war progressed. Wireless and kite balloon work, airship and aircraft-carrier service, the working out of combat tactics, of dealing with airship and bomber raids over Britain, these and other themes will each claim attention but so will aircraft maintenance and training for all types of essential work in an expanding service. There may be elements which the reader can justifiably claim have been omitted or have been too scantily treated: to acknowledge this is not to excuse it but at least an attempt has been made to leave a clear impression of what it was like to fulfil many of the requirements of service in the Air Arm during World War One.

1

1914: Preparations and War

Little could more starkly stress the degree to which new-born service flying in Britain had a foreshortened infancy before taking off into the buffeting winds of adolescence than an awareness that the year x5w4 saw the first heavier-than-air powered flight in Britain and that the English Channel was first flown in 1909. In 1910, the War Office approved private enterprise flying from War Department land at Larkhill on Salisbury Plain and in the spring of 1911 the Air Battalion of the Royal Engineers was established. The pedigree of this particular unit had been through the balloon detachment of the Royal Engineers which had been in existence since the 1880s and had campaign experience in Southern Africa with balloon observation of the terrain and enemy unit movements. It was also from this unit that Britain's first Army airship was operated in 1907 and when the new Air Battalion was established four years later, its Number One Company operated airships and its Number Two Company operated aeroplanes while the Royal Engineers Balloon Factory became the Royal Aircraft Factory.

In its brief history, the Air Battalion suffered, as the *Official History* records, from 'divided counsels and uncertain policy.'[1] For many wasteful weeks aircraft and airships were seen as alternatives rather than as partners in military flying. This unfortunate situation, arresting the progress of both theory and practice, was removed in April 1912 with the establishment of the Royal Flying Corps on the authority of a Standing Sub Committee of the Committee of Imperial Defence. The new Corps had a Naval Wing, taking due recognition of the Admiralty's proven interest in airships, aeroplanes, seaplanes and even a flying boat, a Military Wing and a Central Flying School at Upavon for the training of pilots.

Immediately absorbing the Air Battalion, the Military Wing of the Royal Flying Corps was to have seven squadrons of aeroplanes (twelve machines to a squadron and a machine for the Squadron Commander) and one airship and man-lifting kite squadron. The airship squadron based at Farnborough was under the command of Edward Maitland, who as an aeroplane pilot had had a bad crash. His somewhat cavalier approach to the hazards of flight led to some extraordinary ballooning mishaps like the one in which he landed with two girl friends on Kensington rooftops and needed fire brigade rescue. Ballooning with Maitland certainly had more alarmingly swift ups and downs than some of his passengers might have chosen.

At Farnborough was based the airship *Beta*. Capable of flying at 40 mph, the hydrogen-filled *Beta* simply drifted in the wind as a free balloon when her somewhat unreliable engine failed and the mechanic was labouring at its repair. *Beta*'s operational ceiling was about 2,000 feet. When landing under her own power, she could be manhandled in calm weather by merely two men on the ground hauling on the rope thrown out for them. The degree to which *Beta*'s progress allowed for improvisation is clear in the memoirs of Brigadier-General Sir Robert Pigot: 'you could stop and ask the way from a passer-by on the road below just by turning into the wind and throttling down. We used to fly over all the events of the day like Ascot Week and the Fourth of June at Eton and *Beta* came to my wedding. Unfortunately she broke down on this occasion over the house and landed in the park nearby. I have a photograph of my wife climbing over the fence (in her wedding dress) to greet the crew.' In his memoirs, Sir Robert laments the lack of interest shown from the military establishment at Aldershot in what was happening in the air so near to them at Farnborough. A great effort was made to prove the utility of airships and aeroplanes in army manoeuvres at Cambridge in the summer of 1913. As the pilot of the airship *Delta*, Sir Robert records a successful five-hour night reconnaissance, the 'enemy' troops and more particularly transport on the roads being clearly visible: 'Our report served very well to spoil the whole manoeuvres.'[2]

The Airship Squadron had man-lifting Cody Kites in addition to its airships and balloons. Made of bamboo and canvas with a span of about 14 feet and attached by 2,000 feet of cable wound onto a winch, a pilot kite, in a wind of at least 20 mph, would readily take to the air. Five hundred feet below it, the first of the larger lifting-kites was run up the wire until it came to a stop on its own bobbin. At intervals of 50 feet other lifting-kites were run up, each on its own correct-sized bobbin, to achieve the required lift. The carrier kite itself was put on the wire when the pressure gauge on the lorry had reached a certain figure. Attached to it was a basket in which the pilot sat. He had two ropes, a red one and a white one, which were attached to the top and to the bottom of the kite respectively so that he could control the kite's angle to the wind and thus by pulling the white rope he went up and by pulling the red he came down. Observation work could be undertaken for as long as there was sufficient wind to keep the carrier kite aloft.

J.N. Fletcher in 1912 was a cadet at the Royal Military Academy, Woolwich. At the end of his course at the School of Military Engineering, the Head of the Air Battalion Royal Engineers came to Chatham to recruit two replacements for men recently killed in a balloon accident. Fletcher, who was second under-officer in his batch 'volunteered to set an example' but found himself too heavy for the kites, never getting further than 20 feet off the ground. Fletcher describes the airship he flew after passing a ballooning course as like a very well-proportioned pear; the fabric was the skin of animal bladders and held hydrogen gas and

from the pear-shape hung enough wires to hold a 'car' of wood and canvas in which there was a pilot, engine and engineer. The envelope was kept permanently filled with hydrogen from 12-feet long, 6- to 8-inch diameter steel cylinders holding gas under high pressure. The inflated dirigible was kept in a tall oblong shed.[3]

A clear illustration of the path by which a fascination with both flight and engines led to the RFC is shown by the early career of T.E. Guttery who was to be drafted to No. 3 Squadron at Larkhill on Salisbury Plain.[4] With the fortunate start of many hours in his uncle's engineering workshop in Cradley Heath, the next step on leaving school was his local engineering works. Inspired by the Bleriot cross-channel flight in 1909 and by making flying models which were initially using twisted elastic as their motive power before he devised a relay system to lengthen the duration of the flight, Guttery and some friends actually made their own aeroplane. It did lack certain all too essential elements, an engine, housing for engine assembly and testing and not least, somewhere from which it could fly! The line of development was no cul de sac but an avenue to the RFC. Guttery had become totally convinced of the application in war of the flying machine. There were opportunities in the newly established RFC for young men with his interests and experience and, after recruits' training, he was appointed as an air mechanic. As No. 3 Squadron was equipped with Nieuport, Deperdussin, Bleriot and Bristol monoplanes and Avro and Bristol biplanes, he was not to lack for variety in engine maintenance work.

W.J. Smyrk, as Guttery had done, experimented with gliding aero models and with kites. Having served his time as an apprentice press tool-maker, he enlisted as a mechanic in the RFC in July 1912, his regimental number being 253. As a second class mechanic his weekly pay was 14 shillings from which two shillings was docked for extra messing and washing. During the celebrated August 1912 Military Trials of aircraft suitability for war, Smyrk took the opportunity of a flight with

This Short S 86 Pusher was a Navy aircraft that took part in the Army manoeuvres near Rugby in September 1913, when this photograph was taken. Later in its service life it became a seaplane at the RNAS school at Eastchurch. (Squadron Leader J.C. Andrews)

S.F. Cody in his *Cathedral* which surprisingly won the trials. It was built of bamboo struts lashed together with string between every knot and painted with shellac. The string was to prevent the bamboo from splitting.[5]

Smyrk had an amusing recollection of the Commanding Officer at No. 3 Squadron, Major H.R.M. Brooke-Popham, who had a passion for looking after his own motor car. Someone had walked off with one of his small adjustable spanners colloquially known as a 'King Dick' but Brooke-Popham searched in every shed and enquired of all and sundry for what he called his 'King Willie'.

Though an engine fitter, Smyrk did rigging too and this involved making-up spare flying and landing wires. At that time stranded wire was used, considerable skill being needed for splicing and binding and attaching to the turn-buckle or connecting joint.

From a very different geographical location, South African Kenneth van der Spuy, a scientific assistant at an observatory on the outskirts of Johannesburg, was dimly aware that 'something deep within myself demanded adventure, an exploration into new and more exciting fields'.[6] He, like many others, was fascinated by the journals *The Aeroplane* and *Flight* and he applied in 1913 for the South African Government advertised course of flying instruction at Kimberley, established so that a flying arm to the South African Defence Forces could be created. Van der Spuy, a particularly tall man, was, in view of this, fortunate to be among the ten selected candidates for instruction at a school staffed initially by a Chief Pilot Instructor, a mechanic and one man who did everything else that there was to do. The candidates repaired the aircraft, even constructing one, and serviced the engines. There was no work on the theory of flight, behaviour of engines, meteorology, navigation, indeed there was not much flying because the Chief Pilot Instructor had a phobia about wind, had too many pilots to train and the aircraft were frequently rendered unserviceable by crashes in at least one of which van der Spuy was nearly killed by his instructor. Nevertheless, South African military flying had been born. Its first batch of pilots, van der Spuy among them, was sent to the RFC to complete training at the Central Flying School at Upavon. Here, van der Spuy met men whose path to flying was not only from Army and civilian background but also from the Navy.

Serving as a lieutenant in the submarine *C1*, R.J. Bone[7] knew that some of his fellows had engaged in gliding activities from the Portsdown Hills overlooking Fort Blockhouse. His opportunity to engage in the activity which featured so much in conversation occurred when *C1* was docked at Sheerness. From here it was easy for him frequently to visit the airfield at Eastchurch with its factory where the dynamic, eccentric, Horace Short was designing and building a pusher biplane. Among the enthusiasts gathering at this hive of flying activities was the wealthy Frank MacLean who purchased a series of Short aircraft and actually paid for the tuition in flying for the first four naval officers eager to take up the opportunity. Bone himself learned on a Bleriot monoplane machine at the Eastbourne School of Flying, the machines being so difficult for the pupils to handle that it was only under conditions of complete calm that the pupil was allowed to run the machine along the grass, throttling back immediately there seemed a likelihood of leaving the ground. A gust took Bone into the air on one occasion to the apoplectic fury of the watching instructor. The submariner continued with dual control instruction on another machine, having ignored the summary termination of his lessons after so hazarding the monoplane, and took his internationally recognised Royal Aero Club aviator's certificate a few weeks later on a pusher Bristol biplane.

There was some wider significance in the way Bone persuaded a reluctant Admiralty to authorise his transfer to the flying branch. He produced a Frank MacLean aerial photograph of a ship sunk off Beachy Head. The water was clear and the sunken ship easily visible. The potential utility of such photography was obvious. The good fortune of

Seasonally amphibian! The Short S 41 was first flown as a landplane in April 1912 before being converted as a seaplane. Following satisfactory take-off and landing trials, it was taken aboard HMS *Hibernia* for the Naval Review that year. Later, Commander Samson used it to survey potential sites for Home-based seaplane stations and it was then reconverted as a landplane and took part in the autumn manoeuvres in East Anglia. (Group Captain R.J. Bone)

conditions obtaining at the time of the photograph, won what had seemed an unlikely transfer. A fortnight later at the Central Flying School at Upavon on Salisbury Plain, the naval officer found himself dining in company with men arrayed in a rich diversity of mess kit. There were sappers, gunners, infantry officers from many regiments and cavalry officers too. A 'certain inarticulate Major' was in charge of administration. In this manner, the former submariner recalls the course run by Hugh Trenchard. The station was commanded by Captain G.M. Paine, 'a naval post captain who was extremely energetic on the ground – but never flew'.

A course on seaplanes at the Isle of Grain led to a posting to Great Yarmouth where Bone prepared for the imminence of war on French pusher biplane seaplanes but also had a memorable experience of flying over the July Naval Review by both day and night when the illuminated ships were an unforgettable sight.

In an awareness of the infancy in 1913 of flying for military purposes, one should note that even then experimentation along productive lines was taking place. Not merely were there manoeuvres involving cooperation with artillery, infantry and cavalry, each of course in the sphere of observation and report, but there were efforts to mount machine-guns, work to

1913: Staff and pupils at the Central Flying School, Upavon. The Commandant, G.M. Paine, RN, is in the centre of the second row. Second from the left in the same row in Major H. Trenchard, later Marshal of the Royal Air Force. (Group Captain R.F. Barton)

mount cameras from which successful photographs were taken, night-flying endeavours, bomb dropping trials, endurance flights and consideration of how an airship might be attacked by an aircraft. There was, too, the celebrated feat as early as 1911 of taking-off from the deck of HMS *Africa* as well as wireless experimentation first undertaken from airships but then from aeroplanes, significantly developing the speed and hence the utility of reconnaissance reporting.

The military potential of aircraft and the link being forged between sport and war is nicely illustrated in a letter from the A.V. Roe Co. Ltd in Manchester to a young man at Lancing College who had enquired about Avro biplanes. 'The particulars sent herewith will give you an idea as to the range we cover; from the same single-seater to the immense gun-carrying seaplane. For your purpose we would strongly recommend the swift little single-seater in which the wings are folded back so that it can be housed in any ordinary shed. This is a machine which will go a long way towards popularising aviation.'[8]

A paper prepared at the end of August 1912 by Captain Murray Sueter, Director of the Air Department at the Admiralty, clearly illustrates that the Navy saw a wide range of work being undertaken by aeroplanes and airships of the Naval Wing – distance reconnaissance work with the Fleet at sea, reconnaissance of the enemy's coast from detached cruisers or special aircraft ships, protection of British dockyards, magazines and oil storage tanks from enemy air attack were among eight specified areas of work though, rather strangely in view of the distinguished early efforts in this area, there is no reference to bombing.[9] Some senior officers in the Army were no less convinced of the vital part which Military Wing aerial observation would play in land warfare. General Sir James Grierson, having used information obtained from the air with decisive swiftness to achieve victory in the 1912 Army manoeuvres, declared: 'Personally, I think there is no doubt that, before land fighting takes place, we shall have to fight and destroy the enemy's aircraft. It seems to me impossible for troops to fight while the hostile aircraft are able to keep up their observation. That is to say warfare will be impossible unless we have the mastery of the air.'[10]

On the eve of the outbreak of war, the Admiralty won independent control over naval flying with the establishment of the Royal Naval Air Service in July 1914. Whatever may be said about a failure to judge accurately the nature of the approaching war at sea and on land, the War Office and the Admiralty at least were aware of the outstanding prospective importance of their respective flying services, though the role of the RNAS had not been precisely defined – unlike that of the RFC, a Corps of the British Expeditionary Force and hence bound for France – and this was later to occasion much debate, particularly over Home Defence.

WAR

'After dinner Major Trenchard (Royal Scots) mustered all hands in the ante room and told the Military Officers that they would leave the school on the morrow. This was the first intimation we had of the International crisis.'[11] Lieutenant G.R. Bromet, at the Central Flying School Upavon, thus described in his diary for 29 July 1914 his personal involvement in the developing crisis. The Military Officers duly departed for their respective squadrons and on 31 July 'Lieutenants Hooper and Bromet, Sub-Lieutenant Tompkinson and Sub-Lieutenants RNVR Barr, Cripps and Wanklyn left the school for Eastchurch, Isle of Sheppey.' At Eastchurch, crowded with both a Military and a Naval Flight, 'all the cabins were full, everybody on the alert and sentries all over the place, armed to the teeth and looking out for German airships.'

Bromet was elated to be posted to a newly designated seaplane station at Westgate-on-Sea. He felt 'very important during my interview [at Sheerness] with the Inspecting Cap-

tain of Aircraft and left his office armed with several charts, £50 in gold and a burning desire for civilians to know and appreciate the fact that I was on active service.' As the newly appointed Intelligence Officer to the advanced seaplane base of Westgate-on-Sea, Bromet made haste through seaside holiday hordes and a crowded train to get to his post. It was the first day of August. Quartered in St Mildred's Hotel, Bromet then got a temporary wireless station operational in the hotel grounds and another officer arranged for accommodation for the ratings in a roofless building normally used to store bathing machines in the winter. On 2 August, the Commanding Officer, Flight-Commander Babington and another officer arrived in Short seaplanes and quickly the new station was established with sufficient security to protect their flying machines but in such a way, using the cooperation of the police, 'as to offend nobody.' The restrictions necessarily imposed on civilians in the neighbourhood of the new station excited the alarm of many and the resentment of some. The Post Office and a small army of Boy Scouts greatly assisted the work of the busy Intelligence Officer and then a company of West Kent Territorials came to take over security duties. 'We got no [war] news at all until midnight of August 4 when a wireless signal reached us to the effect that hostilities between England and Germany had commenced. The Senior Naval Officer Nore Patrol made the signal to "kick off" and we knew at once that war had indeed begun ... In the hotel lounge cheers were given, drinks went round and the band played the National Anthem.' In such fashion the RNAS readied itself for war, while the RFC as an integral element of the British Expeditionary Force embarked for France.

RFC Headquarters left Farnborough at 11.15 a.m. on 11 August. Boulogne was reached via Southampton at eight o'clock on the evening of the following day. O.G.W.G. Lywood, the Wireless Officer, recorded in his diary: '13.8.14 Left in train for Amiens fine reception by population of villages passed through – arrived Amiens about 11 a.m. rode to Aerodrome installed wireless.'[12] Destination was Mauberge and an aerodrome about four miles from the station. For Saturday, 22 August Lywood records: 'First casualty in RFC Sergeant Jillings shot through thigh whilst over German's lines.'[13] ... '25.8.14 Left Mauberge Germans driving our firing line back – covered about 15 miles to Landrecies, bathed in river.' ... '26.8.14 Left early passed le Cateau arrived Saint Quentin about 8 p.m. Rained like hell. On the way to St Quentin a German plane flew overhead with five of our own over him – lined up firing party but no opportunity to fire.' The retirement continued and on 29 August: '3 bombs dropped on us so had to leave.' Lywood was having to leave Compiègne, but with the victory on the Marne, the opportunity for which had been brought about by an aerial reconnaissance report of the eccentric course of Von Kluck's 1st Army, he was to take part in the advance towards the Aisne.

Transport vehicles for at least one squadron, No. 5, had had to be requisitioned and included a large furniture van and a red Thorneycroft van holding bombs and ammunition though conspicuously advertising 'H.P. Sauce the World's Appetiser'. These vehicles and others were bedecked with flowers by French civilians and made a colourfully unmilitary progress towards Amiens. One machine of No. 5 Squadron came down at Senlis and the unfortunate pilot Lieutenant R.M. Vaughan, suffered the indignity of arrest until French enquiry and the authority of the mayor led to his release spurred on his way by the embraces of the civic official's daughters. The first useful reconnaissance by No. 5 Squadron was a report on 21 August locating massed German Cavalry ten miles beyond Namur. On the following day, anti-aircraft fire was first experienced by British pilots but it was rifle fire from the ground which brought down one machine, killing both pilot and observer.[14] Warrant Officer Guttery's memoirs record for this month the hazard of British machines being fired on by their own troops and the temporary security measure of painting Union Jacks on the sides of fuselages and undersides of wings, an identification soon to be replaced

The end of the retirement from Mons. Lorries of No. 4 Squadron, RFC halted near Chantilly, September 1914. (Air Vice Marshal O.G.W.G. Lywood)

by red, white and blue roundels to avoid the slight similarity from a distance of the German Cross and the Union Jack.

During the retirement, No. 5 Squadron's red H.P. Sauce van was a helpful indicator for pilots searching for their temporary airfields but not all vehicles kept up with the pace of retreat. One tender took a wrong turning and brought captivity to its driver and three occupants when it was caught by a German cavalry patrol. Guttery contests the Official Historian's claim for No. 2 Squadron of the first enemy machine shot or forced down. He quotes an account by No. 5 Squadron pilot Lieutenant Wilson which describes his observer, Lieutenant Rabagliati, forcing down an opponent by rifle fire on 25 August. Guttery quotes from Wilson's diary: '29.8.14 Lunched at hotel in Compiègne, many pilots of RFC collected. Harvey Kelly [Lieutenant of No. 2 Squadron] posing as successful warrior, relating his method of downing Huns and showing small plaque taken from machine downed by Rab and 398 [25.8.14]. Stopped him in full career and claimed first Hun for 398. He had landed beside our prey and attended its burning! H.K. handed the plaque gracefully to me "Your bird I think".'

Among the distinctions earned by RFC personnel at this time was a French decoration for Corporal Harry Jameson: 'I got the medal which is called in France the Medal Military [sic]. It seems to be very highly prized by them. I got it for working the wireless in an aeroplane over the German lines, a shell from one of their anti aircraft guns exploded near us and blew part of our main inlet valve away and cut the pilot's hand. The pilot was Lieutenant Lewis now a Captain, and he is doing some very fine work with the wireless.' Jameson's Médaille Militaire was in fact presented to him by Brigadier-General Henderson in command of the Royal Flying Corps in France at that time.[15]

So precipitate was the great retreat from Mons that it is recorded in Guttery's memoirs that two of his officers landed and borrowed two cavalry horses to deliver more swiftly the intelligence they had learned but on return to their machine found it under shellfire and were fortunate in being able to take-off safely. It was intended, however ineffectually, to form a defensive laager of the transport vehicles around the parked aircraft if the squadron were to be in danger of being overtaken. Such a measure was taken but the anticipated night attack did not occur and in point of fact the worst damage to the squadron's machines was done by torrential rain and high winds in mid-September as the Germans took their stand on the Aisne.

On 5 August, Lanoe Hawker, newly transferred from the RE to the RFC, wrote from the Central Flying School at Upavon to the girl he wished to marry, that he hoped he would 'get thro' in time to do some good.'[16] The officer, who was to be the Flying Corps's first fighter pilot Victoria Cross recipient, wrote a week or so later that he had 'spotted what I was doing wrong and got the hang of the thing and did my first solo.' On 23 August he was still 'not at home in the air yet. I feel like being on a young horse that is just about all I can manage.' Hawker was at this time occasionally depressed by the thought that his future plans and his

hopes for marriage might somehow not be realised: 'How I welcome the coming (soon I hope) distraction of active service – the more dangers the better – death can have no terrors against faith in a future life – and I would far rather not come back than to return a failure ... I shall fight long and hard and refuse to believe that I shall live ... to fail.' Hawker went overseas with No. 6 Squadron in October, his letters making several references to the unpleasantness of being among the bursts of anti-aircraft shellfire. He confessed to being 'apprehensive of Archibald, as we were barely 4,000 [feet] and could only climb slowly'. Hawker described the noise of the burst of anti-aircraft shell as 'a horrid metallic sort of noise rather like a short burst of a powerful Claxton [Klaxon] followed by a metallic bang, leaving a yellow puff from high explosive (the more usual) or white from shrapnel.' (The use of the word Archibald, or more usually Archie, for anti-aircraft fire was drawn from the Music Hall song 'Archibald, certainly not!')

A qualified civilian pilot, D. Corbett Wilson, was unsurprisingly welcomed into the RFC when he volunteered immediately he had returned from Italy where he had been on holiday. He champed at the bit, eager to get into active service but was 'hedged round with Captains and Military ways.'[17] From Farnborough he wrote on 8 September: 'was out twice today, took Dowding, my Captain for a turn', then a few days later: 'Trenchard, our Colonel, tells me that the authorities over there wire for the machines they require and he has to send off what they ask for, and as yet there has been no demand for Morane monoplanes; they've got it into their heads, I fear, that they are very hard to land, whereas with care and practice they are splendid ... I like the machine immensely and think it most practical for war. You get a very fine view out of them; they are fast and good flyers and we have three good ones and they won't send them.' Corbett Wilson's keenness, which had included the personal pressing of his case at the War Office, was rewarded in mid-October when he took a new 80 hp Bleriot to France. An early reconnaissance flight from RFC HQ ended before it began owing to a combination of unfortunate circumstances: 'a fourteen stone observer, all tanks full, a rifle and ammunition and our heavy clothes and the ground was bad and I had to start down wind or rather down side wind while the machine declined to fly, tail went down and she settled down and flopped on one wing.'[17]

This officer's letters in October and November 1914 illustrate well some of the work done and the problems encountered in the early months of flying under active service conditions and they also give in Corbett Wilson's case an indication of a pilot's feelings about his work. The machine he flew to France was soon condemned as dangerous as its unseasoned wood warped on getting damp. The French-built machines, he considered, were better. 'Some of our people go out each day observing for batteries, telling them by means of lights dropped how their shots are going. I haven't done that. I think it sounds a very difficult job. On reconnaissance we go out over a country agreed on beforehand, and I just dodge about as my observer wants me to. He enjoyed his flight today; it was so clear, and he got on to some good things ... It's funny to see shrapnel bursting, sometimes you think they are near the machine when they're probably a long way away really .. I wish you'd send me out a revolver, not too heavy ...' Corbett Wilson found his work 'all very interesting' but helping the artillery range upon a target was often dull and irritating: 'especially when they don't fire in answer to us when we signal.' Climatic conditions were a frustration too: 'We've hardly done anything lately, the weather has been vile.' In windy weather he reported. 'There is a poor old Henri Farman outside, tied to earth by every device of man. I'm not sure it is not better off than in this flapping tent. Of course it [the tent] is of the oldest and rottenest. Most of the machines are out in the open so we must be thankful our Bleriots are in somewhere. The fact is the Bleriots won't stand being out long, they run very quickly to seed.' ... 'Took 50 minutes to do 20 miles coming home and that very low. At three thousand [feet] I was standing still.' Reference to this inability to make any headway at all against strong wind is made in further letters.

On one particular day he had to test-drop two examples of a new bomb – neither exploded. Snow followed upon the gusting winds and when the weather did improve sufficiently to allow flying, a shock absorber perished letting the machine down on one side, necessitating a replacement, the fitting of which left little time for flying before darkness fell. In the air, goloshes over his ordinary boots and then wearing leather trousers kept the cold at bay and he recognised that his comfy billet at St Omer made him lucky indeed in comparison with those in the trenches. Nevertheless, Corbett Wilson linked the airman to the soldier in his acknowledging the impasse in the fighting in France. On 29 November 1914, he wrote: 'I can't help wishing something would happen for or against in the war. Standing looking at each other all the winter will be dreadful ... What do people in England think of things, how long do they give the war?'

Frustration was to give rise to imagination and Corbett Wilson pressed an idea upon Trenchard: 'My plan was to fly to Berlin and try to blow up the Zeppelin sheds there, also to drop pamphlets in Berlin and through Germany, go on and land among the Russians. With this prevailing wind I could have done it, with eight hours petrol which with a squeeze I could have got by fitting an auxiliary tank in the passenger's place. Of course it was a big chance but Trenchard approved it, but the powers that be say No, not till the Spring ... I really believe it could do an immense amount of good in showing the Germans in Germany that they've got to look out, it should make them think a bit.' More realistic (though he did offer plans for a raid on the more reasonable target of Essen) was an observation in another December letter commenting upon the lack of progress in the fighting: 'I must say at present we can't see any end to it.' As for the Germans, he was becoming rather 'bored' with the newspaper blackguarding of them because after all 'they can't help it, poor people, they don't know any better.'

Four twelve-aircraft squadrons originally

provided air reconnaissance for the British Expeditionary Force. Only two of those squadrons operated a single type of machine, the BE2. The total RFC establishment in France including the Aircraft Park or Central Depot was less than 900 men. A squadron was commanded by a major, and each of its flights was under the command of a captain, most of the other flying personnel being officers. Sixty four RFC machines in all were in France for the first weeks of the war but the significant part the RFC played in those weeks is attested in all accounts of this period which perhaps in retrospect, even bearing in mind the spring of 1918, was the only time in the war when the Germans might have won.

The association of the RNAS with armoured cars began in 1914 when the Eastchurch Wing proceeded to France and a number of motor vehicles were adapted by Commander Sampson for this role. Later vehicles were properly designed and armoured and even landed on the Gallipoli Peninsula though not with any good effect. The car shown here is a Lanchester of No. 15 Armoured Car Squadron, RNAS seen prior to embarking for Russia where it was to see action in support of Romania in 1916. Note the different treads on the front tyres. (L.A. Dell, Sergeant)

During the autumn and winter months with RFC HQ firmly established at St Omer, aerial reconnaissance had supported the Allies in their endeavour to outflank and not to be outflanked by the Germans. The City of Ypres was held and the opposing defensive positions were extended right to the North Sea coast at Nieuport. Behind that relatively small but absolutely critical length of the Allied line held by the BEF, the RFC was to teach itself and to be taught the possibilities of, and the restrictions upon, its role in supporting land forces in a grim struggle. In essence, the struggle was so grim and so prolonged because the iron laws of military technology determined the costliness of assault, but the equally inexorable laws consequent upon Germany having seized the strategic initiative by being seated well within France and Belgium dictated that assaults to throw them out had to be mounted again and again and again. Britain, as the junior military partner in the Allied coalition, had to march to the French trumpets.

For the RNAS in the first months of war, a remarkable variety of work was undertaken. While airships, seaplanes and landplanes

conducted East Coast and English Channel patrolling, scouting seaplanes, a flying boat and landplanes sought to secure Scapa Flow, Cross Channel steamers were fitted out as seaplane carriers and the offensive spirit with which the service was imbued found expression in the work of the Eastchurch Squadron under Commander Samson, the first RNAS squadron to be sent abroad. At first, the squadron operated from Ostend at the end of August and in the three days here Samson demonstrated his force's intrepidity with a motor car reconnaissance inland to Bruges and Thourout. Ostend was patently insecure but chance allowed a further spell of dual nature work for the Eastchurch Squadron when the French asked for their support at Dunkirk which had merely been considered as a staging point for squadrons en route to and from England. From Dunkirk, anti-Zeppelin flights were to be conducted by the aircraft and then, using machine-gun-carrying armoured cars, the squadron was also to carry out raids on the open Northern flank of German east-west communications. Several raids of this kind had useful morale-raising results, notably at Cassel and then in a sort of daring, flag-raising visit to Lille, not long before the city was occupied by the Germans.

The Eastchurch Squadron made its base at Morbecque near Hazebrouck and further scuffles with German troops ensued, armoured cars only just escaping capture as they attempted with Royal Marines to help the French hold Douai.

Aerial exploits there were too: the most notable being raids in September and October from Antwerp on the airship sheds at Düsseldorf and Cologne. The raid of 8 October held high drama as it was mounted from a beleaguered Antwerp in the act of surrender but it achieved spectacular success at Düsseldorf with the destruction of a shed and the Zeppelin within it. As if this were not sufficient, the successful pilot of the Sopwith Tabloid, which was seriously damaged by ground fire, had to land about 20 miles short of Antwerp and pedalled his way to the city by borrowed bicycle. Samson's squadron now had

a retreat on its hands comparable to that suffered by the Royal Flying Corps just over a month earlier. The RNAS, however, was to assist the military on its most northerly flank as the front stabilised and a seaplane base established at Dunkirk began the varied work of land and sea reconnaissance. This, with the bombing of various targets like enemy-held railway stations or docks and harbours, or gun emplacements, was to distinguish the work of the RNAS in this area until the end of the war. There is in the papers of Sir Geoffrey Bromet a hand-drawn map showing Norddeich where a German wireless transmission station lay on a coastline shielded by the Friesian Islands. Bromet, newly appointed to HMS *Ark Royal*, a cargo ship being converted at Blyth into service as a seaplane carrier, was detached to a similarly converted vessel, HMS *Engadine*, for a late January projected raid on the W.T. station. Briefing for the raid was conducted by Erskine Childers of *Riddle of the Sands* fame but this particular raid was abandoned, perhaps as Bromet contends, on the grounds of a rumoured German naval presence in the area.[18]

Much further south, from Belfort, French military authorities approved a raid carefully planned by the RNAS on the Zeppelin sheds at Friedrichshafen on Lake Constance. The raid took place on 21 November, three of the four Avro 504 machines getting airborne and reaching the target unscathed, though one of them was brought down by machine-gun fire from the ground. Each machine carried four 20 lb bombs and though such bombs may seem tiny even by 1918 standards let alone those of World War Two, a considerable amount of damage to sheds, a Zeppelin and a gas works was effected. The *Official History*, having printed extracts from one of the pilot's logs, rightly praises the planning of the raid and the groundstaff's careful preparation of the machines. It was a splendid achievement reflecting credit on all concerned and though a seaplane raid on Christmas Day 1914 launched by escorted carriers did not achieve its objective of attacking the Cuxhaven airship sheds, it did useful reconnaissance of the High Seas Fleet Naval Base at Wilhelmshaven and its

This Short Seaplane No. 136 was one of the seven which attempted to bomb the Zeppelin sheds at Cuxhaven on Christmas Day 1914, the observer carried on that occasion being Lt Erskine Childers, author of *The Riddle of the Sands*. Shipped aboard HMS *Ark Royal*, No. 136 was flown in support of the earliest stages of the Dardanelles campaign in 1915 and is shown here at this period being recovered after the undercarriage collapsed when it was taking off. (Air Vice Marshal Sir Geoffrey Bromet)

approaches as well as demonstrating again the determination of the RNAS to take the war to the enemy. Of the seven machines which successfully left the water on take-off, only three, in due course, returned to the mother ship. The crews of three of the missing machines were picked up by a British submarine, and a fourth pilot recovered by a Dutch trawler was not detained in Holland for long.

Geography determined that the German to England threat from the air, launched as it was from advanced bases in occupied territory, would be a good deal more serious than anything the British flying services could manage in bombing Germany and despite the achievements earned in raids launched from the Luxeuil region later in the war on Saarland industrial towns, this imbalance of threat would remain until awesomely redressed from the middle years of World War Two.

2

Home Defence

The Aeroplane as a Counter to Aerial Bombardment

While it does not fall within the remit of this book to describe and evaluate the means by which the Government strove to develop and coordinate means of defence from land and air against the airship and aircraft raids, work which in any case has been magisterially laid out by Cole and Cheeseman,[1] it could in a certain sense be suggested that active aircraft defence of the UK began from RNAS units based in Belgium bombing the sites in German-occupied territory where airships were based. Reference has been made to the bombing of the Zeppelin sheds at Friedrichshafen, but then, from St Pol near Dunkirk, the RNAS, in the person of Flight Sub-Lieutenant Warneford, achieved the first air-to-air success over an airship, *LZ 37*, in June 1915.[2] In the

following August, an official RFC communiqué confirms a reference in the log book of H.A. Buss, the pilot of one of the machines which attempted by bombing to destroy the back-broken airship *LZ 12*, towed through the water to Ostend. '10.8.15 Dunkirk to Ostend. 4 bombs dropped on Zeppelin in harbour at Ostend. Heavily fired upon and machine struck by piece of shell at 9,000 feet.'[3]

Distinction for one of a pair of Morane-Saulnier Parasols of No. 1 Wing, RNAS, at St Pol in 1915, the one on the right (No. 3253) was flown by Flight Sub-Lieutenant Neville but is is better known as the machine in which Flight Sub-Lieutenant R.A.J. Warneford flew on the night of 7 June 1915 when he destroyed the Zeppelin *LZ37* over Ghent, the first such success and one which led to an immediate award of the Victoria Cross. Warneford died in a crash just a few days later, 17 June 1915. (Lord Braybrooke)

Leefe Robinson's Victory. In a sixteen-airship raid, Schutte Lanz *SLII*, a German Army airship of wooden construction, was destroyed in a great conflagration over Cuffley. None of the sixteen-man crew survived. The British pilot's success made him a national hero and he was awarded the Victoria Cross. (per Dr J.L. Tasker)

As far as the UK was concerned, the very commencement of the aerial defence of London has been recorded at a personal level in the well-known story of a young RNAS pilot, E.B. Beauman. Reporting on instruction to the Admiralty on the day after the British declaration of war, he was told by Captain Murray Sueter, Director of the Air Division at the Admiralty, that he was now 'the defence of London from air attack'. Beauman, who had just flown a Caudron, a machine type of which he had no experience, on an unfamiliar route from Eastchurch to Hendon, now, in the awareness that the Caudron had neither armament nor observer, was unsurprisingly at a loss as to how he was to operate offensively against an enemy airship the ceiling of which was far in excess of the Caudron's capabilities. In response to his anxious enquiry as to a method of attack, Sueter replied non-committally: 'I leave that to you'. It is intriguing to speculate whether he expected Beauman to have inferred that duty called for a self-sacrificing ramming of the enemy. Wing Commander Beauman recalled another somewhat ad hoc measure at Hendon and one not notably successful in having anti-airship observation from a captive balloon. The first enemy 'sighting', an ap-

parently flashing light, proved to be the star Vega, a discovery made too late to prevent the take-off and subsequent crash of another determined pilot.[4]

Airship raids over Britain began in late January 1915 with the bombing of Yarmouth and various places in North Norfolk. Though the East Coast air stations were now instructed to be prepared and had aircraft standing by ready to attack the huge silvery shadows, ghostly but for their throbbing engines in the night air, they had little forewarning of the approach of enemy raiders other than by the airship incautiously using wireless. And, in any case, the aircraft could never match the airship's ceiling, already securely achieved. These serious disadvantages were progressively to be tackled and with some success but they remained depressingly dominant. Aircraft in some number took off in attempts to intercept but with infrequent airship sightings, let alone attack possibilities. Responsibility fell in the main on the RNAS coastal aerodromes and even when the machines of the RFC training stations, piloted by more experienced aviators than the pupils of course, were drawn into the fray, no more success was earned.

In the autumn of 1915, the RFC deployed aircraft at selected aerodromes around the perimeter of London in an expansion of the endeavour to defend the capital from the air attacks first launched on the city in August. The first recorded aerial sighting of an enemy airship over the capital has been described by Marshal of the RAF Sir John Slessor, who as a 2nd lieutenant, was one of the pilots appointed for the night defence of London in September 1915. The well-known story, here described to the author by Sir John, recalls that the newly-established aerodrome of Suttons Farm (later named Hornchurch, renowned in the Battle of Britain) had two pilots sharing defensive duties from that aerodrome. The spin of a coin decided who should carry out the first night's duty, Slessor winning the honour and the loser retiring to the local hostelry. In the early hours, a telephone call from the War Office alerted Slessor from his makeshift sleeping arrangements in the hangar. Despite misty conditions, he decided to take-off though he had been specifically instructed not to do so unless he considered the conditions fit for flying.

'I was climbing to my 10,000 feet which one thought was a fabulous height in those days and took a hell of a long time to get there, and suddenly I looked out (and there was practically no black-out in those days) and there lit up by the glare of the lights from London was this enormous thing about, I suppose, 1,000 or 2,000 above me. It looked like a cod's eye view of the Queen Mary. I immediately started to climb to it. We had no guns, we had these ridiculous little bombs we were supposed to drop on top of these damned things and so the thing was, in those days before Buckingham [incendiary] bullets, one had to go above the Zeppelin to have any chance of dealing with it and when I was climbing towards him, I suddenly saw a trail of sparks come out of each of his four engines and he then started to move forward and cocked himself up to an almost unbelievable angle. I had no idea that they climbed like that and he just left me standing. He climbed far faster than the poor old 2c could and that was the last I saw of him!'[5]

The first airship to be destroyed from the air over the United Kingdom was the Schutte-Lanz *SL11*, spectacularly set ablaze on the night of 2/3 September 1916 over Cuffley in Hertfordshire. Lieutenant W. Leefe Robinson, in a BE2c from Suttons Farm, ignored the danger of anti-aircraft fire and attacked the airship from behind and below with incendiary-bullet fire from his Lewis gun. He emptied one drum into the airship. The bullets seemed to have no effect. He changed drums. Before the second had been emptied, a glow appeared at his aiming point. 'In a few seconds the whole rear part was blazing . . . I quickly got out of the way of the falling blazing Zeppelin and being very excited fired off a few red Very's lights and dropped a parachute flare. Having very little oil and petrol left, I returned to Sutton's Farm landing at 2.45 a.m. On landing I found I had shot away the machine-gun wire guard, the rear part of the centre section, and had pierced the rear main spar several times.'[6] Leefe Robinson's exploit was soon to be repeated by 2nd Lieutenants Tempest and F. Sowrey with victories over Potters Bar and Great Burstead near Billericay respectively but there were other successes in combination with anti-aircraft fire. It seems that fifteen British air-to-air victories over airships can be claimed but, as might be expected, this number includes some made for anti-aircraft batteries.[7]

Under Defence of the Realm Acts, blackout conditions were imposed upon London. The effectiveness of these provisions could only be assessed from the air. Professor G.C. Cheshire volunteered to take part in this assessment as a member of the crew of a free-balloon to fly over the capital. The flight took place on 16 November 1916, the departure being from Wandsworth Gas Works, with a Naval lieutenant, an Army captain and Cheshire, newly transferred to the RFC, crewing. Once airborne, they found that the night was so dark that the lights which showed could not be identified to their ground location. Drifting over the countryside, the Naval lieutenant's ambition for a record distance for a night-flight led him to pay scant heed to the fact that the wind was currently from the south-east so that his anticipated land-fall in Scotland was, to say the least, optimistic. The mountains of North Wales, still less the Irish Sea, held little enchantment for the RFC officer. Moonlight and shifting clouds suddenly revealed the River Dee and the City of Chester. Gale force winds were hurrying them towards the estuary of the Dee. The Irish Sea and almost certain drowning beckoned but the Naval officer with quick decision saved two lives but sadly not his own. He pulled the rip-cord which removed a complete panel of the envelope, losing in an instant most of the aerial buoyancy and causing swift descent. The basket hit the sand just less than a hundred yards from the sea at Point of Ayr. Cheshire and Captain Ford were shaken, not seriously hurt but the Naval officer pilot was to die from the spinal injuries he had received.[8]

THE GOTHA RAIDS

It might be anticipated that the experience gained from the British successes coupled with incendiary ammunition and improved aeroplane performance, complemented by the strengthening and greater sophistication of the ground defences would together have rendered the United Kingdom more secure from the aeroplane bombing attacks of 1917–18. Sadly, this is not the case. It was seldom that sufficiently early warning of their approach enabled fighters to intercept them and have the chance of shooting them down. The decline of the airship threat resulted not just from the improvement in Home Defences but from their incapacity to bomb effectively from a height at which they were safe from attack and, by no means least, their vulnerability to adverse weather conditions. The German twin-engined Gotha and multi-engined Giant bombers presented a very different challenge. They were only rarely successfully engaged after interception.

The daylight aeroplane raids of 1917 commenced in May. Gotha bombers hit Folkestone severely and in the following month London was attacked; 162 people were killed and 432 injured as the result of a raid on 13 June. Such was the alarm occasioned by these raids that the War Cabinet requested its special advisor on Air Defence matters, Lieutenant-General J.C. Smuts, to investigate means of improving

Not the most fully alert gun team manning anti-aircraft defences! Officers relax at RNAS Westgate: H.A. Buss, A.B. Gaskell (with telescope) and R.H. Mulock (Major H.A. Buss)

Home Defence. The General's swift response in July 1917 led to the radical reorganisation of Home Defence including increased provision of anti-aircraft batteries and the additional protection provided by fighter squadrons temporarily withdrawn from the Western Front. Quite apart from these measures, the slow German bombers were also at risk on their return to their bases as they could be caught by fighters based at Dunkirk. The long return flight in daylight exposed the bombers to continued attack from defenders whose response was improving all the while. The German answer to this was to abandon daylight raids and open a night-bombing campaign. In late August, Dover was raided and then in September, with more tragic effect, Chatham too before the capital itself was attacked.

On 7 July, an Armstrong Whitworth FK 8 of No. 39 Squadron from Hainault pursued the daylight raiders. The observer, Gerald Stoneham, recorded in his log after the German raid: 'Followed 22 Gothas to London-Southend and out to sea.' From a height of 14,000 feet they had managed to get off 37 rounds at one enemy machine: 'Hit one bus', but the shooting was from too great a range to be effective. It was almost certainly coincidence that precisely one day earlier, the crack No. 56 Squadron, which had been withdrawn from France for service in Kent for the emergency of the Gotha raids, had returned to France. Stoneham wrote little about the raid to his mother but a week later he regaled her with the news that 'I had to be pall-bearer at an RFC funeral on Friday and the victim had been dead about a month – the result being that we nearly all fainted – it was as bad as the trenches and we had to march $2\frac{1}{2}$ miles beside the coffin. Thousands turned out and made the usual demonstration – how the public love funerals.'[9]

From Stow Maries in Sussex – a Home Defence airfield though not one of the new ones established to cope with the night raids on the South East – Flight Commander A.B. Fanstone at the end of January 1918 travelled the short distance by road to see the remains of one Gotha bomber which he, from the air, had seen burning on the ground the previous night.

Home Defence over Essex: This Bristol Fighter of
No. 39 Home Defence Squadron based at North Weald,
piloted by Lt P. Thompson with Lt G.T. Stoneham as
observer is photographed from the air during daytime
but in fact its night markings (no white used) and the
landing flares under each lower wingtip confirm that the
German bombers were now coming over at night and
hence the task of intercepting them fell to squadrons
trained in night-fighting work. (Squadron Leader G.T.
Stoneham)

'There was not a great deal left and it was still
burning – a quite uncanny smell of roast flesh
for the bits of the three Germans were still
there. I got a bit of the goggles off one and one
or two other little odds and ends. Last night
again we were busy – of course we get the best
of fun in these raids – gallery view of the bombs
bursting and so on and our guns flashing on the
ground and the shells bursting in the air from
the safer height of 10,000 feet or more – of
course the worst of this game is that these
Gothas are not like Zeppelins – you can't see a
machine in the air until you are right on it – so
all one can do is to go up and down on our beat
hoping to see one loom up in sight – but unlike
the Zeppelins it is all chance if you get in touch
with one. One of our fellows however last night
encountered one and didn't get the best of it
apparently for his machine was badly shot
about when he got down – another got lost in
the mist and landed some distance away
damaging the machine.'

Salvaging Victory. Probably the victim of anti-aircraft
fire, this Gotha was shot down shortly after crossing the
coast of Kent on the morning of 22 August 1917. Of ten
raiders, three were shot down, this one falling near
Margate at Hengrove golf course. There were no
survivors in the three-man crew. Illustrated here is one
of the engines being hauled clear. It had fallen some
distance from the golf course, attracting the attention of
a mixed crowd – an RNAS working party, an RFC
observer, Army personnel (some on horse-back),
civilians and a policeman. (Major R.E. Nicoll)

Fanstone's strongly accented individuality is
attested in his letters by numerous details, from
his landing on the Thames estuary for duck
shooting to flying with a farmer's ferret on
board. His longest spell in the air (two hours
50 minutes) in a BE12b, at night, still failed to
find him a Gotha but he had 'plenty of fun in
dodging our own shells and searchlights – I was
picked up seven or eight times by searchlights –

Lieutenant A.H. Bird of No. 61 (Home Defence) Squadron with his fitter and rigger at Rochford in October 1917. The aeroplane is a Sopwith Pup and is probably B 735 which he flew for some six months and in which he attacked a Gotha over Essex on 12 August 1917. (A.H. Bird)

29 October 1917. Lt A.H. Bird has just landed following his first solo flight, in a BE2c (2492) with No. 61 Home Defence Squadron at Rochford, Kent. The broad strap hanging over the cockpit is the loosened seat belt. (A.H. Bird)

rather a strange experience to be suddenly blinded with a blaze of light and do a dive or a turn to get out of its way or signal down the "friend" sign. One of our fellows came to grief last night – crashed and burnt to death – but probably his own fault.'[10]

More fortunate was A.H. Bird who was dazzled by the reflection of a searchlight on his windscreen as he was taking off just before midnight on 21 May 1918. His log laconically records the crash: 'Undercarriage and bracing wire broken on taking off and running into flares through searchlights blinding me.' Bird must have been frustrated at coming to grief in such a manner. His careful thoroughness led him always to test his own ammunition for defects such as sunken caps, swollen cases and thick rims and he always filled his own ammunition belts. He designed and had made a

Home Defence of a sort: a new role for the Air Arm. It is impossible to estimate the effect of leaflet dropping to undermine enemy morale but perhaps it could be proved that War Savings in British towns upon which such leaflets as this one were dropped, did show marked increase as a result of the rain of paper or card. (H.R.H. Ward)

SKY
THE
BATTERSEA
WAR SAVINGS WEEK
Jan. 28th to Feb. 4th, 1918
BUY WAR SAVINGS
CERTIFICATES
& WAR BONDS
And so play YOUR part in Civilization's Great Struggle.
Our Gallant Soldiers, Brave Sailors, and Daring Airmen
WILL DO THE REST
BRITISH
NAVAL
AIRSHIP
DROPPED
FROM

The RFC takes part in fund-raising for the war. This Sopwith Camel (B6416) of No. 10 Training Squadron, Shawbury has been adorned with patriotic exhortations as well as an RFC badge and the name *The Straffer* behind the cockpit. The career of this machine as a fund-raiser came to an abrupt end when it nosed over on landing at Ludlow. (A.H. Hemingway)

special safety-belt with a quick-release fastener after he had nearly fallen from the cockpit when looping his machine. The dazzle of that searchlight and the resultant crash did not finish Bird for he and his rigger and fitter so efficiently tuned and prepared his Sopwith Camel for inspection at Stow Maries in August 1918 that the examining officers judged it the best kept and equipped machine on display.[11]

Throughout the winter of 1917 and the spring of 1918, while the country continued to be subject to aeroplane raids and to a lesser extent airship raids, the recommendations on Home Defence made by Lieutenant General Smuts in July and September 1917 were progressively implemented. Home Defence was increasingly effective and in what proved to be the final raid in May 1918, seven Gothas were brought down. The challenge of night-fighting required a top-level response – the deployment of squadrons with active service experience and an expanded training programme. By October 1918, some 16 night-fighting Home Defence squadrons were operational. The response outmatched the challenge but, if the 1915–18 scale of operations retrospectively seems puny by contrast, a kinship is undeniable with the significance of the desperate drama of the 1940 Battle of Britain.

1915–16: The Western Front

Major L.G. Hawker, VC. The Battle of the Somme

The British offensives on the Somme and from the Ypres Salient in the central years of the war, no matter how much they may today be the subject of debate, were the hard school in which the RFC learned its support role. The RFC learned so effectively that to talk of air power being a reality four years after the initial reconnaissances over the BEF's retirement from Mons in August 1914 is a sober statement of fact.

Before the battle of Neuve Chapelle in March 1915, the first systematic utilisation of aerial photography for active service military purposes had been employed. Tactical bombing, almost in its first days of infancy, also received a degree of formalisation. From the photographs taken and maps then drawn, a supposed enemy HQ was located for bombing as well as the rail lines servicing the area behind the German trench system. The system had also been photographed in order to plan the attack.

The *Official History* records some successful observation of the progress of the British infantry on the first day of the battle, 10 March. The weather, however, was bad and, in any case, as a certain Corporal James McCudden, an

St Omer, the main RFC airfield in France, around March 1915. The BE2b in the foreground belonged to No. 4 Squadron as did the Martinsyde S1 scout being wheeled across the field (rear left). The other aircraft is an Avro 504 (unit unknown). The observer for the BE2b (No. 705) during the Battle of Neuve Chapelle was A.J. Capel. (Air Vice Marshal A.J. Capel)

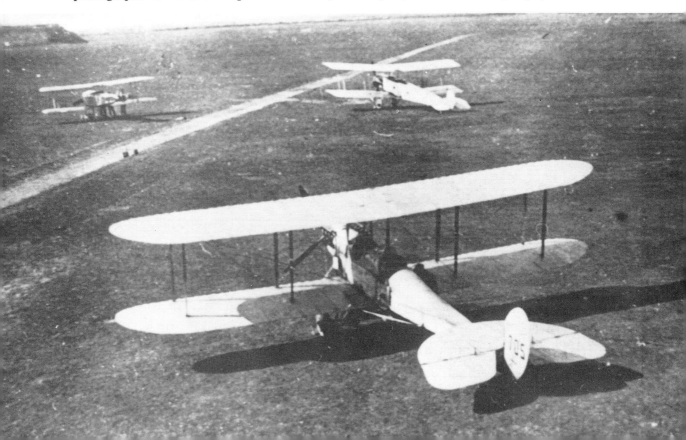

observer/gunner to Lieutenant Corbett Wilson wrote in his memoirs, 'one could not follow what was going on much, as there was so much smoke'.[1] A.J. Capel of No. 4 Squadron, also in support of the offensive, confirms in his log that both cloud and mist affected observation between 10 and 13 March.[2] Nevertheless, aircraft equipped for wireless transmission helped to locate the position of enemy gun batteries. Despite the limitation of the effectiveness of RFC reconnaissance in infantry cooperation, much was being learned and the results were put into effect with striking speed. Photography, map-making and tactical bombing had already been established as essential but, in the continued drive to command Aubers Ridge, recognition strips of white cloth were laid out to mark infantry progress and some wireless messages were transmitted from aircraft to ground reception. Intelligence gained by this means also helped the artillery fire on German batteries and rail-mounted guns which were spotted from the air during the April/May German offensive further north at Ypres. This was also where a pilot of No. 5 Squadron, Captain L.A. Strange, witnessed, again from an aircraft, the deadly yellow gas cloud which heralded the opening of chemical warfare on the Western Front.

As would be expected, only the notable successes left an influential imprint on history as it was being recorded. The log of A.J. Capel an observer at this time with No. 4 Squadron (BE 2), notes what would seem to have been the more usual occurrence: 'Attempt at reconn. in morning, attempt at reconn. in afternoon. Clouds' ... 'Landed to get fill of petrol' ... 'Landed with engine failure. Came back in car. No reconnaissance.' Again and again clouds prevented effective work, then on 21 March 1915, after further engine trouble, and landing at an airfield for repair and being heavily archied over Lille, he was returning to St Omer when: 'On arriving home saw arrow on ground and set out to chase Taube. No luck.' Plugs oiling up and a broken rev-counter afflicted him on the final day of March but, apart from his April Fool joke of dropping a football on Allied positions on the first of the month, he

Bailleul, 1915: No. 4 Squadron's Officers Mess. (Air Vice Marshal O.G.W.G. Lywood)

was increasingly being involved in photographic work. Again there were problems, not merely in the thick-gloved handling of a bulky camera and the changing of plates, a major challenge in itself, but in for example the engine throwing out so much oil that it was sprayed on the camera's filter. Small wonder the evident satisfaction with which he recorded on 26 May that he took eight photographs over the Ypres Salient and: 'They were quite successful and got the right place with every shot.'[3]

In September, the first really large-scale British offensive took place, the battle of Loos, a battle which with cruel reasonableness illustrates that the British High Command had to dance to the tune selected by the Grand Quartier Générale of their numerically far superior coalition partner. The RFC was heavily involved in the necessary preliminary work of photographic reconnaissance, artillery registra-

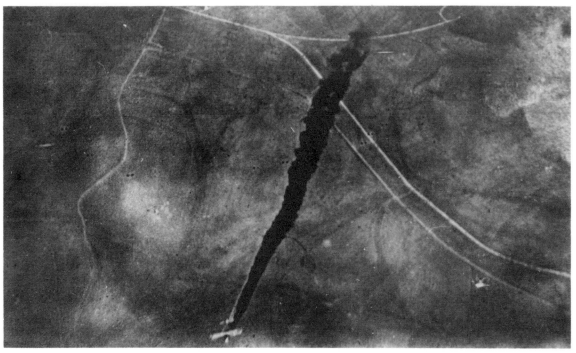

Even if this photograph were to have been faked, as is possible, it may quite properly represent the grim fate likely to be endured by aircrew in a machine well on fire. The aircraft is an Allied pusher emitting a long trail of black smoke as it dives to its doom. The period must be early in the war. (C.E. Townley)

tion and bombing. Then, on 25 September and in the days to follow, the RFC attempted to peer through the swirling veil of smoke, gas, rain and cloud to report the grim evidence of a lack of significant military progress. The means worked out for the hard-pressed infantry to indicate their position to the RFC and for them to display signs which showed the direction from which British further progress was being arrested, were not successful. The white strips for this purpose were either not being put out or not being seen from the air, though brave efforts to make up for this by the use of a signal lamp operated by RFC personnel with the infantry had some success, till the two men concerned were put out of action.[4]

Writing from Paris at the beginning of October and from here escaping censorship, H.V.C. de Crespigny revealed a range of emotion and sensitivity as he criticised the administrative work of the General Staff for the Battle of Loos. 'The battle was the grandest yet the most awful sight I have ever seen and one to be remembered for ever. Complete villages were burnt to the ground and the country made desolate for miles around. One cannot help feeling sorry for the poor country people who are absolutely ruined ... it is not a civilised war but absolute murder of innocent people. Lens and Arras which are truly beautiful cities are now nothing but heaps of ruins.' So much for any wartime or retrospective illusion of protection to the senses being brought by physical removal from the ground level of battle but it is interesting to note by contrast that de Crespigny seems to view with equanimity the depletion by casualty of his own Officers Mess. The loss of two men from his squadron (11), Captain C.C. Darley and Lt R.L. Slade, whose Vickers FB5 had fallen victim to Max Immelmann in his Fokker *Eindekker*, draws from de Crespigny: 'strange to say one looks on it as a matter of course, and in a very short time it is forgotten'.[5]

In fact, British losses in the air in 1915 could not be forgotten; they were serious. The British workhorse machine, the BE2 of pre-

1914 Geoffrey de Havilland design and under mass production in a way not accorded to any other British machine, was being used on all fronts for all types of work. With improvements to its original design and with achievements to its credit, it was nevertheless now being completely outmatched by the new German monoplane, the Fokker E.I with its interrupter-geared forward-firing machine-gun. What became known later as the 'Fokker Scourge' precipitated the development of an effective British response. The design and production of a fighter were essential.

BE2s and other machines undertaking aerial reconnaissance work needed protection, and German reconnaissance had to be prevented. From the winter of 1914/15, it had become the practice for squadrons in France to have one or two single-seater scouts with some form of armament that enabled them to act as fighters, not merely faster reconnaissance aircraft. In terms of new development, the first successful RFC single-seater fighter as such was the DH2 pusher biplane. No. 24 Squadron, equipped with these machines, went out to

France in February 1916 to challenge and, in fact, overcome the Fokker monoplane and the German two-seaters in the struggle for aerial supremacy.

Captain L.G. Hawker was a pioneer of aerial fighting. At first from No. 6 Squadron and later as a major commanding No. 24 Squadron, Hawker, piloting both two-seaters and the single-seater Bristol Scout, had initially experimented with a carbine for armament. Later, to overcome the problem of being unable to fire through the propeller arc, he used an oblique mounting for his Lewis gun and mastered the technique of flying his Bristol Scout so as to give him the angle to fire his gun. It was not just in his own tally of successful combats (nine victories) that his achievement is to be measured nor in his engineering skill in invention, adaptation and improvisation of armament equipment but in his personal leadership which quite evidently inspired his men and raised into reality those words too readily used on some occasions that this man was truly loved by all who served under him. The Squadron History pays eloquent tribute to his 'genius for leadership and passion for efficiency',[6] listing his inventive devices or 'gadgets' as Hawker called them, his rocking fuselage for ground training in aerial machine-gunnery, the ring sight, the aiming-off model for making allowance in aim for the high-speed movement of the target and fur-lined thigh boots for warmth.

In a letter of as early as 6 March 1915, Hawker provides an indication of the determination in the air which was to become so characteristic. 'We got underneath one of the German aeroplanes [an Aviatik] and I fired my revolver, but he didn't seem to mind so I took my observer's rifle and leaving go controls – (the beauty of these machines) fired at him with that. This woke him up and he hastily turned right about and made off down wind for home.'

Entente Cordiale and an exchange of caps! Officers of No. 6 Squadron RFC, and Escadrille MF 33 of the French air service pose at Poperinghe in March/April 1915 in front of a Maurice Farman Shorthorn. (Major L.G. Hawker VC)

This same letter provides an indication of the almost constant disadvantageous factors for the British airman, the prevailing wind from the west. 'It didn't take 10 minutes getting there but over 1½ hours getting back.'[7]

Hawker's letters to Beatrice, the girl he hoped to marry, of course contain much affection for her, but they also reveal much of his own introspection and bouts of depression. Intriguingly in such personal letters, they show a preoccupation with flying matters in concentrated detail. He writes about the BE2c and what he called its 'party trick' of tail sliding (i.e. stalling). 'Any ordinary machine, when you pull the elevator back and point its nose to the sky, ceases to be a flying machine and behaves rather like a bit of paper, till (unless it is inherently unstable) it eventually gets more or less nose down and gathers speed again when the pilot, if sufficiently skilled, again takes control and brings the machine back to its normal flying angle, (this not infrequently happens to a greater or less extent when the pilot loses control in a cloud). With this beast however, as soon as she starts to slip back, the tail seems to stay where it is, while the whole front of the machine falls like a stone (most alarming), till she points more or less nose down and then as she gathers speed again up comes the nose and she resumes her normal flying angle. This is a fairly harmless 'stunt' as it doesn't strain the machine, but I suppose really ought not to be done as it is nothing but a 'stunt' and war is not the time to show off.' The remainder of the letter contains a confession he had not dared tell his mother, that he had done a loop but 'all sorts of funny things fell out, signal lights, cartridges, mud, paper, oil and petrol and I was watching anxiously to see if my passenger would follow.'

During April 1915, Hawker always carried a rifle in the air. Its place in the two-seater was just to the right of his legs, the stock once neatly deflecting a piece of shrapnel which had come through the fabric of the fuselage. On 19 April, he dropped bombs on a Zeppelin shed and his skill in attempting to do the work while using a German kite balloon to shield him from anti-aircraft fire earned him his DSO. In the same month, he recorded the results of ground fire while engaged on two low reconnaissance flights: 'picked up fifty bullet holes thro' my plane ... one chipped the propeller, one a strut, one through my exhaust pipe, one thro' my tail skid and one into my leg. It fell out when I took my sock off and I have sent it home as a souvenir.' He was acquiring a considerable reputation but the high praise he was receiving from officialdom in no way diminished his popularity in the Flight which he commanded. Despite this, his letters to Beatrice's mother show the other side of the hero he was becoming. Her son was a friend of Hawker's. Of his death, Hawker wrote: 'Gordon is still very much in my thoughts and I am just beginning to be able to think of him without agonies of grief – specially so, of course, in my prayers when one naturally contemplates the beyond.'

His rifle, however skilfully handled, had limited use against German aircraft armed with a machine-gun. In his biography of Lanoe, his brother T.M. Hawker quotes from a letter which graphically illustrates Hawker's deter-

In a letter Lanoe Hawker very briefly refers to his achievement on 25 July 1915 in taking up a Bristol Scout fitted with makeshift armament and driving down three enemy aircraft, one in flames, in the course of a single patrol. It was for this feat, unparalleled at the time, that he was to be awarded the Victoria Cross. (Major L.G. Hawker, VC)

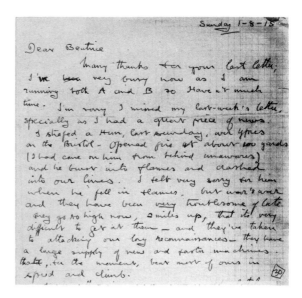

mination in using a rifle even under those circumstances.[8] In June, he had a machine-gun fitted to his Bristol Scout and thrilled to the experience of diving at 120 mph firing it, then, on 1 August, Beatrice is given 'a great piece of news. I strafed a Hun, last Sunday, over Ypres on the Bristol – opened fire at about a hundred yards (I had come upon him from behind unawares) and he burst into flames and crashed into our lines. I felt very sorry for him when he fell in flames but war's war and they have been very troublesome of late.' Hawker was referring to the height the German machines could reach while British reconnaissance flights over the German lines were being attacked by new German machines faster in speed and rate of climb. He was giving some details from his exploit on 25 July of attacking three German aircraft, forcing one down behind German lines and destroying another. The supreme accolade of the award of the Victoria Cross was to be the result of his aerial success on that day, the feat being recorded in the very first RFC communiqué circulated within the Corps. There was a special feature to the investiture: he 'had to trot round twice' in order to receive his two awards of the Distinguished Service Order and the Victoria Cross.[9]

Hawker had a new challenge. He was appointed to command No. 24 Squadron then working up in England and equipped with the

Senior NCOs of No. 24 Squadron, from the left: Sergeant Lampard and Flight Sergeants Little, Wakeling, Allen and Travers. (Major L.G. Hawker VC)

February 1916 in snowy France: An air mechanic of C Flight No. 24 Squadron has his usual task of swinging the propeller of a DH2 with its somewhat unreliable Gnome Monosoupape engine. The squadron, commanded by Major Lanoe Hawker VC has recently arrived in France. It was the first single-seater fighter squadron. The pilot here preparing himself for take-off is Captain A.M. Wilkinson. He shot down at least five aircraft and was awarded the DSO and Bar and was Mentioned in Despatches for his 1916 work with No. 24 Squadron. Note the chocks in place in front of the wheels and the mechanics holding the wings steady until the moment to draw the chocks away. (Major L.G. Hawker VC)

new DH2. He wrote to Beatrice from Hounslow of 'busily fighting a Squadron into form, I think fairly successfully'. In France, early in February 1916, the squadron almost immediately lost two men in flying accidents, something which was keenly felt after an unusual fatality-free four months of training in England. Hawker stressed the need for caution and the reward for the qualities nurtured in training was earned in the outmatching of the feared Fokker monoplane in late April and May. The achievement by the designer, Geoffrey de Havilland, and the men who flew the machine was recognised at no less a level than that of the Commander of the 4th Army, in whose sector No. 24 Squadron operated. Sir Henry Rawlinson reported on 23 May 1916: 'I cannot speak too highly of the work of these young pilots, most of whom have recently come out from England, and the de Havilland machine has unquestionably proved itself superior to the Fokker in speed, manoeuverability, climbing and general fighting efficiency.'[10]

'One of my chickens so terrified one of these terrible monsters [the Fokker monoplane] that he dived straight into the middle of a town' was the correct description Beatrice was given of one DH2 victory where the British pilot had not even had to fire. However, Hawker was greatly distressed by a pilot error made by a well-respected Flight-Commander, Captain Mitchell, an error leading to yet another accident fatality. A deep melancholy temporarily afflicted the Commanding Officer: 'Truly one learns only by sorrow; it is the only education the soul gets, and it requires a terrible grief that shakes the very foundations of one's being to bring the soul into its own.' Leave seems to have cheered him up and perhaps the degree of remoteness brought by command was less in Hawker's case despite his renown because 'my chicks are always very suspicious when I come back off leave, and anxiously enquire if I have "done anything rash" as they put it – bar a newcomer they are all bachelors and confirmed women-haters of 20 years experience or thereabouts and therefore very amusing. As the Colonel truthfully remarked, it's a school I run

Major Lanoe Hawker VC in 1916 as Commanding Officer of No. 24 Squadron in France. (Major L.G. Hawker VC)

and not a Squadron – there is only one older than myself and the majority are not yet of age. They are a splendid lot tho' and I am very fond of them.'

Dates, walnuts and even flowers came from Beatrice. Hawker in his hut with its pink chintz curtains, a hut he shared with a Flight Commander, was anxious to create a special atmosphere for his visitors. He asked Beatrice for twelve pinks, their heads wrapped in dry tissue paper and some wet paper or moss round their stems. (How would this have been viewed by T.O'B. Hubbard, another Squadron Commander, who considered one of his officers a 'cissy' merely for papering the inside of his Nissen hut?) Later, Hawker acquired a puppy of somewhat mixed blood, Bulldog, Great Dane and Pointer.

On the eve of the Battle of the Somme, Hawker brought the brevity of operation orders to an art form. His instructions simply stated: 'Attack everything'.[11] In October, he noted the squadron's victories totalled 55 and that an average of 70 to 80 flying hours had been clocked for each success, but his last letter to Beatrice (22 October 1916) recorded yet again the onset of depression occasioned not least by the fact that death, wounding or necessary rest periods or promotion, left him so few of the old faces in his Squadron Mess. He himself was killed on 23 November 1916 in a prolonged combat with the German ace, Manfred von Richthofen. The full impact of his loss is of course incalculable but few men in command could have exemplified better the qualities of professionalism and humanity which were the very essence of Major L.G. Hawker.

THE SOMME

By whatever yardstick the Battle of the Somme were to be measured – as the inevitable price to be paid for victory two years later or the cruel consequence of unimaginative military leadership, the 'Big Push', launched on 1 July and maintained until mid-November, drew the RFC into a tremendous material expansion of its developing role in support of the Army.

The statistics of the Somme are etched into our consciousness of the fairly recent past indelibly in soldier form. The figures are grim. They do not need the exaggeration they are frequently given but they should be particularised, as is so seldom done, to make specific reference to action in the air.[12]

On 1 July, the Order of Battle was composed of 27 squadrons with 421 machines (another 216 were in aircraft depots) and four kite balloon squadrons with fourteen balloons, a huge increase even over so major a battle as Loos in September of the previous year with twelve squadrons and 161 machines. Eight more aeroplane squadrons and eight more kite balloon squadrons arrived on the Somme at subsequent dates. During the course of the battle, 782 machines were struck off charge of squadrons and of 426 pilots available on 1 July, 308 were killed, wounded or missing. In the balance, 164 enemy aircraft were destroyed with a further 205 driven down damaged, while a total of 17,600 bombs was dropped, the tonnage of 292 not seeming impressive by later standards, but 19,000 photographs were taken, from which 420,000 prints were made and 8,612 targets were registered by air observation.

In comparison with the contribution of the air arm in France in the previous year, let alone with August and September 1914 the figures are simply staggering.

Among the innumerable individual documents which might be taken to represent the potential personal reality of RFC service in the 'Big Push', and quite deliberately eschewing those which record death, there is a brief letter from Captain R.E.A.W. Hughes Chamberlain, one of Hawker's Flight Commanders in No. 24 Squadron, to an Australian who had served with him on the Somme in No. 11 Squadron, H.V.C. de Crespigny, newly appointed as Commanding Officer of a training squadron in the New Forest. Hughes Chamberlain wrote from a St John's Ambulance Brigade hospital at Etaples. Having congratulated 'Creps' on his appointment, Hughes Chamberlain wrote: 'I attacked several Huns and got between cross fire of 2 and got one right thro' the foot. As I was well over their side, it took 20 minutes to get down from 11,000 feet going 90–100 m.p.h. foot spurting blood the whole time. Well I made a good landing and was operated on 2 hours later – I have been in frightful agony ever since and had two more operations and there is only a slender chance in saving my foot. Oh Creps I've seen hell – I have not slept yet.'[13]

As the colossal military build-up in the sleepy Somme villages massed men, guns and munitions in unscarred terrain during the early summer, the British strove to maintain a ceaseless aerial offensive over the German lines. From the time of his appointment to command the RFC in France in August 1915, Colonel H.M. Trenchard had determined on the implementation of such a policy as soon as his

Forced landing imminent: Lt Borton, an observer of No. 12 Squadron at Avesnes, practises aerobatics in the spring of 1916. (Sir Robin Rowell [Borton's pilot!])

resources in men and machines allowed its progressive introduction. To this end, in May 1916 he reorganised the structure of the RFC in France, each of the British Armies being supported by a Flying Corps Brigade. A Brigade was formed of a 'Corps' Wing, the squadrons of which were primarily concerned with reconnaissance, artillery cooperation and contact patrols, and an 'Army' Wing of fighting

Albert Ball, one of the outstanding fighter pilots of the war pictured here as a lieutenant in No. 60 Squadron at Savy in September 1916. He had just passed his twentieth birthday. (Air Chief Marshal Sir Charles Medhurst)

squadrons.[14] Air superiority above the Somme and the Ancre from the spring of 1916 would deny the Germans full knowledge of the preparations for launching the battle and considerably hamper their capacity to interfere with these preparations. Accordingly, the daily programme was for ceaseless offensive patrolling over the German lines, unremitting attacks on all German aircraft and kite balloons, the latter of which could be attacked, though seldom successfully ignited, with the recently developed Le Prieur rockets which were attached to the interplane struts of biplanes and electrically fired by the pilot.

One man whose name is synonymous with success as a fighter pilot in action at this time and in the spring of the following year is Nottingham's hero, Albert Ball. With 44 confirmed victories, a DSO with two Bars, a Military Cross and, to crown all, though sadly as a posthumous award, the Victoria Cross before he reached the age of 21, Ball became the most celebrated RFC pilot of his time. In action, he attacked with seemingly reckless ferocity of purpose, preferring to fly on his own sometimes hell-bent into a formation of hostile aircraft. His trust in God held him free from anxieties about his safety and his example inspired others. Several outstanding pilots like McCudden and Bishop[15] wrote of their admiration for a man whose individualism was carried to unusual lengths. He actually built his own hut at one time to be nearer his machine. The hut, which he kept spotlessly clean and tidy, was where his particular friends dropped in to chat, listen to gramophone records and apparently share his addiction to chocolate. Commencing in two-seaters, Ball graduated to scout machines, the bulk of his victories being earned in Nieuports and SE5s.

Not one whit less essential than the offensive patrolling was the accompanying reconnaissance and photographic work being conducted to assist in the detailed planning of the infantry assault and the artillery programme, prepared from the aerial location and subsequently aerial-assisted registration of the enemy artillery positions. At a time when Army Commanders were denied ground-based information of infantry progress by reason of the spacial, numerical, decibel and destructive scale of the modern battle, the work of the RFC in recording and reporting on the progress of the infantry in the assault, became of transcending importance.

The duties of No. 3 Squadron in photographic reconnaissance and in assisting with the registration of British guns on German targets before the opening of the Somme offensive are detailed in the log of T.L.W. Stallibrass,[16] an observer flying in Morane Parasols. On 1 May, Pozières Mill was registered and eight direct hits scored. On the following day, new trenches north of La Boisselle were noted receiving British shelling, though a rainstorm led to Stallibrass's aircraft getting lost over the trenches and being fired on from the ground by both British and German infantry. Two days later, German ground fire hit their Morane: 'overhead compass broken, wireless drum and also a bullet through the floor between us – returned and strafed back.' New trenches at Mametz Wood were observed but heavy antiaircraft fire here hampered their work. Then, on 5 June, there was photographic work: 'a special job for III Corps to take La Boisselle trenches at 2,000 feet', a job which may have had a relationship to the mine prepared ready to eliminate a section of those trenches. German wiring was commanding their attention too before their assistance was called for in registering the guns on the opening of the bombardment preliminary to the launching of the offensive. New trenches and wire were observed: 'tried new oblique photos', and he noted that British gas shelling appeared ineffectual with 'gas going too high. South of Fricourt the gas was blowing over our own trenches'.

From the air, 1 July seemed 'a very cloudy morning. As we neared the lines an immense cloud of smoke and dust was hanging over La Boisselle – this being the result of the large mine exploded by the British which partly destroyed Hun front line, and formed an enormous crater. Clouds were low, and the earth was greatly hidden by smoke from shells, and shrapnel white smoke drifting – our guns

An RFC observer with an infantry soldier's viewpoint! It was recommended that aircrew maintained contact with artillery or infantry units with which they were cooperating and T.L.W. Stallibrass, an RFC observer who had been a cavalry officer, is doing precisely that as he takes the risk of surveying no-man's-land from a forward position. Stallibrass was an observer with No. 3 Squadron from December 1915 to September 1916. (Captain T.L.W. Stallibrass)

putting up a heavy barrage which lifted well when timed to do so, and kept ahead of our infantry.' With Captain Miles as pilot, the Morane had left the ground at 7.07 and was to patrol the awe-inspiring scene for nearly three hours, landing at 9.58. The infantry attacking from Montauban to La Boisselle and Thiepval 'could be plainly seen crossing no man's land and falling down under heavy machine gun fire. The noise even from the air was intense. Between La Boisselle and Ovillers La Boisselle our troops had apparently omitted to clear the dug-outs and lost heavily when the German came up from below and took the British troops in the rear.' Stallibrass paid tribute to the Commanding Officer of one German battery who kept his guns in action despite very heavy British fire which progressively knocked out all but one of his guns.

On 2 July, in a British attack at 4 p.m. on La Boisselle, led by 'an Officer or NCO who was about 10 yards in front', the troops 'reached the line and could be seen getting through the wire, and hand to hand fighting with the Hun ... the fighting round the crater must have been severe as many dozens of bodies could be seen lying about outside crater on the white chalk, and also inside crater.' Under shrapnel bursts, wounded or killed men could be seen rolling down the steep incline of the inside of the crater.

On 14 July, a day of British infantry success, Stallibrass's log describes the attempted introduction of cavalry into the attack. A machine from his squadron was instrumental in successfully strafing German infantry well-entrenched near High Wood who would otherwise have transformed cavalry incapacity into cavalry casualties. 'All the cavalry then retired.'

Routine and technical problems as well as high drama are recorded in another log book

Officers from No. 3 Squadron (at Lahoussoye) bathe in the Somme in the summer of 1916. (Captain T.L.W. Stallibrass)

entry of active flying service over the opposing trench systems scarring the Ancre, the Somme and their sub-valleys. 2nd Lieutenant J. Duncan of the 3rd Battalion Border Regiment did not qualify as a pilot until 4 July 1916, his log book recording in training a 'complete crash on landing' as late as 6 June. By 11 July, he was in active service with No. 9 Squadron (BE2c) and he lists numerous artillery patrols as being 'too misty for observation'.[17] Over several days he noted that the batteries of French 75 mm guns were not answering his signals, he tore his lower wing on telegraph wires, his engine failed

Grim annotation of a picture of aircrew at rest during the battle of the Somme. Over the whole battle, pilot wastage worked out at a rate of 300 percent and T.L.W. Stallibrass's photograph shows a group of relaxed officers from 'B' Flight No. 3 Squadron. All the men shown here were to become casualties. The two officers on the extreme right and the officer whose legs alone are showing are unidentified but from the left is 2nd Lt M. Lillis, 2nd Lt W.B. Young, 2nd Lt F. Ballard and then, with his back to the camera, 2nd Lt R.D. Vacasour. (Captain T.L.W. Stallibrass)

and he ran into a shell hole on landing, his camera broke, his negatives were weak because of poor light, no ground signals were put out to help him communicate with the battery with which he was working, his exhaust valve rocker-pin broke necessitating a return to the aerodrome and his machine stuck in the mud in attempting to take off.

During a temporary attachment to No. 20 Squadron, BE2c pilot Leslie Horridge wrote to his parents in July that he 'has been up six times in the last three days but have not yet carried out a reconnaissance as after climbing to about 10,000 feet the weather has always turned out unfit so we have come down again. It takes one just about an hour to get to 9,000 feet with a passenger and two Lewis guns and 400 rounds.'[18] Four further days of dud weather followed and Horridge was posted back to his own squadron, No. 7, and from here he attempted to distinguish between being shelled in the air and the same experience at ground level. 'In an aeroplane there is always the feeling that it is a personal matter. They are not firing at a line of trenches but at you.' Safety in aerial combat, Horridge suggested, was largely based on seeing your opponent before he saw you. This was certainly true for Horridge in a BE2c with the observer in the front seat, restricted in both vision and field of fire. 'A Fokker will dive down from behind and perch on your tail if you don't see him. If you see him first you have the advantage as your observer has a clear range of fire over the tail. The thing to do is to keep turning as the Fokker has to point his whole machine at you and he can't turn as quick as you. If you try and get away by diving you will be done in. All fighting is done at close range. It is not much use firing until the range is at the most 200 yards. Personally the only thing I care about is a shot in the petrol tank or a direct hit from an Archie and then the fall is the worst part. Anyway it is all luck and you can't do anything to alter it.'

It was not *all* luck – skill and the performance capability of the opposing machines played a dominant role. Skill, courage and presence of mind, perhaps indeed aided by luck, had in fact saved two men in the sort of

A letter describes bombing: Hugh Chance a No. 27 Squadron Martinsyde Elephant pilot, writes to another pilot of a raid on 6 September 1916 when Aulnoye railway station buildings, facilities and engines were visited and we 'fairly buggered the place up'. The letter goes on to relate that five pilots had been lost in the last week or so and later in the same month Chance's machine suffered engine failure, was forced down and he was captured. (Sir Hugh Chance)

circumstances feared by Horridge but this had been earlier in the year further north over Arras where pilot and observer had faced the imminent likelihood of immolation in an aircraft on fire and with the crew denied for whatever reason, the parachutes which might have secured safety for them. An account by the observer in the stricken machine survives. Lieutenant J.S. Castle the pilot and Air Mechanic E. Coleman, the observer (No. 11 Squadron) in their Vickers FB5 'pusher' (where the crew sit forward of the engine) had had two

Ill-directed Archie, France, 1916. This photograph was taken through the tail booms of a Vickers FB5 'Gunbus' being piloted by Maurice Le Blanc Smith of No. 18 Squadron. (Major M. Le Blanc Smith)

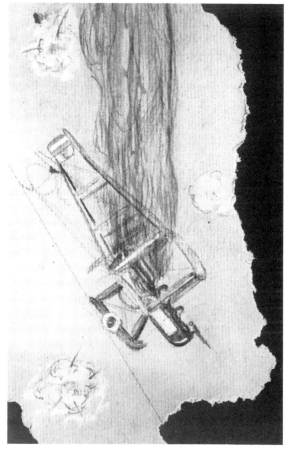

brief combats interfering with their photo reconnaissance when the observer heard 'a tremendous noise under our tail booms and thought an Archie had burst, at the same moment Lieutenant Castle nose-dived straight down. I thought he was diving into a Hun below but being unable to see anything turned round and faced Lieutenant Castle and discovered at once why he had dived; the engine had caught fire and a circle of fire appeared round the propeller. We were falling very fast and the fire continued and everything flammable began to burn. There was no time to strip my gun so I unfastened it and threw it out in one piece ... Then I also flung my camera

On 31 March, 1916, Lieutenant J. Stuart Castle and his observer, Air Mechanic Ernest Coleman, were shot down in a Vickers 'Gunbus' of No. 11 Squadron by enemy aircraft. Their aeroplane caught fire but Castle managed to retain some control and effect a forced landing despite being badly burned. Both airmen were taken prisoner. This illustration was a working sketch by the artist 2nd Lieutenant C.E.B. Bernard (West Yorkshire Regiment), himself a POW. (J.S. Castle)

over the side but as it was so light it passed between the top and bottom planes striking the propellor which it evidently broke as the remainder of the descent was accompanied by terrible engine vibration ... I burnt my maps which was quite easy as it was only necessary to place them near the flame and the cellulose caught fire at once.' Coleman then described that he was preparing for the worst, had his legs over the side and was ready to jump as the fire spread. He looked round to see what Castle was doing and saw him signalling his observer to remain. Coleman could see and guess the pilot's plight: 'the flames were burning his face and the heat and flames were nearly suffocating him, the petrol was running under the nacelle and forming a burning pool at the rudder controls.' Somehow, Lieutenant Castle brought the machine down to a satisfactory landing, the crew losing not a moment in getting out and clear of the burning machine. Castle's flying coat was still aflame and his face and one foot were badly burned. Rudimentary but kindly treatment was immediately given by their captors, the men of a German anti-aircraft battery, before the officer began his imprisonment with a spell at Douai hospital while the mechanic was transported to a camp at Giessen.[19]

No. 11 Squadron during the later stages of the Battle of the Somme was re-equipped with the superior FE2bs. A new pilot, C.L. Roberts, was shot down on his twelfth or thirteenth flight on 17 October.[20] In poor weather on an early morning patrol the British machines were intercepted by three or four flights of Germans. 'Our leader made a left wheel to meet them, I, flying in the outside high right position was left behind. This was the moment the Huns were waiting for. They closed. A flight of five overhauled us quickly, coming in on our right flank, below and behind. I put my nose down as much as I dared to catch up formation. The leader straightened out to bring me into line. We sailed into a cloud. When we came out we had lost formation and three Huns pounced on my tail. Before I could stall sufficiently for my observer to get a deflection sight on them, they got us. My observer was shot through the heart as he stood exposed with his feet on the nacelle sides. He fell back dead. The Hun came in closer and let off a drum of ammunition, spattering the wings and engine all over the place. A half spent bullet hit me with a kick like a mule in the back of the leg above the Achilles tendon. I dared not look. I thought my foot had been blown off.' The involuntary jerk Roberts gave to the rudder bar as he was hit threw his machine out of the line of fire but soon the hostile aircraft were back on his tail again. He

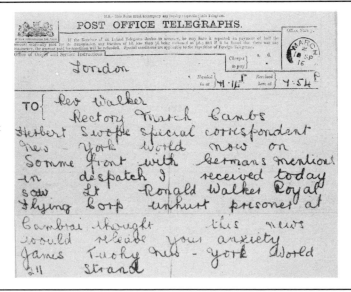

The Rector of March in Cambridge received this telegram which would have relieved him somewhat from the anxieties resulting from the War Office telegram ominously reporting his son as 'missing'. The American War Correspondent Herbert Swope in his position of 'neutrality' successfully used diplomatic channels to get the German authorities to drop a false charge against Lt R.D. Walker and his observer of using incendiary ammunition. (Colonel R.D. Sherbrooke Walker)

himself was slightly wounded in his other leg and the aileron controls were shot away, preventing him from banking. Merciful clouds then enveloped him at least for fleeting moments. He risked catching fire in keeping his engine on though it was firing on not more than five of its twelve cylinders. He attempted to make his limping way westwards but the German machines maintained their attack. 'Occasionally bullets would slash a few more holes in the canvas of the wings and I would hear myself saying "Christ! Jesus! Good God!"' which I realised I had been shouting ever since the affair began.' Losing height, he came under German machine-gun fire from the ground. 'I could see the bullets from machine-guns on either side of me meeting [sic], in an apex a few yards ahead of me as the gunners traversed, following the lines of my flight.' Roberts's machine hit the shell-holed ground of no-man's-land with the pilot somersaulted out, stunned and actually being brought to consciousness by the nearby explosion of a shell. Shelter under the wings of the FE2b proved less than satisfactory so this unhappy haven was exchanged for a dugout, one of a line of such positions in the course of being constructed in a new, advanced front line. He was near Serre where so many men of the Coldstream Guards had fallen just a month earlier and the tank had made its initial appearance upon the battlefield. Awaiting capture, he did what he could to dress his wounds and even began to collect German souvenirs. Despite his fear of entombment, sleep overtook him once he had plucked up courage to descend the steps to the bottom of the dugout but again shellfire wakened him as the roof half-collapsed. He clawed his way out as darkness drew in, returned to his crashed machine to take a spar as a crutch and tried to make his way along a sunken road he judged to be running in towards the British lines. Hobnailed boot marks in the mud encouraged him to believe that a British patrol was out looking for him; dead German and British soldiers lay together, evidence of close fighting. Discarded food tins were German and unfortunately they proved the most reliable clue as to the identity of the

Dancing in Captivity. 2nd Lt C.L. Roberts was shot down and captured on 17 October 1916. He spent the remainder of the war in captivity, his talent for dancing enhancing numerous camp concerts as 'Professor Lumbago'. A fellow prisoner illustrates Roberts's autograph album with this sketch and 'Njinski Roberts', under the name Robert Sielle, became a professional dancer after the war. (C.L. Roberts)

nearest troops. First a sleeping German sentry and then a man wearing not a pill-box cap but an unknown steel helmet were encountered. Roberts was tentatively challenged in French and believed that the concern of the figure that they should not stay – 'Vite! vite! obus!' – betokened well. In fact, the two men made their hurried way to a group of soldiers shading their cigarettes with cupped hands as they waited beside the entrance to a roadside dugout. Descending the dugout, Roberts came face to face with a composed self-possessed German NCO and active service for a young English airman was over.

4

1917: The Western Front

Bloody April. A Fighter Pilot – P.F. Fullard

The Battle of the Somme saw a tremendous expansion in numbers of men and machines committed to an offensive itself on an infinitely larger scale than any mounted hitherto. RFC casualties had risen alarmingly but Trenchard's offensive policy was continued into 1917 even with the loss of material superiority in terms of machines during the autumn of the previous year. His policy, with its special relationship to the new offensive at Arras, was to lead to exceptionally serious losses in March, April and May. Historians of the air war have written of the central month, 'Bloody April', in terms which might link it tragically to 1 July

1916 for the soldier but the seriousness of the losses did not come with cataclysmic suddenness nor did it affect the maintenance of Trenchard's 'spirit of the offensive'.

The statistics of the losses in the air make sobering reading, something like 316 RFC pilots and observers posted as missing or killed in April 1917 and 224 RFC machines destroyed. Certainly, the principal responsibility

France, April 1917: Facing the Music. The weather allows a sing song before lunch. In this group are the following officers of No. 25 Squadron: Wilson, Tingle, Grieg, Moody, Roulstone, Hardy, French and King (Ernest G. Green)

for such losses must be borne by the offensive policy, the ceaseless patrolling of the German lines and rear areas, reconnaissance, photography, artillery registration, bombing, escort duties, offensive patrols being maintained day after day. There was too the special coincidence of the Arras offensive, the inadequate training of some of the new pilots needed so urgently and hence posted too early to active service squadrons, and then of course the superiority of the German fighters, principally the Albatros D.III, the effect of their shrewdly concentrated organisation, aerial tactics and the skill of the German pilots. The latter, under inspiring leadership, fought a strategically defensive battle with a tactically offensive spirit and their action, shared to some degree by the German ground defence, resulted in the rich aerial harvest which Germany reaped in the spring of 1917.

It is noteworthy that numbers of RFC personnel recall the experience of the spring months of 1917 in a matter of fact rather than in a sensational way.[1] Writing home on 1 May of his morning's photo reconnaissance being delayed three times by enemy aircraft attacks and of the 17 replacements needed in three weeks, A.B. Fanstone regarded it as 'our bad luck still continuing . . . things should improve shortly.[2]' Lord Balfour of Inchrye, who served with No. 43 Squadron (Sopwith 1½-Strutters), has recalled that 'every morning we would go out and we'd see these coloured Albatros playing about like puppies in the sky waiting for us in our poor old Sopwiths which we were taking on offensive patrols. Most of our casualties were with fairly new pilots. They couldn't keep in formation. We used to say that if your engine was not giving full power, if for some reason you couldn't keep up, put the nose down and get below us and you'll be comparatively safe because, what we did when the German circus dived on us, we just went round and round in a circle. We were two-seater fighters and all the observers' guns in the circle were concentrated on the diving Germans. We gradually edged the circle (each chasing each other's tail) towards our lines and with any luck we'd get over. Sometimes with casualties,

sometimes without. They were very trying, very hard times. Trenchard came round the Squadron and we thought he was going to tell us how sorry he was for our casualties and what fine chaps we were. Not a bit of it. He said: "You never finished your job, get on and do more than you are doing" and very nearly told us all off. He did it in a very charming way and it was far better for morale than trying to condone the casualties and console you.'

Lord Balfour, having thus described something of what was expected and then the manner in which the need to survive drained the intention and left a compromise, made particular reference to the attempt to capture Vimy Ridge during the Allied offensive. Flying low over the German trenches he was so severely shot up by ground fire that he was forced to crash-land just within the British trench system on the slope to the ridge. After there had been, only the night before, a debate in the Mess as to whether crash-landings should or should not be undertaken strapped in: 'I remember quite well saying to myself, shall I keep my seat belt on or off.' Balfour had earlier been against the consensus to unstrap but he 'flicked open the belt just as we hit. I was thrown right through the struts in front (the sort of place I would have found it hard to crawl through if I'd tried to). I shot straight through onto the ground and of course the engine came back and had I not unstrapped myself and been thrown out I'd have been squashed to bits. My observer did a sort of parabola over the top and hit his head and I'm afraid the poor chap was out for the rest of the war.'[3]

It goes without saying that not all machine losses were as a result of enemy action. An RNAS pilot named Pierce (No. 3 Squadron RNAS) recalled that at Bertangles in early March 1917, convivial parties with Nos 18 and 32 Squadrons RFC had led to the naval pilots being introduced to the game of 'Cardinal Puff' and following one such party 'some DH2's had failed to take-off and two had crashed.'[4]

Some accidents were attributable to technical reasons of faulty manufacture or even

An unknown RNAS pilot displays two individual answers to the intense cold which not infrequently caused frostbite in flying in open unheated cockpits at high altitude. (Lord Braybrooke)

maintenance. Structural failure could occur without the intervention of damage by enemy action and in times of great emergency and constant activity it is not to be wondered at that aircraft did not always get the meticulous servicing required. Pilot fatigue must have been a relevant factor and accidents may well have resulted from a failure to follow the correct procedure preliminary to take-off, such as inspection of the aircraft controls and checking that bombs, machine-guns and ammunition were as required, that the engine was firing properly both when stationary and then after taxying to get into the wind. There had been of course more to check, with camera, photographic plates and map before take-off and then, once airborne, there was the wireless aerial to be reeled out carefully (or it would snap), the transmitter and call signs to be checked and the test-firing of the machine-guns. Even then, quite apart from enemy action there were physiological problems – low temperatures for everyone and for some, like Lieutenant Hyde (No. 54 Squadron), feeling 'dud' above 18,000 feet as his log book clearly relates,[5] evidence, one can presume, of altitude sickness.

The winter of 1916/17 had been very severe. It had been intensely cold and in a list of hints to observers, they were advised to carry a hot baked potato to keep the hands warm, hands which were already protected by silk gloves beneath the flying gauntlets. A heavy leather flying coat and fleece-lined thigh boots helped to offset the sub zero temperatures at high altitudes. Silk socks were recommended to be worn beneath one or two pairs of woollen socks and then even overshoes were suggested when walking to one's machine across wet ground to keep the flying boots dry.[6] Obviously, individual judgement was influenced by the availability of some of these items and by personal preference or need. Sir Victor Groom (No. 20 Squadron) remembers that 'the issue goggles also had a face mask as the eye pieces were surrounded by fur-lined leather. The helmet also included an extension which buttoned across to fit and cover the chin, only the mouth was not covered. Notwithstanding this, the colder altitude was so intense that we covered our faces with whale oil before donning our helmets. It was also fashionable in No. 20 Squadron in 1918 to wear a lady's silk stocking, begged from one's girlfriend, over the head under the helmet with the leg of the stocking round one's neck.'[7] Thawing out after a flight was an agony particularly clearly remembered by Major Le Blanc Smith.[8] The cold winter

must have seemed cruelly prolonged with flurries of snow, heavy cloud and low temperatures even on 9 April, the opening of the Spring Offensive.

Filling in sad detail to the stressful anxiety for families of men being posted as 'missing' at this time, the parents of Hugh Welch, killed on 28 March 1917, had to wait until 1919 for a well-founded account of their son's death, though some information had been gleaned by the interrogation of the German fighter pilot responsible, who was captured soon afterwards. A French priest wrote: 'I plainly saw from my house, as did many villagers the fall of your brave boy's machine. It had been struck in aerial combat by a German aviator who was

Tragic formalities: The next of kin of Ronald Collins in correspondence with the Admiralty. Sub-Lieutenant Collins had lost his life in a take-off accident as a pilot of a Sopwith Triplane in No. 10 Naval Squadron on 28 April 1917 at Furnes. (Papers of R.F. Collins)

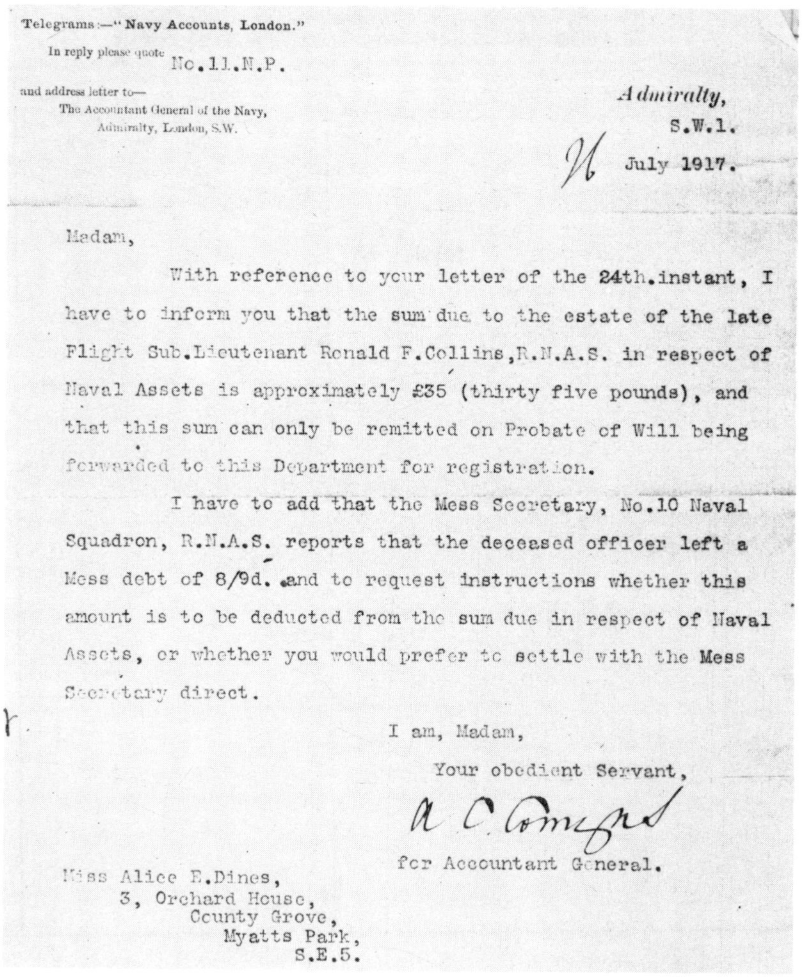

Telegrams:—"Navy Accounts, London."

In reply please quote No. 11.N.P.

and address letter to—
The Accountant General of the Navy,
Admiralty, London, S.W.

Admiralty,
S.W.1.
July 1917.

Madam,

With reference to your letter of the 24th instant, I have to inform you that the sum due to the estate of the late Flight Sub.Lieutenant Ronald F.Collins, R.N.A.S. in respect of Naval Assets is approximately £35 (thirty five pounds), and that this sum can only be remitted on Probate of Will being forwarded to this Department for registration.

I have to add that the Mess Secretary, No.10 Naval Squadron, R.N.A.S. reports that the deceased officer left a Mess debt of 8/9d. and to request instructions whether this amount is to be deducted from the sum due in respect of Naval Assets, or whether you would prefer to settle with the Mess Secretary direct.

I am, Madam,

Your obedient Servant,

for Accountant General.

Miss Alice E.Dines,
3, Orchard House,
County Grove,
Myatts Park,
S.E.5.

German success. The end of a Sopwith Pup which has crashed in occupied territory (probably Belgium). Three RFC and five RNAS squadrons flew the Sopwith Pup and it was particularly popular with its pilots. The one which fell victim here, in the absence of any dating on this captured photograph, was probably destroyed in mid-1917. (G.J. White)

attacking it. I seem yet to see as upon the day of the accident whole pieces of fuselage fluttering in the air just like pieces of paper, and the remainder of the machine together with the body of your regretted son fall to the ground in a few seconds. The village doctor who was just then passing, could but verify the fact of the death of your son on approaching the debris of the machine. Some difficulty was experienced in extricating your son from the position in which he had fallen. The whole [sic] was buried in the ground more than 18 inches deep. But all was done decently by the Germans. The body was taken to an inn nearby and the people of the house prepared a bed and a room to place him in.'[9] The Germans had organised a simple military service, refusing to accept the French request for a more elaborate funeral in case it were used for patriotic demonstrations.

Narrowly escaping that unfortunate pilot's fate, Lieutenant Hyde (No. 54 Squadron, Sopwith Pups), a month later had a very demanding baptism of fire. His log shows that on escort duty on 28 April 1917, his flight was attacked first by six hostile aircraft, a number increasing to at least 12.

The German attack on his machine took him by surprise. He attempted to go into a spin to shake off two Albatros D.IIIs on his tail. His dive took him to 180 mph, bringing with such speed a serious risk of losing the wings. Flustered and indeed frightened, he neglected to switch off the engine to curtail his speed as he hurtled towards the ground. Rectifying his error and again attempting to spin as the enemy aircraft persisted in their attack, he was fortunate in being able to recover and head for home.[10] Also from No. 54 Squadron, Russell Smith, a Canadian and an original member of the squadron, had a remarkable but not unscathed escape in April. Russell Smith had not been taken by surprise by the German aircraft rising to meet him. He had 'dived on the leader in a collision course firing continuously. The two outside planes fanned outwards in climbing turns and the leader soon pushed his nose down and passed under me.' The Sopwith Pup's engine now started to misfire, it was running out of fuel, so Smith closed the throttle and put the machine in a spiral dive. Regaining control, the pilot attempted to glide home as fuel was totally exhausted. The machine in fact came down in no-man's-land but a fair landing was effected. Making quickly for a shell hole, the Canadian, who at some stage in the whole proceedings had suffered a slight head wound, now had to endure German artillery attempts to destroy his machine. He decided to make a rush for the Allied lines encouraged by the cautious showing of a British type steel helmet. When he reached the position, it was entirely appropriate that he should he hauled over the parapet by Newfoundland troops.[11]

The battles of Arras and Vimy co-ordinated with a huge French drive under their new Commander-in-Chief, Robert Nivelle. An offensive which had been planned to achieve decisive success, earned for the British no more than early inconsequential gains without the development of any prospect of a real breakthrough. The compelling reasons for the later re-mounting of a British offensive in 1917 do not concern us here nor does the argument over its continuance under abominable conditions in the autumn and early winter of 1917. Messines and its mines in June and the stages of the 3rd Battle of Ypres from the last day of July to early November gave air units their own distinctive knowledge of the Ypres Salient, a knowledge which was so vital in that no matter what aerial harassment of German troops was undertaken, correctly reported information and photographs were of higher utility. This was something which was then a matter of debate, but with hindsight can be seen as a matter of certainty. The location and strength

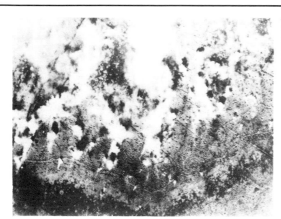

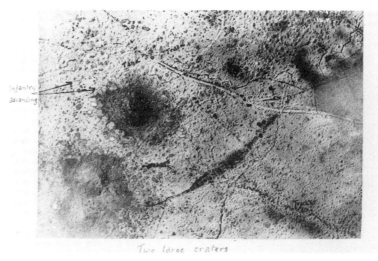

The Battle of Messines 7 June 1917: The Artillery Barrage. A total of 2,266 guns and howitzers were brought into action for this preliminary bombardment. (Captain C.E. Townley)

The Battle of Messines, 11 a.m. 7 June 1917: several of the nineteen huge mine craters can be seen, infantry are noted and tank tracks make their marks as indicated by a contemporary annotation on this photograph probably taken by an RE8 of No. 42 Squadron. (Captain C.E. Townley)

Date and Hour.	Wind Direction and Velocity.	Machine Type and No.	Passenger.	Time.	Height.	Course.	Remarks.
24.5.17 / 5.30		F.E.2D 1936	Self	40m	8500	Aerodrome	Morning on No 2 Scds
24.5.17 / 8.0 p.		A6351	Solo	1h.0m	9000	Aerodrome	
25.5.17 / 9.45a		A1936	Solo	1.45m	8500		
						Total solo for week ending 25.5.17 ——— 6hrs 0	
						Total solo in air ——— 21 hrs 36	
						Total time in air ——— 33 hrs 32.	
						[signature] Major	
						Commanding No. 46 R.S.	
						Royal Flying Corps	
						Proceeded to B.E.F. May 29 1917.	
						Posted to No 20 Squadron June 2 1917	
		FE 2D	Solo				
3.6.17 / 9.20		A ?	Chester	30	2000	Aerodrome	Landing + getting used to aerodrome
/ 12.0		A 6380	A. Chester	50	4500	St. Omer	Practice formation Flying
/ 3.0		6377	A. Chester	1h.10	9000	Ypres – Comines	Line Patrol
4.6.17 / 9.20 a.m.		A6374	A. Lloyd	2.30	10000	Contre Patrol – Becelaere – Gheluvelt	Offensive Patrol
5.6.17 / 1.47 p.m.		A6420	A. Chester	2.45	10000	Theatre Patrol	Patrol
6.6.17 / 7.55 a.m.	E M	A6430	Lt. Kennard	2.36	6000		Line Patrol
7.6.17 / 4.18 p.m.	S M	A6427	Lt. Tennant	1.43	7000	Contre Patrol	Offensive Patrol
7.6.17 3 p.m.		A6403	Pte. Lloyd	?	?	Last seen going down apparently under control in German territory	

of preparation for German counter-attack were top priority information which from September the RFC increasingly provided. That some pilots were well aware of this is made clear in a letter of A.B. Fanstone (No. 12 Squadron, BE2d) written on 29 April 1917. 'Photography alone is very important work during such operations as are going on now. When new maps of trenches etc., have to be made daily – for instance a day or so ago I came down with my 36 plates – an hour later there were excellent prints from them – and our Intelligence Officer was busy telephoning through to Army H.Q. many important points – points that would be modifying tactics etc., perhaps six hours after I took the plate – as one instance a photo showed a German bridge over a river, cut.'[12]

In a hard fought struggle to secure a measure of aerial superiority, the skies saw combat in

'Last seen going down apparently under control': tragedy in classic form. Within one week of joining No. 20 Squadron, B.S. Marshall was sent on patrol six times, witnessing the opening of the Battle of Messines on 7 June 1917. On that same day, he was shot down and killed, his observer, Private C. Lloyd, surviving and being taken prisoner. Note that the final entry in Marshall's log book is written in another hand. (The papers of B.S. Marshall)

greater numbers than hitherto but bad weather conditions continued to exercise a baleful influence on flying. Concerning the elements, it is worth reminding ourselves of the dangers for the British dawn patrol as sudden attack too frequently struck from where it could be least detected, the sun. To beware the 'Hun in the sun' was indeed essential in all hours of daylight. In addition to this there was the difficulty of coaxing a faulty engine or damaged machine against the prevailing Westerly wind on the homeward flight which might also, in the late afternoon, be into the dazzle of the setting sun. Equality or better still, superiority in material and human resources was vital but the disadvantages brought by geography and natural factors were constant.

To revert to the point that serious losses should not be seen retrospectively to have affected the work of a squadron, Sir Archibald James, who had commanded No. 6 Squadron throughout the months of the 3rd Battle of Ypres, has written: 'We had 52 flying casualties, killed, wounded and prisoner. These losses in no way affected the morale of the squadron.'[13]

Lieutenant Cripps of No. 9 Squadron, who had been in action at Aubers Ridge in 1915 with the Welch Regiment, had his first active flying service over the Ypres Salient and in particular the Langemarck area in August 1917. His log book shows the wide range of work upon which all Corps squadrons were engaged: artillery observation, contact patrol, ground strafing, infantry protection, photography and offensive patrol, dropping bombs and also sacks of pamphlets over the German lines. Some indication of aerial opposition is indicated by reference to 'dozens of Huns about'. The diary of the same officer balances these dangerous activities with references to badminton, rugger and soccer, vingt et un, bridge, a concert party (The Diamonds), a trip to St Malo, tea, shampoo and a champagne dinner in Dunkirk. Several German raids on this airfield, Proven, are recorded and the way in which the strain of war was eased by off-duty pursuits is shown on 6 September. 'I saw an F.E. brought down in flames. It was a ghastly sight and we saw the two occupants fall out. I played badminton in the evening.'[14] Sporting activity was vigorously pursued by many, too vigorously by P.F. Fullard the fighter pilot whose record of success was ended by breaking a leg playing football at Bailleul. Enjoying gymnastics and taking a horse over jumps, A.B. Fanstone was dismayed that a posting from No. 12 Squadron to No. 8 might mean his missing the opportunity of playing on No. 12's newly-constructed tennis court. He had put that to right within a week by

A survivor from the airman's great fear. An unknown, badly burned pilot in No. 3 Ward of No. 2 British Red Cross Hospital at Rouen. (Mrs I. Smythe)

flying over to arrange a tennis match between the two squadrons. (The away team, dressed in flannels, arrived by air.) Another pilot, the non-smoking Hugh Walmsley, kept himself fit by running round his airfield at Boisdinghem.

Sport, a time-filler, so useful and so easily arranged, was an element in achieving a corporate identity as well as being enjoyable relaxation or a means of achieving fitness. Number 8 Naval Squadron, commanded by G.R. Bromet and attached to the RFC from the squadron's formation in October 1916, actually started a riding school and built a swimming pool: there was athletics with Bromet himself running the quarter-mile as well as playing soccer for the squadron. 'Naval Eight', as it became known, also had its own concert party in which the Commanding Officer to follow Bromet, Chris Draper, was a leading singer.

With the British in 'Naval Eight' were Australians and Canadians. Bromet remembered them as 'absolutely marvellous but not always easy to handle, though they are really simple people and if they can get confidence in you and think you are working for joint advantage then you get their loyalty and support. Life outside their work is free and easy and you can wink at a lot of things and exactly the same way with your own men. You've got to remember that in those days there were only a handful of regular NCO's and other ranks in my Squadron but they were all people who had been dragooned into the RNAS at Wormwood Scrubbs [a service training establishment beside the prison]. They came straight from all walks of civilian life and were all ages – some of them older than me of course, but there again there was a wonderful spirit of loyalty and happiness in between the pilots and their ground airmen.' Sport in 'Naval Eight' was completely inter-rank and from both social and military aspects the squadron seems to have been fortunate. The Commander of the RFC in the field, Major General H.M. Trenchard, renowned for the loudness of his voice, was ready to accord equal standing to a Naval squadron. 'Boom Trenchard gave us the best of everything, gave us a good airfield, gave us a good squadron alongside us, he made it the duty of his Staff to see we got everything we wanted for our comfort and efficiency and he visited the squadron regularly.'

Particularly remembered by Sir Geoffrey Bromet were two of his Flight Commanders in 1917, Charles D. Booker and Robert Alexander Little, both Australians and both killed in 1918 with Booker having achieved nearly 40 victories and Little with 47 to his credit. Booker was a Flight Commander when he was nineteen and 'simply revelled in air fighting. When he wasn't in the air he was the most quiet self-effacing little man you could possibly meet, absolutely lovely character but he was never happy unless he was in the air so you can imagine the inspiration he was to the Flight which he had. Now Little was a swashbuckling little Australian, a deadly shot, good sportsman in every way. I don't suppose you would class him as an extremely good pilot but he was a frightfully dashing pilot. On the ground he was never still, he had a dog and he used to go out rabbiting or shooting, a wonderful young man but in his way quite different from Booker.' Of the Canadians, Bromet mused: 'wonderful chaps, breath of the wide open spaces, great pilots, likely to destroy a Mess or anything in five minutes at a Guest Night.'[15]

One of the most celebrated of Canadian pilots, W.G. Barker, was remembered in a different context in a personal experience account by a BE2c pilot, his Flight Commander

in No. 15 Squadron, Eardley Davidson. Seeing the danger to British infantry after a trench raid had won them possession of an isolated sector of a German position in the Hulluch area, Barker repeatedly dived low over the Germans who were progressively working their way inwards upon the British with grenades and mortars. The BE2c, with no forward field of fire, was put into a dive in such a way as to allow Barker's observer on three occasions to draw the enemy's attention and to fire upon them. 'How he himself failed to be shot down passes my understanding. He was on routine patrol, had no orders to attack targets on the ground. It was the highest order of bravery.'[16] Barker was in fact to earn a Victoria Cross in 1918.

In an official pamphlet *Fighting in the Air*, issued by the General Staff in March 1917,[17] the over-riding importance of offensive action and of securing surprise was emphasised to pilots. Individual skill in manoeuvre was stressed, too. Pilots were expected to know the fuel capacity of their machine and its speed at all heights. The significance of wind direction and of constantly maintaining a good look-out and of taking advantage where possible of sun, cloud and haze were all spelled out in detail. The performance and armament of enemy machines had to be studied and German tactics evaluated. With regard to general principles, flying in formation had to be perfected and correct fighting tactics followed. 'When surprise is impossible, advantage must be taken of the handiness and manoeuvring power of the scout to prevent the enemy from taking careful aim by approaching him in a zig-zag course, and never in a straight line ... When within about 100 yards the zig-zag course must be abandoned and the moment when the enemy is in the act of shifting his aim, should, if possible, be chosen. He can then be attacked in a straight line with a burst of rapid fire or it may be possible to place oneself below him and fire at him more or less vertically at almost point blank range.' There is advice on swerving to avoid a collision, on machines acting in pairs or threes or in a group. All of these recommendations made sound sense but no study of the

A smiling group of pilots from No. 1 Squadron at Bailleul in July 1917, from the left, Captain P.F. Fullard (Flight Commander 'C' Flight), Lieutenants H.G. Reeves, C. St Lavers, W.W. Rogers, J.B. Mawdsley, H.S. Preston and T.T. Gibbons, the Recording Officer. The officer being sat upon, Lieutenant F.M. MacLaren, was later killed, as was Lieutenant Reeves. (P. Wilson)

A sergeant pilot, G.P. Olley, who like McCudden provides an example of promotion to officer status from 2nd class air mechanic rank. Gordon Olley joined No. 1. Squadron in 1915 as a dispatch rider but through sheer persistence became a gunner on patrols over the lines. He then learned to fly and as a sergeant returned to No. 1 Squadron. A fighter pilot in 1917 under the leadership of P.F. Fullard, his Flight Commander, Olley shot down thirteen enemy aircraft and was awarded the Military Medal. By the end of hostilities, he was a captain on test pilot duties in Norfolk. He was to become a pioneer civilian airline pilot between the wars and claimed to have flown a million miles. (P. Wilson)

1918 and elegant convalescence. Philip Fullard (left) with W. Campbell, also from No. 1 Squadron, who with a score of 26 was second only to Fullard in terms of victories in the squadron. Fullard was still recovering from his football injury and Campbell was also unfit for flying but, as an instructor, was at the School of Aeronautics, Reading. (Air Commodore P.F. Fullard)

This Nieuport Scout Type 27 (No. B 6789) was Fullard's machine from the time he returned to No. 1 Squadron after his eye troubles until his football accident in November. He scored his final fourteen victories in this aircraft. In the cockpit in this photograph is W.W. Rogers who, as successor to Fullard as Flight Commander, carries the distinctive streamer from each lower wing. Rogers was to shoot down a further three aircraft with this scout. (Air Commodore P.F. Fullard)

handbook on its own would make an outstanding fighter pilot.

On 9 May 1917, the RFC lost its most celebrated fighter pilot, Albert Ball. His mantle was picked up by other Nieuport pilots, the Canadian, Billy Bishop and the Irishman, Mick Mannock. The exploits of these three high-scoring pilots were to become well-known, as a result no doubt of their being awarded the Victoria Cross but it is a striking fact that their score in the little French scout was surpassed by the comparatively unknown P.F. Fullard.

In Fullard's relatively short and quite outstanding Great War active service there are exemplified some of the elements which, in combination, first kept a man alive and then alive long enough to be successful as a fighter pilot. These diverse elements would include sound flying experience before active service or before becoming a scout pilot. In all probability, they would include some prior skill in handling motorbikes, cars or horses. Mechanical aptitude was likely to be an attribute. More certainly still, being a good shot and having instantly swift reactions, control under stress, a capacity for absolute concentration and a passion for perfection in the supervision of one's aircraft, engine and armament were characteristics, and then, possessing that indefinable but undeniable extra faculty of aerial awareness of both opportunity and danger, the 'airman's eye'. To add to this in Fullard's case one must pay tribute to his qualities of leadership, qualities which help to account for the low casualty rate on patrols led by him and, of course, for their high rate of success. It might be pointed out too with regard to his shooting that he has said that he liked to get sufficiently close to the enemy machine to see his bullets striking!

In a period of six months, Fullard shot down perhaps as many as 48 enemy aircraft. Remarkably this period included a leave and a sick leave, following, of all things, temporary blindness in the air, and commenced in May 1917, a month during which the RFC lost over 115 machines of which 46 were scouts – only one fewer scout than in April. He was awarded a Military Cross and Bar, and the Distinguished Service Order and it seems that he may have been recommended for the award of the Victoria Cross but the picture is still incomplete.

In the completion of that picture may lie something at the very heart of an enquiry into the nature of the fighter pilot ace, the accented individuality of such an individual. Perfectly capable of self-analysis and with acute reflective observations that shed the self-deprecation which one authority considered hampered his later advance in the Royal Air Force, Air Commodore Fullard has stated quite simply that he was 'a brilliant pilot' – he had after all flown solo after less than three hours' instruction – and 'totally without fear.' He had, however, had a serious public brush with authority in criticising the policy of attacking balloons and it is at least possible that this may have had inhibiting consequences upon the initiation or momentum of the upward progress of any recommendation of a Victoria Cross award.

As a further illuminating pointer to Fullard as a fighter pilot, he has vehemently denied to the author that he was subject to the stress one might almost assume would be a part of the daily life of a scout pilot. It does seem that he may have been a man who was exceptionally skilled and who simply put that skill daily into practice with professional thoroughness and efficiency.

When he arrived at No. 1 Squadron based at Bailleul, he was not quite 20 years of age. He had had a happy and successful schooling in Norwich, at King Edward VI's, a small public school. He had captained the school hockey and soccer 1st XI and played cricket for the school. In 1914, he had actually played centre half in Norwich City's reserve football team. He was well-travelled and was interested in steam engines, motorbikes and flying, the latter of which he had watched at Hendon. The continuation of the war beyond what had generally been anticipated was to influence him away from taking up his Exhibition place at Brasenose College, Oxford. Instead, learning that a Royal Aero Club certificate of flying proficiency was a stepping stone to acceptance into the RFC and that the £100 it would cost to qualify by civil flying training would stretch his widowed mother's resources, he enlisted in London in the Inns of Court Officers' Training Corps. In due course, he was commissioned into the Royal Irish Fusiliers. In 1916, he applied for transfer to the RFC. This application resulted ultimately in an interview during which he was asked questions on sailing and on motorbikes. He was accepted, trained at the School of Aeronautics at Oxford and on satisfactory completion of the course there, undertook flying training first at Netheravon and then at Upavon. He also attended a machine-gun course at Hythe. In December 1916, he received his Wings and was appointed as an Instructor at Upavon. In retrospect, this may have been vital in giving him the opportunity to extend his own competence before it would be tested under active service conditions. This testing came in the last days of April and the beginning of May 1917 when, from Bailleul, he had his first experience of flying the type of aircraft recently allocated to No. 1 Squadron, the Nieuport Scout, a French designed and built single-seat scout with a Lewis gun fixed above the centre section of the upper wing in order that the bullets would clear the propeller. He had written home from Upavon: 'They would not let a dud man go to Scouts' but his diary record of making himself familiar with the Nieuport admits that he found it 'most frightfully heavy handed. Not a bit like a Pup.' Doing stalls, turns and spins, he found the Nieuport unwieldy but practice made taking-off and landing easier.

Examination of his log book shows that his first offensive patrol was on 4 May but, with flying opportunities reduced by poor weather

'Comic Cuts': The internal reports issued by RFC HQ in France to keep personnel informed of the varied work undertaken and achievements earned. Several men celebrated then or later are included in this communiqué of August 1917. (Air Commodore P.F. Fullard)

ROYAL FLYING CORPS COMMUNIQUÉ.—No. 102.

During the period under review (17th to 23rd August inclusive), we have claimed officially 51 E.A. brought down by aeroplane and 45 driven down out of control.

Over 36 tons of bombs have been dropped during this period.

August 17th.—The weather was fine and a great deal of work was done, while the hours flown made a record.

Sixteen reconnaissances and six contact patrols were successfully carried out; seven of the former and four of the contact patrols were by the 5th Brigade.

Our aeroplanes continued to attack troops and various other objects with machine gun fire. No. 34 Squadron fired nearly a thousand rounds at different targets.

Artillery Co-operation.—Artillery with aeroplane observation successfully engaged 126 hostile batteries for destruction; 30 gun-pits were destroyed, 73 damaged, 52 explosions and 14 fires caused.

375 zone calls were sent down and 79 were observed to be answered.

Artillery of the First Army successfully engaged 22 hostile batteries for destruction, destroying five pits and a battery position, damaging 19 gun-pits and causing 17 explosions and three fires. 101 active hostile batteries were reported by zone call and fire observed in 35 cases.

Seventeen hostile batteries were successfully engaged for destruction by artillery of the Second Army; four gun-pits were destroyed, four damaged, and six explosions and four fires caused. The 236th Siege Battery obtained 11 O.K.'s and 13 M.O.K.'s on a hostile battery on which it was ranged by Lieuts. Dowdall and Legg, No. 53 Squadron. With observation by Lieuts. Glaischer and Ferguson, No. 6 Squadron, the 221st Siege Battery entirely destroyed a hostile battery.

Artillery of the Third Army successfully engaged 42 hostile batteries for destruction; 20 gun-pits were damaged and 16 fires caused. Lieuts. Bentley and Kennedy, No. 59 Squadron, ranged the 40th Siege Battery on a hostile battery on which eight direct hits were obtained, three pits being damaged and two explosions caused.

Artillery of the Fourth Army obtained sixty O.K.'s on battery positions. Twenty-three hostile batteries were successfully engaged for destruction: 11 gun-pits were destroyed, 28 damaged, 16 explosions and four fires caused. The 133rd Siege Battery was ranged on to a hostile battery by Lieut. Wills, No. 52 Squadron, and obtained nine O.K.'s and three M.O.K.'s, destroying one pit, damaging one and causing two explosions. This battery, with the same observation, damaged a pit and caused an explosion in another hostile battery position.

Artillery of the Fifth Army obtained 30 direct hits on battery positions and successfully engaged 22 hostile batteries for destruction; 10 gun-pits were destroyed, 10 damaged, seven explosions and three fires caused. 113 zone calls were sent down and 29 were seen to be answered.

With Balloon Observation.—Artillery successfully engaged 14 hostile batteries for destruction and dealt with 27 other targets. Eleven of these batteries were engaged by artillery of the Second Army, which dealt with seven other targets. Five of the shoots were carried out in conjunction with aeroplanes and four fires were caused.

Artillery of the Fourth Army successfully engaged one hostile battery for destruction and dealt with six other targets, and artillery of the Fifth Army also successfully engaged one hostile battery for destruction, neutralized three and dealt with six other targets.

Enemy Aircraft.—On the evening of the 16th, when on a bomb raid, five D.H.4's of No. 25 Squadron were attacked by eight Albatross Scouts, and in the fighting Lieut. Stubbington and 2/A.M. Leach shot down one of the German scouts in flames, while 2nd-Lieuts. Hancock and Algie shot down another out of control.

A D.F.W. was engaged and destroyed by Capt. Mannock, No. 40 Squadron, and an Albatross Scout was driven down out of control by 2nd-Lieut. Gedge and 2/A.M. Blatherwick, No. 42 Squadron.

An offensive patrol of No. 20 Squadron engaged eight Albatross two-seaters near Menin, and one was driven down out of control by Lieut. Luchford and 2nd-Lieut. Tennant. In another engagement between an enemy formation and machines of No. 20 Squadron, one of the enemy aeroplanes was driven down out of control.

Captains Fullard and Hazell, No. 1 Squadron, each drove down a German machine out of control.

2nd-Lieuts. R. Curtis and D. Uniacke, No. 48 Squadron, dived at a two-seater, but lost sight of it and found themselves in the midst of Albatross Scouts, while several more were lower down. One which they attacked crashed in a field and burst into flames and another was driven down damaged, probably out of control.

When on a reconnaissance, Major Joy and Lieut. Leathley, No. 57 Squadron, shot down an Albatross Scout out of control, and Lieuts. Musgrave and Brooke of the same Squadron who were bombing, also shot one down out of control.

On the 17th, a patrol of No. 48 Squadron encountered and fought several formations of E.A. In one big fight 2nd-Lieuts. K. Park and A. Noss saw three E.A. attacking a Camel, so dived at them, but were then immediately attacked by two more from behind. 2nd-Lieut. Noss fired a drum at one and it fell out of control. Two of the German machines dived past the Bristol Fighter, so they followed one down and destroyed it. After this, seven more enemy scouts attacked, but one was hit by the Observer's first burst and turned on its back and fell out of control. The front gun then jambed and the pilot turned west, and one of three Albatross Scouts which continued to attack from behind was shot down completely out of

and even after escorting a bombing raid over Courtrai and Tournai, it is noticeable that he chose to fly again in the evening for an hour of practice. He wrote in his diary for 11 May: 'I had to practise contour chasing to Ypres and back. This means balloon strafing, a damn rotten prospect. Go over trenches at 25 or 50 feet and zoom at balloon and return same way.' Escort duties on 26 May led to aerial combat between Nieuports and Albatros machines with Fullard getting his first victory. 'He stalled into my sights, not seeing me.' Two days later, he was successful again and the diary ends, leaving the log to continue the record of remarkable success.[18]

With No. 1 Squadron closely behind the Ypres Salient, involvement in the RFC support of the Battle of Messines and then later in the 3rd Battle of Ypres brought concentrated German opposition in the air and Fullard thus had a scene in which he could display his truly remarkable talent. He exercised positively pernickety care over his Lewis gun, the ammunition and its drums, allowing no round even with the slightest misshapen configuration to be inserted in a drum. Not unrelated is the professional caution that characterised his own combat flying and his shepherding in close formation of the pilots of his Flight once he had achieved the responsibilities of a Flight Commander on a permanent basis. For a man who eschewed unnecessary risks it is interesting to learn that he lost a whole month of flying through taking a risk at the beginning of September: as a result of testing the handling of his Nieuport in a prolonged spin, the rapid change of air pressure damaged a blood vessel and caused temporary blindness. At the time he thought he had been hit by a bullet. He managed to pull out of a dive at low level until a measure of vision returned, enabling him to land.

In the resumption of his remarkable career in October, Fullard had a further close call with bullets hitting his oil tank and setting alight his Very cartridges and also striking his goggles and penetrating his flying coat. Fullard himself in his personal war account prepared for a Staff College Lecture in 1924 wrote of the marked

AIR HEROES.
British Captain's 42 Huns.
THRILLING STORIES.

London, Monday.—The "Daily Mail" to-day reveals the identity of two of the crack British airmen whose exploits have created so much interest lately.

Bag of Four in One Day.

Captain Philip Fletcher Fullard, D.S.O., M.C., aged 20, is a fair, curly-haired, good-looking boy, clear-eyed and fresh-complexioned, with regular features. He went fresh from school into an officers' training corps. He has flown in France for about six months and during that time has brought down 42 enemy machines and three balloons.

In a single day (says the "Daily Mail") he brought down four German aeroplanes — his record day's "bag." On another occasion he and another airman brought down seven enemy machines before breakfast, Fullard accounting for three of them. Up to the middle of October the squadron to which he belongs had brought down 200 enemy machines, and their number now stands at about 250.

The outstanding feature of Captain Fullard's record is the few casualties his "flight" has suffered. For three months he worked with the same flight of six pilots without a casualty among them, and in that time they brought down more enemy machines than any other flight in France. His achievements are widely known among the flying men at the front, and the French call him "the English ace."

Goggles Shot Away.

He had a narrow escape when fighting a German two-seater, his goggles being shot away from his eyes. The Very lights in his machine caught fire and set the woodwork of the aeroplane alight, but he managed to get his burning machine back to the British lines.

Captain Fullard respects the fighting capacity of the Boche airmen, and he considers they are good in a tight corner.

After emerging scathless from many a tight corner in air fights he broke his leg six weeks ago while playing football at an aerodrome.

Captain Fullard is the son of the late Mr. Thomas Fletcher Fullard, of Hatfield, and Mrs Fullard, who now lives at Rugby. He was educated at Norwich Grammar School, and in 1915 joined the Inns of Court Officers' Training Corps. Passing high in his examination, he was offered a commission in the Royal Irish Fusiliers, but was selected as suitable for flying work, and joined the Royal Flying Corps. He went to Upavon and was given a post as instructor there. In April, 1917, he was sent to the front. He has gained the D.S.O. and the Military Cross with a bar.

Celebrity status. Until 1918, very few airmen were fêted in the British Press apart from VC winners. *The Daily Mail* led in a new approach, making good copy of the deeds of 'air heroes' and of course, such reporting, as had already been realised in France and Germany, was part of the necessary morale boosting drive on the Home Front undertaken by Government and private agencies. The cutting here was from *The Glasgow Times* 7 January 1918, one of many kept by Fullard's proud mother. (Air Commodore P.F. Fullard)

inferiority of the Nieuport against its German fighter opponents, so how can one account for the superb victories by No. 1 Squadron during the months of May to mid-November 1917? The account provides an answer which would not be contested today: 'Our continued success was due to the fact that many of us had worked together for some months, and in addition to having the utmost confidence in each other, each of us knew what the tactics would be in given circumstances. Formation flying, which is of course based largely on confidence and anticipation, was our great forte, our compactness and drill alone often intimidating superior formations to the extent of making them hesitate to attack us until the opportunity was lost.'[19]

Fullard, as has been mentioned, denied in retrospect that he felt stress and apprehension during his period of active service but it is sobering to read his own account written so soon after the war that, while his leg was being set and re-set after his football injury, 'my nerves gave way completely, and I suppose it reacted on my body, so that it was not until September 1918, that I was able to resume Light Duty.'[19] It seems that the strain, not perhaps personally detected – and Fullard has spoken of his lack of imagination – had been accumulating during months of Offensive Patrol work and leadership responsibility.

Certainly one element in the build-up of stress is the actual duration of and the number of occasions he was on operational flying duties. In the very month of his introduction to active service, he flew on 20 of the 31 days and on seven of these he did more than one patrol. Bailleul where he was based was not far behind the Allied lines so there was no appreciable period in a patrol when he could dismiss the possibility of combat.

The record of Fullard's confirmed victories shows that he shot down two enemy aircraft in May, five in June, nine in July, 12 in August including three in one day, 12 in October and finally two in November. No. 1 Squadron's communiqués are naturally bald statements – like No. 4 for July which *inter alia* states simply that on 13 July 1917: 'Capt. Fullard attacked one E.A. [Enemy Aircraft] nose on, firing about thirty shots, E.A. dived vertically. Shortly after he dived on a formation of six, one of which rolled on its back and went down vertically with smoke coming out.' And for 22 July 1917: 'Capt. Fullard attacked two E.A. scouts – he fired a whole drum at the first one, which got into a spin and was still spinning when about 1,000 feet from the ground.' However, behind the official bureaucracy, behind the statistics, there lies irrefutable evidence that the squadron's loss when Fullard was invalided home was immeasurable, as was the loss of Hawker to his squadron though in Hawker's case of course it was more tragic. As his Commanding Officer, Major Barton Adams, wrote to Fullard's mother: 'No. 1 will lose its finest and stout-hearted pilot ... He was the "crack" pilot in France.'[20]

Fullard's injury was sustained three days before the final British offensive of the year, that of Cambrai from 20 November 1917. There, the use of tanks in large numbers and on suitable ground heralded, not an end to the war, but certainly a revolution in the technology of war, the full impact of which would not be felt until 1940. However, German counter-attacks gave a hollow tone to the bells ringing from English parish church towers when early success had led to precipitate rejoicing. From several points of view, it has to be accepted that RFC support of the ground offensive at Cambrai was limited while that of the German air units drawn into an emergency and assisting in rolling back the British infantry from their new gains was quite remarkable. Poor weather for flying restricted the work in the air but in the British case, a lack of detailed planning for the use of aerial observation and misguided emphasis upon tactical support duties rather than artillery registration and reconnaissance reporting were matters of policy which still occasion debate today.[21]

Home Establishment

Training, Research and New 'Manpower'

In a book with the declared scope of this one, it would be expected that within the vast area of Home Establishment service there would have to be a restriction upon the number of topics which could be covered. One topic, Flying Training, selects itself as being of fundamental significance while others have been chosen more subjectively because they represent interestingly important aspects of the necessary support in Britain of the services of the Air Arm overseas. Re-emphasising that consideration is being given to men and not to policies, to personal experience and not to the machine related to that experience, this chapter will concentrate on the training of pilots, observers and non-flying personnel in specialist trades. From this primary concentration there will then be some reference to men involved in research and experimentation before something will be described of the work of those women who responded to the extension of the flying services which enabled them to serve.

FLYING TRAINING

In the first place and especially when one considers the competing claims of the Navy and the Army for voluntary enlistment, one can hardly but be impressed at the rate of expansion of the RFC during 1915, an expansion naturally still further developed in each year of the war. As early as September 1914, a small number of pilots was withdrawn from France and thus provided pilot training instruction by those who had been on active service. The Central Flying School (CFS) at Upavon, even after establishing an annexe at Netheravon in the first weeks of the war, proved unable to cope with the numbers of men awaiting their flying training. Requisitioning the existing civil

aerodromes of Brooklands and Hendon and using the aerodromes vacated by squadrons which had departed for France proved quite insufficient for the expansion of training facilities. The countryside had to be scoured for sites for the newly established reserve squadrons in which men could receive their first instruction before proceeding to CFS at Upavon. From mid-1915, the reserve squadrons found themselves responsible for the provision of advanced as well as preliminary training. The prime mover in encouraging this growth had been Lord Kitchener, Secretary of State for War, a man with a vision for which some carping contemporaries as well as some historians have given him less than due credit.

In contrast to the much improved teaching methods he himself was later to use as an instructor, S.F. Vincent learned to fly at the end of 1915 and the beginning of 1916 under what seemed even at the time to be disadvantageously primitive circumstances. At Brooklands, he was taught on the Maurice Farman which did not have proper dual control. The pupil sat behind the pilot, put his feet on a duplicate set of pedals to control the rudder and 'in order to control the aircraft fore and aft and also laterally the wretched pupil had to stretch forward and put his arms round his instructor's body to put his hands on two handles branching out from a control column which moved up and down for the lateral control and forwards and backwards for fore and aft control. His head was more or less jammed up against his instructor's neck and he was squinting round one side of his large "crash helmet" which was then worn by all.' After complaining of inadequate teaching, Vincent was transferred to another instructor who quickly told him to go solo and so from an

A Maurice Farman clearly showing its 'Longhorns'. The female curiosity (even in the cockpit) was understandable, the machine having had to make a forced landing. The Maurice Farman Longhorn was the RFC basic trainer up to 1917. (Air Vice Marshal H.V.C. de Crespigny)

unaccustomed front position and never having handled the throttle lever before, off he went. One steady trip, a good landing and Vincent's first solo flight ended his dual instruction. The very next morning he qualified for his Aero Club Certificate on the completion of two figures of eight in the air, a landing, repeating the performance and then doing what was called an 'altitude test', that is cutting the engine out at 500 feet and landing on or near a designated mark. The right-hand turns of the figure of eight he had never previously experienced during dual instruction and only an improvised wriggle of an S-turn prevented his overshooting the landing mark. He had, however, satisfied his examiner, got his Civil Licence and was commissioned into the RFC as a 2nd lieutenant, antedated to the date of his reporting at Brooklands. During his training there, Vincent had managed to avoid a feature of Brooklands which to the pupils became

almost as celebrated as the motor racing track inside which the airfield and its ancillary buildings lay – the dreaded sewage farm which also lay within the perimeter of the track. He has recalled the cheers from watchers as one unfortunate landed his Maurice Farman Shorthorn and overturned it on landing on the scarcely suitable surface of a treatment area. He was left hanging by his flying belt just above the uninviting terra less than firma but had to release himself to make his personal landing for fear that petrol and fire might bring him to a still more fateful end.[1]

It may be an apocryphal story but in J.A. Aldridge's typescript recollections[2] of training in May 1917 he records that some of the instructors at Northolt carried a wooden mallet to lay out any pupil who panicked into physical rigidity under instruction. One instructor who had experience of his pupil suddenly becoming 'frozen' in that state of tension when all rational thinking, all understanding and all control over physical movement had gone was Eardley Davidson. After considerable flying experience in France as well as a period instructing in Britain, Davidson was appointed to command a Training Depot Station at Easton near Stamford. Here, in a DH6, his pupil was suddenly clutched by panic. 'His eyes were glazed with fear and while gliding in he tried to land while still thirty feet up. The machine had dual controls but he pulled back the joystick with frenzied force, too great for me to counter. I turned and struck him half insensible with a blow to the face. Falling back he let go of the controls and allowed me to push out of the impending stall.'[3] A crash was averted.

During his own training, Davidson had listened to the explicit instructions that a qualified pilot gave before the man then made a demonstration take-off. 'Always remember you fellows, if your engine begins to fail as you leave an aerodrome you are sure to wish to turn back downwind to return. Don't do it. You will stall and crash, ten to one if you do.' The odds he had forecast proved accurate; his own engine failed, he tried to turn, stalled, crashed

A Martinsyde Elephant scout as shown on the film from a camera gun. Loaded with film (and not bullets!), when the machine-gun trigger was pressed, a photograph was taken and the aim of the gunner could be assessed from the result. (R.D. Best)

Left. Gunnery practice. A student, Lieutenant R.D. Best, aiming a camera gun at a moving target. Note the means by which the gun is given elevation. (R.D. Best)

Right. The bomb-dropping tower at RFC Thetford in Norfolk. The trainee would occupy the nacelle at the top of the tower looking down on a roller map the movement of which simulated the aircraft movement in flight above countryside. How was the trainee's judgement on bomb release assessed? (R.D. Best)

and killed himself providing a sad object lesson unlikely to be forgotten by Davidson and all who witnessed the tragedy.

The sensitive, introspective Davidson upon whom deaths in training preyed, found that it took him almost super human control to compose himself and explain a training accident death to a distressed family without letting slip into speech the recent picture of the fire-blackened 'ghastly contortion that lay ulcerating in [his] imagination'.

Specialist courses were introduced in the second half of 1915 so that, quite apart from flying competence, pilots (and observers) were receiving instruction on the Lewis gun at Hythe and, at Reading, the large numbers of candidates for the RFC had to pass through courses in engines, rigging, map-reading, reconnaissance, signalling and cooperation work with Army units. There was too a wireless school at Brooklands. Early in 1916, a clearly standardised attempt was made to improve the level of expertise being reached by men in the

Cadet Wing attempting to get their 'ticket' to fly. There were requirements for at least 15 hours solo in the air, having completed a cross-country flight of 60 miles with two intermediate landings, and for two landings to have been effected in the dark. Even then, the good intention was that newly qualified officers would continue their training in, for example, bomb dropping, aerial fighting, night flying and formation flying before being sent overseas. The reality infrequently matched this idea. The sheer number of casualties in France and Flanders resulted in men being rushed out to France where the unlearned lessons were demonstrated for them on what became all too regularly an early but final flight, one from which it was tragically too late to take heed. At the close of 1916, the year in which the RNAS Flying Training School for pilots of aeroplanes and non-rigid airships was established at Cranwell, new regulations revised the training requirements not only in the number of hours of solo flying to be completed (now increased to 20), but also in the inclusion of auxiliary tests in gunnery, artillery observation, bomb dropping and photography.

An attempt to raise standards had to be sustained by improved training facilities and, in 1917, new specialist schools were established for example, at Farnborough, for photography and at Turnberry for aerial gunnery. There were also schools for navigation, bomb dropping and for observers. New Cadet Wings were set up to supplement those at Denham and at Hursley Park and at Denham, Bristol, Bath and Cheltenham new Schools of Military Aeronautics were established. Technical training provision for Equipment Officers was something else which received proper expansion.

Flying training was now taking eight months, a candidate starting in a Cadet Wing and progressing to the school of Military Aeronautics, an Elementary Training Squadron, a Higher Training Squadron and finally to a post-graduation course.[4] The RNAS training programme was along similar lines (seaplane stations being involved where appropriate), except that everyone finished up at Cranwell. In the early summer of 1917 an RFC official

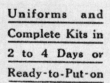
The Fledgling, the magazine of No. 2 Cadet Wing, RFC at Hursley Park. The magazine was first produced in June 1917. There was nothing unusual in an airman, potential or qualified, buying items of personal flying kit from the well-known firm advertising here. (Air Chief Marshal Sir Hugh Saunders)

Airship training flight, from RNAS Cranwell in 1917, the artist, F.W. Verry, himself being an airship pilot. (H.R.H. Ward)

memorandum indicated that it was expected that from just under 6,000 pilots undergoing training about 1,200 would not complete their course satisfactorily and, quite apart from those who had died or had been injured in the attempt, the failure of the remainder could be attributed to sickness or to their unsuitability for flying.

However much the whole programme had been expanded, the unsatisfactory nature of both principle and method in instruction, the high number of casualties during training and the unreadiness of so many of the pilots for active service on completion of their period of instruction attracted the practical attention of Major R. Smith Barry, recently in command of No. 60 Squadron in France and who was now in January 1917 taking up his new post as Commanding Officer of No. 1 Reserve Squadron at Gosport. He introduced a radical change in material and method, changes which he was able to implement through the use of the highly manoeuvrable Avro 504 instead of the antiquated lumbering Farman machines. The Avro 504 was fitted with dual controls so the pupil could fly from the rear seat with his teacher, already proven as a good pilot, instructing from the front cockpit. In due course a tube with a funnel mouth-piece at one end and bifurcated earpieces at the other for the pupil was used to carry the voiced instructions from teacher to student – this became known as the Gosport tube. The instructor, insisted Smith Barry, had too frequently been chosen from those pilots recovering after convalescence or waiting to go overseas or even from those who had not proved themselves useful overseas. Under Smith Barry, No. 1 School of Special Flying was to train good pilots to become good instructors. It may be pointed out, as is stressed by the Official Historian, that Smith Barry was fortunate not merely in having a machine suitable for his new methods but in the fact that the seemingly insoluble problem of spinning, how it occurred and how it could be controlled, had just been solved.[5]

A pilot reporting to Gosport was there for a ten-day period in which he would have six half-hour lessons and unlimited solo flying from the passenger seat instructing an imaginary pupil and becoming familiar, in simulation, with the role of instruction. All sorts of flying manoeuvres were performed during these practice sessions and then a final examination would have to be faced. In the memory of at least one Gosport trained man, A. McL. Mooney, perfection was a constant goal. The Avro 504Ks were all superbly rigged, the engines in tip-top condition and absolute precision was required in all the flying, and Mooney states: 'the Officer's Mess was superb'. Behind almost everything lay the imaginative and practical

handbook (*General Methods of Teaching Scout Pilots*), based on Smith Barry's ideas and which became every would-be instructor's *vade mecum*.[6] Some of the principles enunciated within it reveal the general nature underlying everything, the avoidance of crashes in training, the ability to fly without total reliance upon instruments and deliberately induce problems in the air in order to master them, rather than coming upon them unaware and unprepared in France when other factors were demanding the pilot's attention.

After service in No. 60 Squadron in France, S.F. Vincent joined his old CO, Major Smith Barry, as a Flight Commander at Gosport in the spring of 1917. Vincent has focussed upon an essential element in the system, the pupil being given a reason for everything being done, a proper explanation of what the controls were doing and why. From this fundamental starting point the sort of understanding developed

Distinctively marked Avro 504Ks of 'C' Flight of this South Eastern Area Flying Instructors School when that school was based at Manston and, as one of the Area Commands of the newly formed Royal Air Force, was using the 'Gosport' system. Instructors and mechanics are pictured together. (Air Vice Marshal S.F. Vincent)

The enjoyment of flying clearly expressed on the face of Flight Commander Christopher Draper photographed by his pupil observer Flight Sub-Lieutenant Russell in a Maurice Farman 'Shorthorn' of the RNAS Observers School at Eastchurch. They were flying at 4,000 feet at 9.45 a.m. on 23 June 1917. Air speed may be judged by the fact that the pilot wears his service cap without fear of it being blown off. Christopher Draper later commanded No. 8 Squadron RNAS. A penchant for flying under bridges (the Tay in 1915) was revived in 1954 when Thames bridges in London were similarly treated to prove his unimpaired flying ability. (Sir Frederick Russell)

which was designed to lead to real mastery of the aircraft. As he has related, the experienced pilot arriving at the School of Special Flying may well have felt resentful at the re-thinking which was required at Gosport but very few were not conquered by the sheer logic of the new approach. Smith Barry the visionary, indeed revolutionary, was not to be alone among such men in finding it impossible to secure satisfactory career development within Service conditions. It is tempting to lament this but probably more fruitful simply to extol his achievement.

While Gosport-inspired thinking so much improved flying instruction, the urgent need for yet more pilots, as the Western Front took its toll, put heavy pressure on the Training Squadrons, pressure not eased by the days lost

An instructor, T.L.W. Stallibrass in January 1918 standing beside the standard trainer of the latter half of the war, the Avro 504. He trained men as pilots and others as observers, a total of 47 men in all, some of whom undertook advanced pilot training from him. In 1916, he had been an observer in France and later in 1918 he piloted a DH6 on anti-submarine patrols from Pembrokeshire. (Captain T.L.W. Stallibrass)

A farewell dinner in the Sergeants' Mess. The NCOs at London Colney play host to a departing officer and other invited guests in June 1918. The officer leaving may have been S.F. Vincent (seated at table fourth from the right), the CO of the Special Instructor Flight, the first offspring of the 'Gosport System'. (Air Vice Marshal S.F. Vincent)

A studio photograph of newly commissioned and pilot-qualified, 2nd Lieutenant John Whitworth Jones in his 'maternity' jacket and pristinely clean 'Wings'. (Air Chief Marshal Sir John Whitworth Jones)

— 2 —

Taxying.

The effects of the torque of the engine and of gusts of wind tend to make some machines difficult to manœuvre on the ground. The air speed of the machine being so small, it is necessary to correct any tendency to swing by using the rudder fully and coarsely, at the same time giving it a blast of air from the propeller. The first sign of any tendency to swing should be met in this way, as, if the swing is not anticipated, it is difficult to stop. If the stick be kept fully back the tail-skid is apt to suffer ; if too far forward some machines are liable to go on their nose ; the best way is to hold the stick in its central position.

Taking Off.

In taking off, the object is to get flying speed before leaving the ground. If the stick be kept back the incidence of the planes will be very great, and the moment the air grips the machine she will start climbing, although she may have only just enough forward speed to keep her in the air. The stick should be put fully forward at the first until the tail rises. The planes then have very little incidence and the machine gathers speed rapidly while still on the ground. The stick is then eased back and the climb is started with the certainty of sufficient forward speed. The least tendency to swing while taking off should be anticipated by a full use of the rudder, because until the machine has flying speed the controls are very slow to take effect.

— 3 —

In taking off a cross wind the pilot's object should be to "yank" the machine, tail down, a few inches off the ground, so as to avoid drift straining the under-carriage, and then gather the necessary speed with the wheels a few inches off the ground, instead of actually running along the ground. As soon as the machine has flying speed, let him turn into the wind and climb.

Effect of Controls.

When flying horizontally the elevator controls the fore and aft trim of the machine that is, makes it climb, dive, or fly level ; the rudder controls the lateral direction of the machine, that is, makes it turn or keeps it straight.

When the machine is banked steeply it is now the rudder that controls the fore and aft trim of the machine, that is, makes the machine climb, dive, or fly level ; and the elevator that makes the machine turn or fly straight. At all angles between the horizontal and the vertical, each control has a dual function, in a proportion varying with the amount of bank used. Thus, when the machine is slightly banked, the rudder turns the machine more than it puts the nose down ; when the machine is banked to an angle of 45° the functions of the rudder are equally those of rudder and elevator ; and the functions of the elevator are equally those of elevator and rudder—and so on.

Another simple way of viewing this so-called "Reversion of Controls," is that, for instance,

Pages from a 1918 Flying Instruction booklet. This booklet was produced from notes prepared by Captain E.J.L.W. Gilchrist in September 1917 for the School of Special Flying, Gosport. (T.S. Brooks, Air Mechanic)

Flight Office at No. 212 Training Depot station, Vendôme, France in the autumn of 1918. The wall board was to record the progress of the pupils through the Training Syllabus. (R.D. Best)

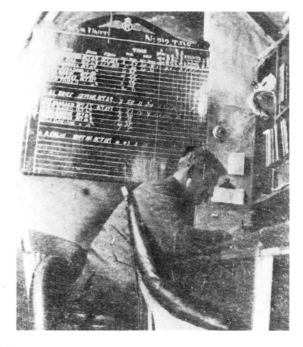

to flying by reason of unsuitable weather in the winter months. Early advantage had been taken by the RFC to train pilots in Egypt, while the RNAS too, with weather conditions in mind, had established a training base in France at Vendôme in the valley of the Loire, the facilities in each case being made available to the sister Service. The successful negotiation, by 1918, of Canadian and US facilities for the RFC training of North American recruits to the British flying services, and the Service

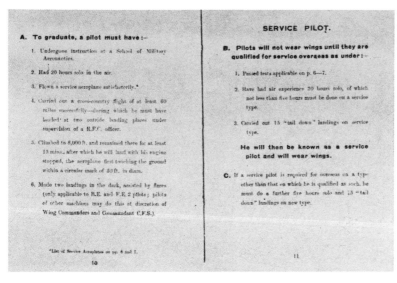

The minimum standards for pilot training as defined in December 1916 are listed in these pages from a Training Transfer card. (R.D. Best)

amalgamation (which brought further rationalisation into the hugely expanded organisation) led to the provision of both general and specialist instruction which was fully capable of sustaining units on active service. Trained pilots were arriving from Canada for example, at a rate of 200 each month in the final year of the war.

An idea of the daily progression of a pupil through his flying training can naturally be gained from his log book. Gerald Court's first flight which he noted as a 'Joy-Ride' was on Boxing Day 1916 and just under a month later he had his first solo flight. He graduated on 22 May 1917. From 'Feeling Controls' in his first week, dual control landings and take-offs in his second and then his 'spirals, figures of 8 and Landing in Circle', he passed through his elementary training at Nos 27 and 28 Reserve Squadrons. In his next stage, at the Central Flying School, Upavon, we can see that he practised 'steep banks', 'turns' and 'glides', 'vertical turns', 'formation flying', 'stalls', 'fighting', 'photography', 'bomb dropping' and Immelmanns.[7] He recorded 'fighting' named, qualified pilots (like Lieutenants T.E. Smith, Brockensha, White, Turnbull, Bayetto and Drew). He had also completed a fortnight at the No. 1 School of Aerial Gunnery at Hythe and was to finish his flying training with No. 56 Training Squadron at London Colney and a final brief return to the Central Flying School before he was sent on active service to No. 60 Squadron at Marie Cappel in October. In logging 75 hours 55 minutes solo flying he had been much more fortunate than many rushed out to the front in the spring of that year: in the most critical weeks pilots had been sent out having completed only seventeen and a half hours. (In 1918 the average number of hours of solo flying in training was 50.)[8]

The initial two weeks at one of the RNAS training schools, Chingford, in 1916 were somewhat depressing for members of 'B' class, one of them recalling that this class merely represented the station at the local church and fulfilled various chores, most memorably, the manhandling of aircraft in and out of the hangars. Ivor Novello was in the class and to his tune for 'Keep the Home Fires Burning' they sang:

Keep poor B class stowing
Though the lorry's going
Tho' the lorry's due to leave the aerodrome
There's another Maurice
Waiting out there for us
We must shove the damned thing in
Or we can't go home

(Incidentally Novello's music proved superior to his flying capacity as he failed the course.)

Higher Training Squadron.

WIRELESS ARTILLERY and SIGNALLING.

1	BUZZING	Eight words per minute (five letters to a word). Sending and receiving. Test to be of three minutes duration.	*[signature]* Major. O.C. "45T." Sqdn.
2	ARTILLERY CODE	Written examination of six questions. "Passed" = 80% correct.	*Nor done* Major. O.C. "No 46 T.S." Sqdn.
3	ARTILLERY PICTURE TARGET	To range three targets correctly, sending their map co-ordinates and using Artillery Code and miniature ground signals without error.	*Nor done* Major. O.C. "No 46 T.S." Sqdn.
4	PANNEAU SIGNALLING	Reading Panneau accurately from the air at rate of four words per minute.	*Nor done* Major. O.C. "No 46 T.S." Sqdn.
5	SENDING ON SILENCED KEY	Clearly readable Tape Record, produced at rate of eight words per minute.	*[signature]* Major. 15.11.17 O.C. "45T." Sqdn.
6	ARTILLERY PUFF TARGET	One series of 10 Puffs to be ranged correctly. Map co-ordinates of target to be sent and Artillery Code and ground signals correctly used.	*Nor done* Major. O.C. "No 46 T.S." Sqdn.
7	GROUND SIGNALS	To send from the air correctly the meaning of 10 out of 12 Artillery Code signals placed on the ground.	*Nor done* Major. O.C. "No 46 T.S." Sqdn.

Higher Training Squadron.
PHOTOGRAPHY.

8	PHOTO-GRAPHY	Take six successful photographs of given pin points	Certified Passed. 11.10.17 *[signature]* Major. O.C. "46." Sqdn.

BOMB DROPPING.

9	BOMB DROPPING	Three flights over Camera Obscura or Bachelor Mirror Limit of error at 2000 ft. 30 yds. range, 50 yds. line.	19.10.17 *[signature]* Major. O.C. "46 T." Sqdn.

GROUND GUNNERY.

	Tests	Date passed	Marks	Signature of Instructor
LEWIS	4	7-8-17	80	
	6	10-8-17	85	*[signature] 23rd Wing.*
	7	22-8-17	80	
	8	9-8-17	85	
VICKERS'	D	14-8-17	85	
	E	14-8-17	85	*[signature] 23rd Wing.*
	F	31-8-17	80	
	G	10-8-17	85	

		Tests	Date Passed	Marks	Signature of Instructor
AERIAL GUNNERY TURNBERRY	LEWIS	9			
		10			
	VICKERS	H			
		J			

GUNNERY IN AIR. With Instructor, hrs. mins.

A Trainee's progress through the various stages of his flying instruction was recorded in his Training Transfer card which accompanied him to all units during this period. Typical entries are shown here in the card of Lieutenant R.D. Best. (R.D. Best)

Sir Austin Bradford Hill, who had these memories of B class, found that the winter weather woefully cut short their flying hours once they did get their opportunity to fly. 'In some weeks instruction was limited to a few minutes, in some there was none at all – and this might continue for two or three weeks so that all the rhythm of learning was lost.' Later at Cranwell: 'one took an examination in musketry, theory of flight and morse code (often aided

Practice and its dangers: the School of Aerial Gunnery, Turnberry in August 1917. The letter writer draws attention to the fact that firing at an aerial target required care in avoiding the aeroplane doing the towing! The writer E.A. Whitehead, managed to hit the targets but sadly was killed within three weeks of his arrival in France to serve with No. 24 Squadron (SE5a) in February 1918. (E.A. Whitehead)

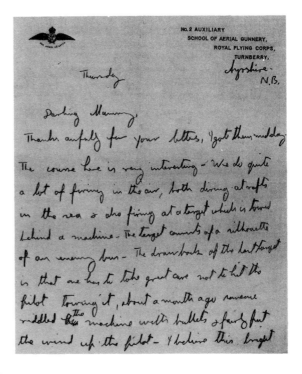

considerably by the petty officer in charge and more than a little petty cheating). We also learned the make-up and action of the internal combustion engine but I cannot recall that we ever practised servicing or looking at it.'[9]

If such detail were not to sound the best advertisement for RNAS training then former RFC Cadet Officer at Farnborough, Sir Charles Illingworth, was not greatly impressed by his experience, 'cold and wet in leaking canvas tents, attending parades, drills, physical jerks, kit inspections, cookhouse fatigues and lectures from Boer War Veterans on the need to avoid venereal disease'. Oxford proved little better in that, after more squad drill or parades in the morning, 'in the afternoon we attended at the classrooms in South Parks Road where wound-disabled subalterns tried with little success to acquaint us with the elements of field tactics and military law, and superannuated aircraftmen instructed us by rote in the science of aeronautics and the mysteries of the internal combustion engine, purveying information which had been familiar to me since the age of twelve.' The inadequacy of the flying training too, in the memory of this former pupil whose own medical studies had been interrupted by the war, seemed an affront. 'Accidents in training were everyday occurrences and every training centre had its funeral fund, deducted from the weekly mess bills. I shudder to think of the wastage of young lives from carelessness or neglect.' Developing this subject and denying that the crashes induced fear among the pupils, Sir Charles makes an interesting point. 'I would complacently take into the air a fragile contraption of lath and piano wire, while the thought of a reprimand on parade or a laugh at my expense in the mess would cause me acute distress.'[10]

That no exaggeration was being made with regard to the numbers of crash fatalities at training establishments is endorsed in a 1916 letter from O.B.W. Wills from Netheravon. 'I am feeling rotten just now as I've just seen the sixth fatal accident in three days ... so we've had two more killed and one terribly burnt today. I rushed up with several more to extricate the men from the ruined aeroplane, but we

A sports meeting at RFC Yatesbury in August 1917. First prize in this greasy pole pillow fighting brought 10/-, 2nd prize 5/-. (F. Brook)

could only get one out and the other was burnt stiff and black in a kneeling attitude, trying to get out.'[11]

One former cadet, J.T.P. Jeyes, has written of watching four successive crashes of new RE 8s at Scampton before he was invited to come forward, not for a dual instruction flight but to go solo. 'Of course I said I would have a try if they thought it was a wise plan ... It had been an expensive morning so far, in both men and machines. Perhaps the debit incurred weighed heavily in their minds. I had certainly not had much flying experience and was not

A casualty in training. Lieutenant Sherah of No. 10 Training Squadron, Lilbourne, was killed when his Sopwith Camel crashed in the spring of 1918. (A.H. Hemingway)

The Fear of Fire: a training accident at Yatesbury in the latter half of 1917. While the fate of the crew of this FE2b (A 873) is unknown, that of the aeroplane itself is all too clear despite the efforts of the mechanics. A fully-laden FE2b carried 33 gallons of petrol! (Air Vice Marshal H.G. White)

outstanding as a pilot.'[12] In the event, neither Jeyes nor the RE8 was put to the test that day.

To balance RNAS and RFC training accounts, R.M. Morris has written of a week at Lee on Solent (RNAS) when six of the FBA flying boats were crashed in flying training by the probationary flight sub-lieutenants or 'Quirks' as they were known.[13] Incidentally, such details explain without further comment why the embryo pilots as 'enemies of the state' were known as 'Huns'. Of course there were Quirks in plenty whose flying did not take machines permanently 'off establishment' – Garth Trace was one. He wrote to a girl cousin that he had 'finished with that goddam Maurice Farman, you know the awful looking abortions one used to see at Hendon and am a qualified pilot on them with 12 hours flying to book', but earlier in the same month, March 1917, he had written from Sleaford: 'We had a good day on the 1st March, 11 crashes, one poor devil went west during his 13th loop, we bedded him out today. It rather put people off doing stunts on the next day, but they were all hard at it again on Saturday.'[14]

The RNAS Observers course at Eastchurch, Isle of Sheppey, perhaps not least because all the piloting was done by experienced men, has earned a warm endorsement in the memoirs of A.J. Price. Reconnaissance, sketching, photography, wireless communication with base (all in code and in Morse), Aldis lamp signalling, aerial gunnery, using a camera gun, firing at small balloons and then bomb dropping were on the practical side of the course but there were lectures on some of these subjects, on naval procedures, on visual recognition of British and German warships and on Navy flag codes.[15]

Because it may stand for the procedural ideal, variants upon which would be followed by so many pupils in the 'accustomed emergency' of a forced landing, this section on flying instruction will be concluded by some lecture notes on the subject. 'Choose a good field

whose longest dimension is in the direction of the wind. After landing send a written message to the nearest Military establishment for a guard. Having posted the guard go to the nearest telephone and phone squadron commander giving name, number and type of machine, cause of landing, whether machine were damaged on landing, number of men and

Salisbury Plain upside down: O.B.W. Wills conveys something of the view and sensation of looping the loop in this sketch accompanying a letter home. He was learning to fly at Netheravon and, as can be seen, used official notepaper for his sketch. (O.B.W. Wills)

A delegation from the Imperial Japanese Navy to No. 4 Fighter School, Freiston, Lincolnshire. The Anglo-Japanese Alliance still holding good: 1. Captain Mellersh, 2. Surgeon Wear, 3. Captain Scott, 4. Lt Com. Ohyeka, 5. Captain Broxbourne Smith, 6. Equip. Lt Com. Kitajinna, 7. Lt Winfield, 8. Prof. Sihara, 9. Captain Findlay, 10. Capt. Hegarty, 11. Lt J.C. Andrews, 12. Major Wilson, 13. Lt Com. Hono, 14. Captain E.D.G. Galley, 15. Rear Admiral Keyoshima, 16. Major H.S. Kerby, 17. Lt Com. Heyeshi and 18. Major Chambers (Squadron Leader J.C. Andrews)

Russian cadet pilots under training at No. 47 Squadron, Waddington, Lincolnshire. (Air Chief Marshal Sir John Whitworth Jones)

material required, exact spot of landing, best route to the spot and position of the nearest aerodrome, whether private property were damaged.[16/17] Quite often pupils would have cause to remember these notes; carrying them out would be another matter!

It will be readily appreciated that a great deal of instruction would be required in the further theoretical and practical education of tradesmen recruits to the air Services. Some of the distinctly separate trades like that of electrician have been mentioned but many different requirements had to be fulfilled: carpenters, pattern makers, sail makers, acetylene workers, sheet metal workers, blacksmiths and more – even shorthand typists. Recruits signed on for four years plus four years in the reserve or for 'hostilities only'. It has been suggested by Fred Adkin in his book *From the Ground Up* that one priority of training for those in the ranks of both air Services was to produce men who were self-reliant and adaptable, who could work efficiently on their own without supervision.[18] This seems a balanced presumption. Certainly the very nature of the work would demand a fair degree of independence, matched by reliability. There is an anecdote in the recall of Sir John Dean which nicely illustrates the problem when such independence was not matched by reliability. Several aircraft were losing their

wheels on take-off at a station which had received American mechanics on training. After some accidents the source of the trouble was fully revealed when Dean requested that the American who had serviced the machine which was to be test flown one morning should accompany him in the flight. He had looked somewhat sickly and had asked if he could re-check the machine. Dean had said no and the mechanic had then pointed to the wheels and

An all too familiar scene at the RAF Training aerodrome at Yatesbury in 1918. The aeroplanes involved are an RE8 which would appear to have landed on top of an Avro 504 which has definitely come off second best. Note that all the figures shown in the picture are American. The RE8 pilot survived to become an Air Chief Marshal [in fact the donor of the photograph.] (Air Chief Marshal Sir John Whitworth Jones)

confessed that no washers were in their proper position behind the split pins.[19]

Farnborough, where the initial RFC training was provided, required some adjustments from those who arrived from comfortable homes. Regulation issue items like a knife, fork, spoon, tin plate and towel were thrown at the recruit after his long wait in a queue, a blanket and a bare barrack floor were his sleeping arrangements, drills and bawled insults filled a good deal of his day. R.S. Smart is in an 'uncomfortable' majority as he recalled that the legitimate arrival on earth of one and all recruits was from the start denied by the ex Guards NCO who introduced them to the niceties of drill.[20] One well-educated 2nd Class Air Mechanic had recognised that the drill and discipline was 'to smarten ourselves up and break our civilian spirits.'[21]

From the raucous roasting of the drill instructors and from physical training too, fitters, riggers and other tradesmen had to pass progressively through a training syllabus during which few relevant theoretical or practical considerations escaped attention. Men who on enlistment or during the period of initial training were able to show that they already possessed skill and experience in their trade might quickly become instructors or be posted directly overseas but the proof of trade competence, even for acceptance onto a course, was not always scientifically objective – a half-crown or five shillings in the hand could work wonders. In any case, to be posted swiftly overseas and so miss the training course would mean that nothing had been learned about Service procedure before departure and such a deficiency could appear glaringly embarrassing in a man whose mechanical knowledge of engines and their maintenance was absolutely impeccable.

The verdict on a lathe test, a sewing test or a filing and fitting test would only be as well-judged as the competence in judgement of the man assessing the candidates allowed. For those whose average competence (or persuasive purse) led to their acceptance on a course and who then tackled the eight-weeks training, they unquestionably increased their utility in a Service entirely dependent upon the technical

The Regent Street Polytechnic in London provided specialised technical training for many RFC Air Mechanics and Ground Tradesmen. Here, potential wireless operators are being introduced to the mystique of electricity. (D.W. Blackshaw)

competence of its support staff on the ground. Such training was for many undertaken at the new factory building in Reading, commandeered by the War Office and diverted from its original purpose of jam production. Technical training facilities were steadily expanded from their early bases at Farnborough, Reading and the Regent Street Polytechnic in London, to their provision from educational establishments in many towns. For some time, the courses were coordinated from The School of Technical Training at Reading and the Regent Street Polytechnic, but for the RFC from the autumn of 1917 Halton Park was to be at the centre of the web of Technical Training provision. For the RNAS, Eastchurch, the Crystal Palace and Cranwell fulfilled a similar role in extending training facilities of a specialised nature and in Cranwell's case, of a general nature too.

The strictness of training did not slacken as the months of war went by. At Cranwell (even in 1918) the huts were inspected at 7 a.m. and windows had to be spotless as did all walls, tables, beds, lockers, floors, showers and wash basins. Each day men were detailed to clean the classrooms at the end of instruction, likewise the Mess tables which had to be scrubbed after meals, the floor then washed and polished and clean cutlery set out. Frank Thorp, has recall of the Duke of York, as Duty Officer, here failing to find dust on his fingers as he ran it along the underledge of a long table and then of the Duke's sad affliction of a stammer rendering him on one occasion quite unable to enunciate 'granted' in response to a reasonable request. It is pleasant to read of Thorp's understanding sympathy with the Duke even though it was his request that had been turned down. The Prince was 'so obviously a good natured person.'[22]

At Cranwell, Thorp, who was training as a wireless operator for anti-U-boat patrolling, passed his swimming test at 6 a.m. in an unheated pool with thick snow outside. In stiff duck trousers and jacket he swam his two lengths and with his satisfactory progress on the course, plus a special test of Wireless Communication, he was passed out directly to the Lighter than Air Section and not to the practical training in bombing and air gunnery at Eastchurch to which the majority of his class was sent.

HMS *President II*, known to the outside world as the Crystal Palace, served as a reception and initial training centre for RNAS ratings. In 1915, G.H. Price found himself 'in the corner of a kind of transept just behind the great organ. All around us slender iron pillars rose into a maze of girders and cross stays which merged into the great vaulted glass roof.' (The huge Cathedral-proportioned structure served as a Training Establishment for a rich variety of units.) Caps off on the Messdeck was one of the first conventions to be learned when Price and his fellows wearing their caps were greeted by deafening clattering of cutlery against plates when they attempted to join more experienced trainees at the Mess tables. Hammocks had to be 'unlashed and slung' and then 'lashed and stowed', to leave the Palace precincts was to 'go ashore', couples of seamen mechanics were to be seen dancing together solemnly to a Naval band – all this and the issuing of kit thrown over a counter for trying on and if necessary

exchanging, were strange ways of living to which the new servicemen had quickly to become accustomed. No maternity jacket for the RNAS of course but a blue jacket with large side pockets, a waistcoat, grey flannel shirt, black tie, a peaked cap, breeches and putties for working though trousers were worn on Sundays and for 'going ashore'. For the winter, there was a blue jersey worn over a white flannel shirt with its square blue-edged neck. Mechanics wore the badge of their trade in red embroidery on the right arm, promotion would bring badges of rank on the left arm. A huge yellow-painted canvas kit bag and a small white-painted ditty-box held kit and personal treasures respectively and the Navy showed a soul unpossessed by the Army in providing a wooden block to mark a man's name, not his number, on his clothing.

Recruits to the RNAS could keep a moustache worn with a beard but not one flourishing in solitary splendour and in the grounds of the Crystal Palace counterfeit prehistoric monsters stonily stared upon the hirsute and the clean shaved, lively but disoriented new occupants of their park. Vaccinations and throat swabs were to be endured, drilling and more drilling paced out. Forenoon parades opened with the reading of prayers by the Chaplain and a stentorian voice would call out: 'Fall out the Hebrews and Roman Catholics'. Rifle exercises, physical drill, knot tying and signalling, lectures on seamanship, even a single experience of descending ropes, these were the exercises which formed the foundation for all Service experience in no matter how specialist a trade.

Every fortnight a pay allotment was issued from a compartmented tray. So ceremonial was this parade that a rehearsal was held but still one recruit betrayed his naivety with a 'thank you'. The response of course was a barked: 'No need to thank anyone. It's yours or you wouldn't get it.' An almost universal vignette of Service life is remembered by the man from whom all these Crystal Palace recollections come, Gilbert Price, and that was of being sent to pick up rubbish. 'Needless to say rubbish was conspicuous by its absence but since it is part of a serviceman's creed that while it is

No. 14 Training Depot Station at Lake Down in 1918. The aerodrome is to the top left. (P.H.L. Archive)

good to be idle it is fatal to appear so, the usual practice was to take up one's position near a piece of paper or cigarette end, and to pick it up on the approach of an officer. When he had gone it would be replaced ready for the next emergency.'[23]

The oddities or inconsistencies in an introduction to Service life are of course remembered. Frank Brook arrived at Farnborough and unluckily failed his motorcycling test as he skidded on oil outside the balloon shed. He came to grief and damaged a new bike. Five shillings offered to the Sergeant secured a second try, further mishaps being avoided, but his oral test on engines showed up certain eccentricities in military procedure. For him the test was rendered easy by the purchase of a motorbike engine instruction manual en route to Farnborough. He read it and then relied upon his retentive memory. What was not lost on him was the ignorance of the officer supervising the test as all his questions came from the same manual and he openly revealed his inability to grasp the real understanding of one candidate who gave an accurate technical response to a question. The answer was not couched in the words of the handbook and failure was the reward for his intelligence. As it happens, the RFC was losing the service as a dispatch rider of a pre-war racing motorcyclist!

It seemed to Brook that there were thousands at the Farnborough School; practically no toilet facilities and interminable queues for breakfast being features he remembered vividly. He noted too the neatly laid tables and curtained windows of a building where everything seemed far more civilised – it was the Sergeants' Mess![24]

No overcrowding or any other inconveniences could detract of course from the pride with which the double breasted tunic was donned and the magic of the embroidered shoulder insignia: ROYAL FLYING CORPS. Wearing a uniform on one's first leave was a very special experience and for none more so than those wearing the RFC metal-badged forage cap, the distinctive maternity jacket, breeches, putties and boots as new airmen. It was not just the uniform: 'It was impressed upon us that the

Royal Flying Corps was the "Right of the Line", and that we should take pride in this by ensuring that our behaviour and appearance, individually and collectively was always exemplary.' H.D. Chalke in writing this retrospectively was aware that he was looking back on days before sophistication had swamped idealism.[25]

RESEARCH AND DEVELOPMENT

Positive attitudes adopted by men in the ranks clearly would be inculcated by officialdom at all levels and hence it is reasonable that we should take some note, even within the theme of this book, of the attitude of officialdom to those aspects of the Service which impinged directly upon personnel. One such aspect might be the matter of the adoption of Royal Aircraft Fac-

tory manufactured machines and the qualities or otherwise of those machines. It was, at the time of the Fokker scourge and then again during Bloody April, a bone of contention and it has remained so. It lies at the heart of the efficiency of the work to be done and the security of the men doing it. Air Vice Marshal Arthur Gould Lee, as a fighter pilot in World War One, may be thought eminently well qualified to expound on the subject of the use of Royal Aircraft Factory machines (though he in fact flew Sopwiths) and in his book *No Parachute* he shows little mercy towards the official policy makers on this and indeed on the parachute question.[26] The question of the rival performance of Royal Aircraft Factory machines and those of private manufacturers is a major topic and much has been written upon it. In this book, the issue will not be further

Above and right: If a pilot were to find himself forced to land behind the enemy lines through mechanical failure or because he had been forced down in action, his overriding responsibility was to prevent his machine from falling intact into German hands. An improvement on ad hoc measures to this effect was the fitting of a small demolition charge, the result of which can be gauged by this example under test at Orfordness Experimental Station in 1918. A device similar to this must have been used by H.D. Ibbotson when his flying clothing caught alight and he was badly burned. (C.H. Shelton.)

ventilated. Instead, concentration will be upon personal experience of research development in the more specialist areas which buttressed the effectiveness of the use by aircrew of the machines they were given to fly. In particular, work at the RFC Experimental station at Orfordness (1917/18) deserves our attention though it should be remembered that earlier experimental work had been carried out at Upavon and then, with technical research going to Orfordness on the Suffolk coast, aeroplane testing was to go to nearby Martlesham Heath.[27]

At Orfordness, three academics in Service guise directed research upon machine-guns and sights, bombs and bombsights, navigation and aspects of flying. Captain Vernon Brown was the Flight Commander responsible for work on machine-gun sights and the development of fighter tactics. Sir Vernon Brown's recollections are full of fascinating detail on the academics, notably B.M. Jones from Cambridge (later Professor Sir Melvill Jones). 'He had many brainwaves among which was the raising of the front end of the Aldis gun-sight of the Sopwith Triplane by about 5° to help compensate for the effects of wind on trajectory when attacking from behind and at a distance of 100 yards.'

F.A. Lindemann, later Lord Cherwell, was not remembered with such respect by Sir Vernon. 'We tested and I think turned down a negative lens bomb sight in a DH4 whereupon Lindemann arrived in a fury and demanded the use of a DH4 to show we were talking nonsense! It wasn't ever adopted I think and as usual when he turned up he infuriated everyone.'

Practical research into pilots blacking out was placed in Brown's hands. He had to make tight turns or circles over a camera obscura which B.M. Jones had rigged up in a hut on the shingle banks. It was found that he passed out at 5 g for ten seconds but could hold $4\frac{1}{2}$ g for about 8 or 9 seconds, not that this was a great problem for the 1914–18 pilot in aircraft of such limited performance. The renowned Major General W.S. Brancker, the Deputy Director General of Military Aeronautics,

came to Orfordness to discuss this problem: 'I took him up in a DH4 and gave him two tight loops. I was then horrified to see by my mirrors no one in the rear seat. On landing Brancker had just come to and was trying to climb up from the floor having been nearly choked by his harness.'[28]

An RNAS officer, H.S. Neville, was unfortunate in testing bombs at the Isle of Grain in 1917. A bomb was required which would be of a weight and configuration which caused it to fall slower than a bomb to which it was attached. It was a primitive ground burst, stand-off weapon. A trigger was operated in the leading bomb as it struck the ground, closing an electrical contact in the second bomb and detonating it before it hit the ground. Fragments from it (or actual shrapnel balls) then spread laterally as well as downward to kill or maim troops in the open. When Neville turned on the petrol tap of his BE2c which was to be used in dropping such a twin bomb, there was a shattering explosion which injured a mechanic who had been making the connections for the bomb, shredded all the canvas from the aeroplane and left the pilot for some time subject to palpitations, giddiness and 'singing' in the ears which rendered him unfit for further active service.[29]

Oliver Wills was engaged upon test flying and research at Martlesham Heath, Orfordness and Butley near Woodbridge and he wrote of his work consisting of 'dropping things and seeing if they go off. It's rather fun'; and then of his dropping of eight bombs and 'nearly killing as many fishermen. But it seems rather absurd wasting perfectly good fishermen when food is so scarce. I must be more careful next time.' In Wills's case the seeming levity must not be taken at face value as his spirit was deeply troubled by the war and Major B.M. Jones, writing to him not long before he arrived at Orfordness, recalled their earlier active service acquaintanceship when Wills had roused him to a 'state of unseemly rage, indignation and dismay' in listening to his views. Wills's work in Suffolk was carried out in the shadow of the death there of a close friend in a flying accident, an increasingly disturbed conscience

Phosphorus bombs 'in' a letter: Lt O.B.W. Wills a BE2e pilot in No. 34 Squadron illustrated his letter (10 October 1916) with a drawing of phosphorus bombs fused to burst in mid-air 'raining' a burning spray to the ground – truly, as he wrote 'the most terrifying looking things of all the horrors'. (Lt O.B.W. Wills)

small number of men.[31] Vernon Brown, F.D. Holder and Robin Rowell were all to be concerned in one area of experimentation upon which debate has focussed ever since – the design and performance of a parachute to be used from an aeroplane when such a life-saving device was in common use by balloon observers on active service.

In January 1917, E.R. Calthorp's Guardian Angel parachute was tested. Photographs show that the escaping pilot or observer, wearing his harness, would have had to clamber out onto the wing and from here, having checked that his connecting lines were untwisted, would

Orfordness, February 1918: phosphorus bomb under test. The time-fused detonation of a phosphorus bomb is observed from the Experimental RFC station on the Suffolk coast from which many such armament trials were conducted. (C.H. Shelton)

and then to shatter the compensatory blessing of esconsing his new wife in a country cottage in the area, there was to be his own death falling from a machine on the penultimate day of the war.[30]

The nature of the work carried out from East Suffolk was wide-ranging. Apart from that which has already been mentioned, it included the testing of electrically-heated flying clothing, of oxygen apparatus, new cartographical delineations to assist in aerial navigation, the further development of oblique photography, night flying and navigational aids, parachute flares, electric landing lights (a Cranwell development) and night photography aided by flares. There was also the flying of experimental aircraft, the search for a means of cutting the wires of a barrage balloon and an attempt was even made to study the problem of aircraft engine noise – all of the projects being investigated by a highly skilled but pitifully

Success with limitations: From Orfordness numerous experiments with weights and dummy figures were made during parachute trials and then on 13 January 1917 as photographed here, Captain Clive Collett, a New Zealander parachuted safely to the ground from a BE2c. (Sir Robin Rowell)

A problem illustrated. The weighty, cumbersome size of the early parachute with its rigging lines too, shows clearly in this photograph taken at Orfordness during parachute trials in January 1917. The whole apparatus is here being carried externally and is further complicated by the weights and release levers which make it in this form quite impractical for general use. (Sir Robin Rowell)

then have stepped off the wing attempting to ensure that neither he nor the lines came into contact with the tailplane. The jerk of his fall on the connecting lines pulled the parachute from the large cumbersome housing. In such a manner, Captain Clive Collett made the first successful jump from a BE2c that month. According to Squadron Leader Holder, the pilot was Captain Gribble but Sir Robin Rowell and Sir Vernon Brown lay claim too, the latter with a telling anecdote of Collett from the rear seat shouting to him before he jumped that he'd noticed the ambulance and fire tender were in place: 'Much good they'll be if my parachute doesn't open but anyhow it pleases the authorities.' Brown found in Guardian Angel dummy drops that the parachute got caught in the tail skid unless a banked turn were being flown and 'that was how I let Collett out on his first drop.'[32]

The Guardian Angel was rejected because it was so heavy, bulky and difficult to operate. Furthermore, the bracket to house the parachute affected the performance of the aircraft. Holder was impressed by the next prototype,

that of Captain Mears, who had been 'in charge of the dogs on Scott's Antarctic expedition and no doubt used his knowledge of dog traces to make a parachute harness which would be safe and easy to manage', but this parachute too was rejected. According to Arthur Gould Lee: 'Nothing more mystified the pilots and observers of the RFC, RNAS, and RAF, during 1917–18 than the dour refusal of their High Command to provide them with parachutes',[33] but this is not something which the present author has found supported in either the recollections or original papers which he has studied. Many men in retrospect like Sir Robin Rowell have quite specifically disavowed any such preoccupation and so one is left not only with the continuing matter of why no parachutes were issued but also whether or not there was a widespread contemporary call for them. That many lives might have been saved by the issue of an effective parachute is incontestable but was one available? Was there a lack of urgency in developing and approving one? Was delay something occasioned by official consideration that its use would be too readily employed, continued combat evaded, an attempt to save a damaged machine not even essayed? Gould Lee's documented indictment is depressingly convincing. He catalogues the early development of the parachute from its successful use from an aeroplane in 1912 and then relates the evidence of official feet-dragging, supporting his case with details of flying officers calling for parachute provision. The sad story is concluded by the statement that the sole active service (personnel) use of the parachute from British aeroplanes in World War One was in the dropping of spies. Scarcely a subject within the general terms of 'air warfare 1914–18' will outlast this as a topic for debate.

AIR WOMEN

It remains but to give due recognition in this chapter on Home Establishment to the expansion in 1917 of the RFC and RNAS to include women. The opportunity came first to those in the Women's Legion who could drive but in fact the recruitment of women was seen to be more fundamentally important than dealing with a particular requirement. The shortage of manpower for overseas service would be made less serious if fit men employed on the Home Front[34] could be released for draft overseas through their work in Britain being undertaken by women. Women might also be employed at bases or on the lines of communication in France. The specified classes of employment included clerical workers (with shorthand and typing naturally being special concerns), cooks, waitresses and domestic staff, the motor transport service, storekeepers, checkers and unskilled labour, the telephone and postal service and 'miscellaneous services'. Accordingly, in July 1917, the Women's Army Auxiliary Corps was established and it was possible from within this Corps to serve with the RFC.

Recruits, unless they were photographers, had to produce certificates of efficiency for the class for which they were applying. When an applicant, even without a proficiency certificate, was thought to be generally suitable, she was invited to take up at her own expense a course of instruction with a firm approved by the War Office. The satisfactory completion of such a course would secure her acceptance into the WAAC and attachment to the RFC where her certificated sisters were already in service.

On 1 April 1918, the Women's Royal Air Force was established, command at the lowest level over its recruits being exercised by Forewomen and Assistant Forewomen while above them were the Unit Officers, or Administrators as they were known.

In the Royal Navy, the newly-established Women's Royal Naval Service early in 1918 had scarcely time for attachment to RNAS duties before the Service amalgamation of 1 April and the formation of the WRAF with its 10,000 service women, a number which rose to 25,000 by the date of the Armistice.

Among the 10,000 was Daisy Howe of Aston Clinton near Aylesbury who had held a driving licence since 1913. She had no difficulty in being accepted into the Women's Legion and then in getting transference to the WAAC to work with the RFC late in 1917. She was to drive the Model T Ford, then a Crossley Tender and finally a Crossley Ambulance, once getting a 15 shilling prize for having the best kept vehicle in the garages at Halton. She lived at home nearby and was thus classified as 'immobile', reflecting the sensible double compromise with regard to women's domestic commitments and the difficulty of providing suitable accommodation for those ready to move to a distant station or depot and thus classified as 'mobile'.

In recalling the military drill to which they were daily subjected, Daisy remembers the stern admonition of Sergeant Major Lucas: 'Now then stand upright with fingers in line with the seam of your . . .' and he then stopped in confusion as the array of legs before him was not trousered and the skirts not seamed in the right place as far as he was concerned.[35]

Jessie Lambert was a 'mobile' General Clerk at No. 7 Stores Depot RAF Doncaster. At her initial interview in Mexborough she had provided a melancholy list of negatives to questions on her qualifications for entry under the various classes. The exasperated Adjutant had thrown down his pencil and exclaimed: 'What

A WRAF Corporal driver (Daisy Home), presumably of an open car in view of the large fleece gauntlets. (Mrs D. Morgan Davies)

Left. Three members of the WRAF in their best 'walking out uniforms'. (Sir Harold Mullens)

WRAFs in working overalls, perhaps storekeepers or clerical staff. (Air Chief Marshal Sir Hugh Saunders)

do you think you *could* do if we take you into the Air Force?' Jessie's response: 'I can do as I am told', must have struck the right chord because she was accepted thereupon as the Adjutant's Clerk. As it happened, the only future occasion when her instinct let her down was in casually taking her great-coat off during drill because she was becoming too hot. She was sternly informed that if 'she started with a coat she would finish with a coat and that was that'.[36]

An unusually youthful WRAF Service was that of Ella Harding who found work as a sailmaker at the aerodrome at Wye near Ashford in Kent when she was but sixteen. With other girls from 8 a.m. till 4 p.m., in both a repairshop and out in the open too, she repaired damaged wing fabric. Soon she was able to do 'all the sewing and stringing of the ribs, doping and then varnishing, then painting on the roundels.' On 8 October 1918, she received her service uniform and so no longer had to show her Industrial Worker pass at the gate.[37] There can have been few younger servicewomen at the time but she and her 'sisters' in the WRAF (and indeed in the WAAC and the WRNS too) were to have no opportunity of a Service career. Clearly, the prolongation of the war would have resulted in a continued expansion of the number of women in the Air Force but the Armistice intervened, actually forestalling the WRAF appearing in wartime France though not with the occupation forces in Germany. The inevitable contraction of the peace-

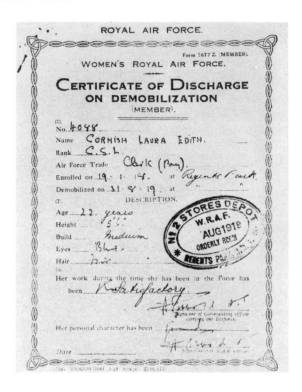

Laura Cornish's year and a half's 'V. Satisfactory' service in No. 2 Stores Depot at Regents Park. (Mrs L.E. Bulcraig, née Cornish)

time defence budget was to have no exception in its impact and the Women's Royal Air Force was demobilised in its entirety in 1920. Fortunately, its imprint upon the nation's defence conscience was sufficiently deep for its ready resurrection a generation later.

6

Active Service

On the Ground, in the Air and Off-Duty

Almost by definition published work on personal experience of the air war concentrates upon flying personnel. Furthermore, as pilots and observers were overwhelmingly holding commissioned rank, a reader's attention is drawn far less to the men in the ranks, the fitters, riggers, wireless operators, dispatch riders, cooks, clerks and lorry drivers, all essential cogs in the wheel of RFC and RNAS effectiveness. In this chapter an attempt will first be made to redress this imbalance, and to enable the men and the NCOs to explain their work, their routine and related aspects of their life on active service.

In the second place, there will be a con-centration upon those areas of operational work to which only brief reference has been made and which clearly require exemplification from the experience of those actively involved in such operations. In this context, wireless communication, artillery observation, kite balloon work and the fulfilment of special duties like the landing of agents behind the enemy lines, will receive attention before consideration will be given to a third aspect, that of the way in

The sand at St Pol was responsible for a German bomb in the spring of 1916 making so large a crater, rather than causing extensive damage to the adjacent hangars as would have been the case had the bomb struck a more resistant surface. (Lord Braybrooke)

which the squadron's life and work were administered.

The Commanding Officer's responsibilities in the administration of a squadron, those of the Recording Officer and then of the Duty Officer for the day when drawn together will make clear at least some of the fundamental factors in the development of good Service morale. Factors which will then require examination as materially supportive in this, would include, for the men just as much as for the officers, the quality of food and accommodation, questions of leave, pay, leisure time and recreational facilities, the maintenance of good health, the unit's discipline and the existence of sound officer/men relationships: to each of these elements some attention must be paid.

GROUND STAFF

It is scarcely surprising that the technical nature of flying work was reflected in the varied job specifications of the men on the ground staff of a squadron. It may be unrepresentative to select figures for 1918 but in that year the establishment figure of 36 other ranks per flight in a squadron included not merely a fitter and a rigger for each of the flight's seven or eight aircraft but armourers and batmen, a blacksmith, a sailmaker for the repair of aeroplane fabric, a coppersmith for fuel pipes and small metal fittings, a storeman, a welder, a compass swinger and an electrician, though no squadron would have its men so fully provided and neatly specified. There were also four motorcyclist dispatch riders and men to drive and maintain the two Leyland workshop lorries and four trailers, the six three-ton tenders, the four Crossley light tenders and the Crossley touring car for the Commanding Officer. In the Headquarters Flight, among other named posts, there were cooks, clerks and a telephonist. These figures are for a fighter squadron whereas for the two-seater squadrons more batmen, more cooks, more motorcyclists, and wireless and photographic sections would need staffing. To indicate in a specific instance that no set numbers can be generally accepted it is clear that for the Battle of Messines in June

1917, No. 6, an artillery observation squadron had 50 wireless operators attached to artillery batteries, certainly a figure above establishment level though figures for the following year could be in excess of this with an Australian squadron (No. 3) having over a hundred wireless operators – not all of them however being Australian Flying Corps men.

Behind the aircrew there stood a far greater number of men whose work helped to keep the machines in the air. In a two-seater squadron, which might have had 36 officers, this would be up to 200 other ranks to ensure that the squadron could operate in the field.

After military drill at Farnborough and postings to Montrose and Thetford, Colin Methuen went to France with his squadron (No. 25), to serve much of his time as a rigger even though he had joined the RFC as an electrician. Wings, struts, controls and wires were his responsibility and he welcomed bad weather as it reduced flying time and thus gave some respite from the hard, monotonous work re-rigging and adjusting the many wires and struts of the FE2b. As a 2nd Class Air Mech-

A man and his responsibility: Frank Brooks, an air mechanic, poses by the tail booms of one of his charges, an early series FE2b of No. 28 Squadron which was forming up at Gosport in 1917. (F. Brooks, Flight Sergeant)

Above. Table to show the new pay structure of Other Ranks in the Royal Air Force. (Rev. Dr T.C. Gordon)

Top right. Table to show the new ranks and pay structure for Officers in the amalgamated service, the Royal Air Force. (Rev. Dr T.C. Gordon)

anic his pay was 2 shillings per day. Promotion to 1st Class Air Mechanic brought this to 4 shillings – still 2 shillings less than the squadron lorry drivers earned though some of them were only 2nd Class Air Mechanics in rank. In fact, there was little opportunity to spend money at Auchel where No. 25 Squadron was based in early 1916 and there seems to have been no canteen though some of Methuen's funds did go to the corporal in charge of the Cookhouse who ran a blackmarket with the locals and sold eggs, fruit and other consumables.

On the subject of pay, the second lieutenant at 10 shillings a day would have a further 8 shillings Flying Pay on all those days when he had been in the air. A sum of 4 shillings was the Flying Pay entitlement of other ranks. A major's pay was 32 shillings per day. He too could qualify for Flying Pay. The relationship of pay to the cost of living can be gauged by noting that the equivalent cost of egg and chips was 9 or 10d and 50 Players Navy Cut cigarettes would cost about 1/3.

To return to the work of a rigger, keeping a machine clean, patching bullet holes in the wings with Irish linen fabric stuck on with strong-smelling dope, replacing struts or binding them with whipcord and then the ceaseless testing and adjusting of the wires, was not work which earned Methuen's respect despite his awareness of its vital importance. He has affirmed that making new control wires with their loops at either end and then fixing and adjusting them was skilled work requiring meticulous attention but he added that one of his colleagues was really a photographer and another a tailor. He himself as an electrician was glad to achieve a transfer in due course to being in change of the workship lorry which supplied light for the hangars of their flight with its petrol engine and D.C. dynamo.[1]

It seems understandable that engines gave inspirational urge to some fitters in ways which

Whatever its previous use, this building at St Pol was obviously ideal for its purpose as an aircraft workshop. There is plenty of space for the aircraft though it is noteworthy that the refinement of drip trays is not in evidence. (Lord Braybrooke)

eluded Methuen with his fabric, struts and wires. A former flight sergeant, W.J. Smyrk, remembers modifying the 110 hp Le Rhône engines to boost their power output. 'They had detachable cylinders screwed into the crank case, and we were able to raise the compression ratio of the engine by screwing them in further, and turning off the excess metal inside. We altered the valve timing and the result was an increased output to 120 hp.' Smyrk's recollections are full of engine-part improvisation in the field and experimentation to secure a better engine performance. He has particular recall of a problem in his early days in France, that of oil freezing. The rotary engines used medicinal castor oil because it would not dissolve in petrol like the mineral oils. In the worst of winter, oil left in a machine would freeze, granulating like sugar. An answer to this problem was to drain off the oil immediately flying had ceased for the day. Next morning, the oil would be warmed before it was put back into the engine and the oil pump primed with heated oil. Oil caused other problems too, rotary engines throwing out a great deal of it

which covered the bottom wings on biplanes and had to be washed clean to prevent it creating drag.[2]

Engine servicing took place under all sorts of circumstances dependent on the permanent and ideal (or other) nature of the squadron's base. Each flight carried two spare engines, making six spares for a squadron. Four had to be kept completely serviceable so that two were going through the workshop at any time. In No. 60 Squadron, Sergeant W.J. Smyrk used to park the four workshop lorries in a square and work from within the centre, the sailmakers making a huge tent which completely covered

The Leyland 3-ton lorry was standard equipment in the RFC with each squadron usually having six but on occasion just four. This example photographed near Amiens in 1917 reveals its solid tyres and it may be noted that it had to be 'swung-started'. (F.E. Waring)

98

the area enclosed by the lorries. The lorries provided the power for lighting, a lathe, a grinder and a little hand-operated shaping machine which had been scrounged in France. A log book for each engine was kept. The rotary engines were only given 25 hours' use between overhauls and then a flight fitter would take them out assisted by the sergeant or corporal fitter attached to that flight. If there were no lifting tackle this could be an awkward job involving manually lifting the engine onto timbers and easing it to a trestle. The same men would see to the replacement but workshop personnel would see to the overhaul. An engine had a major overhaul after 100 hours' service. When a squadron did not have the necessary replacement parts for this, the work had to be done at the Engine Repair Section at Pont de l'Arche on the Seine. Smyrk's recollections of this servicing work have an ironic addendum. 'A Squadron had two Warrant Officers: technical and disciplinarian. They were at loggerheads for most of the time; the technical Warrant Officer wanted the men at work, and the disciplinary Warrant Officer wanted them on parade.' There was more to it than that because on parade, Aspinall the disciplinarian, formerly from the Coldstream Guards, naturally required a formality out of accord with the more easy-going relationships necessary in a workshop.

As would be expected, engines were by far the most important item to attempt to salvage from a crashed machine, no matter what efforts might additionally be made to recover a machine-gun or the instruments. Lorries and their trailers were taken on lengthy journeys to rescue the engines or whole aircraft or elements of an aircraft which had crashed or made emergency landings away from a squadron's base. Even from no-man's-land salvage parties endeavoured to secure engines, and frequently they had the assistance of the Army. The party would be under the command of a Technical Sergeant Major and if the machine was in no-man's-land, a rope would be attached to the aircraft at night and it would be dragged by muscle power towards the British trenches. This could attract shelling, making the whole

expedition singularly unpopular with the battalion holding that sector of the line.

In the spring of 1918, a No. 58 Squadron FE2b bomber crashed just behind the British front line. Its six-cylinder 160 hp Beardmore engine would have cost over £1,000 at 1918 prices. An engine fitter, Air Mechanic Percy Young, was one of the party equipped with field dressings, steel helmets and gas masks and sent up the line by tender to the region rearward of the crash. Along the communication trenches they approached the second line and from here, the men crawled out. Under a certain amount of shell and machine-gun fire, fortunately not designed for them, they cut off the engine bearers and the propeller, secured rope to the engine and got the assistance of men from an infantry section to drag the engine into the second line. In due course, it was manhandled from here to an awaiting tender for return to the squadron.[3]

In a general emergency there were no demarkation disputes between trades: gales which overturned aircraft and ripped through the canvas and wood-framed Bessoneau hangars were one such hazard. High winds in January 1918 affected the Dunkirk area: 'At

Under active service conditions aeroplanes were normally housed in Bessoneau hangars, canvas covered, wooden-framed structures designed to be transportable while providing the necessary weather proofing for storage and workshops. Here a working party at St Pol is clearly in high spirits either because erection is almost complete or alternatively a move to new pastures is under way. (Lord Braybrooke)

2nd Class Air Mechanic Frank Waring serving as a motor dispatch rider in 1917 at Corbie on the Somme near Villers Bretonneux. His motorcycle is a 3½ hp P & M and from the records he kept he considers that he covered a million miles during his two and a half years carrying messages over the roads of England, Belgium, France and Italy, never once failing to reach his designated destination. (F.E. Waring)

11.30 p.m. good breeze sprang up and an anchor watch was called out about 12.30 a.m. A hangar went west into ditch behind and at 1.30 our hangars showed similar signs so the duty watch was called out to strengthen all ties. Oh what a sad night. Parts of the trusses were snapped at the base like carrots and the curtains or coverings refused to go where wanted and got their own back by ripping in all directions.'[4]

COMMUNICATIONS

Operation Orders from RFC Headquarters and then from the Brigades and from Wings were sent by motorcycle dispatch riders like F. E. Waring who wrote home to describe a journey of 280 miles through melting snow and pelting rain in late February 1917. His journey was interrupted by a hob nail puncturing his front tyre. He then ran out of petrol in a small town which seemed to have just a single British officer in it. Fortunately the officer supplied two gallons of petrol but Waring's destination was in 'a wilderness of valleys and hills with apparently no direct roads leading to it. I took several experimental paths, one leading me to the bottom of a valley in a field where I stuck and it took me ages till I got out.' The dispatch was finally delivered, an acquaintance was met who shared his billet in a barn and egg and chips in an estaminet was enjoyed but on the return journey the following day, Waring's bike chain broke. He repaired it, but the chain jumped off time and again during the final miles of the journey and the magneto gave but a faint spark because Waring's chain tinkering had allowed the engine to cool. The bike had to be pushed for a kilometre till an empty house was reached. From the roadside there he stopped a car, a Staff car in fact, and he was given a lift to the next town. On telephoning his RFC depot, he was advised to stay the night at the point he had reached. Finding accommodation there, he was picked up by a mechanic with a motorbike and side-car together with petrol and a new chain. His bike was relocated, repaired and the remainder of the journey completed.[5]

Dispatch riders answered the needs for confidential intercommunication. For general business, the field telephone was available between RFC units and their Headquarters. At 9th Wing Headquarters, the Signal Office was manned on a shift system from 8 a.m. to 7 p.m. and 7 p.m. to 8 a.m. by two men, one of 1st and one of 2nd Class Air Mechanic rank. They operated a magneto switchboard accepting and dispatching messages which were later to be confirmed in writing. Accepting all particulars of departures and return of every squadron's flights on patrol, they took this information directly into the adjacent room of the Commanding Officer and entered it on the foolscap sheets of a running schedule attached to the top of the CO's sloping desk. Every machine was booked out and, on return, booked in. Telephone operators on duty at dawn had a secondary, incidental task. Before proper meteorological reports were available, E.H. Boon recalls that from Boisdinghem at dawn an aircraft took off and rose to 10,000 feet, flying into the wind. It was the job of the telephone operator on duty to make with the naked eye a visual assessment of the wind speed and its direction at various heights as the machine climbed. The telephone operator's verbal response was then accepted as a rough guide by anyone making a request for a weather report.[6]

WIRELESS OPERATORS AND GUN SPOTTING

Wireless telephony, despite the determined experimentation conducted in 1918, was not developed to a sufficient degree for wide use by the air Services during the war though Victor Tait who had been transferred from the Canadian Infantry has described the hard work carried out at Biggin Hill in Kent to make progress in this area. A major problem was the wireless aerial, at that stage lengthily pendant from the machine, 120 feet with a $2\frac{1}{2}$-lb lead weight at its end. The dangers from this wire if an aircraft were suddenly to manoeuvre let alone be in combat before the wire could be wound in, are all too clear. No. 22 Squadron (Bristol Fighters) was the first to be equipped with sets which allowed the Flight Commander to communicate with pilots of his flight in the air but, in the circumstances of the German Spring Offensive, capture of the sets could not be risked and so they were not used until May. Only one other squadron was similarly equipped, No. 88 and there was still no means of satisfactory two-way communication from ground to air before the end of the war.[7]

It was by wireless, using Morse, that aircrew transmitted intelligence to the ground and in

The Somme. An RFC sergeant of No. 3 Squadron's Wireless Section monitors messages being transmitted from wireless operators attached to the gun batteries. These operators (of 2nd class air mechanic rank) would be living and working under conditions considerably worse than the relative comfort of this sergeant's shed which must surely be 'well to the rear'. (Captain T.L.W. Stallibrass)

Two Wireless Operators attached to an RFA battery, 2nd Air Mechanic Trott and 2nd Air Mechanic Saint, strike a formal pose for a souvenir photograph. (Sir John Saint)

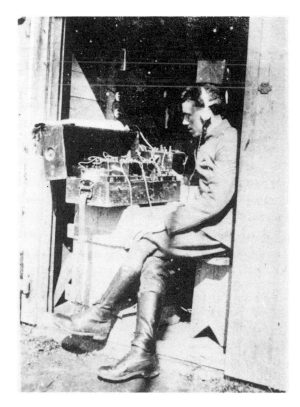

particular to wireless operators attached to Royal Field Artillery or Royal Garrison Artillery batteries. One of these wireless operators who achieved promotion from 1st Air Mechanic to commissioned rank was H.D. Chalke. He had taken an intensive course in Morse code by both wireless and Aldis lamp, a course run from Farnborough Town Hall, and he had then trained at Brooklands. In the late summer of 1916, after one further posting in England, he reached the river Lys to work as a wireless operator from a large brewery, Fort Rompu. His accommodation was in a summerhouse within the grounds of what looked as if it had originally been a manor house. Chalke has written that RFC wireless operators were treated by Royal Artillerymen as colleagues but infantrymen could be less tolerant, aggrieved at the 'cushy' billets operators sometimes enjoyed.

Less congenial was Chalke's next posting to an RFA battery Headquarters behind the ruined village of Bois Grenier. Here he lived and worked in a rat-infested, louse-ridden lean-to against a farm wall, rejoicing on the great days when they marched to a nearby town for baths in the large vats of a disused brewery, the luxury of clean underclothes, of the steam cleaning and ironing of his tunic and trousers. Chalke's wireless room was a corner of the battery's telephone exchange. Here, with headphones on, he sat awaiting his call sign among the cacophony of Morse from the other machines of his squadron and neighbouring squadrons. Concentration was essential but frustratingly difficult.

'The 30 foot mast, in eight sections, had been erected near the receiver, with the aerial as nearly at right angles to the front as possible, sloping down to a five foot pole. The large copper mast was placed under the aerial and covered with earth.' The 'Wireless Set Receiving Mark 3' in its portable wooden box was efficient though it was still a crystal set and not one using the newly developed thermionic valve. Having turned the dials to the approximate wavelength and adjusted the crystals to give the clearest signal possible, a switch was turned to bring in a closed circuit where there was less interference.

For essentially important RFC-observed artillery shoots, Chalke would have had warning of the approximate time he would be receiving the observer's signals. On hearing the call sign from the aeroplane, the sign was acknowledged by the laying out of white cloth strips. Using a field telephone, the battery would then be informed to standby and then to fire. The clock code system by which the pilot reported by Morse code the accuracy of the shelling will be described later but the letters 'O.K.' meant 'a direct hit', 'C.I.' stood for going home and 'R.U.F.' for 'Are you firing', if no burst was detected. Atmospherics and enemy action, involving the aeroplane's incapacity to align its aerial parallel to the ground and fly a figure of eight course, which together enabled the clearest signals to be transmitted, were two factors which influenced the quality of the signals being transmitted and hence the accuracy with which they could be recorded.

The onerous responsibilities upon RFC wireless operators in the field and the great care with which they had to work are clearly indicated in instructions among the papers of 1st Air Mechanic D.W. Blackshaw. 'You are well in the danger zone. Be careful what you say. In calling up units and formations, on no account ask for them in clear but by four letter code call.' The dangers and discomforts are made clear in Blackshaw's diary written before and during the November 1917 Battle of Cambrai. His RFC wireless station was operating from a churchyard. His aerial was cut down twice as they were shelled. In their dugout everything was soaking including the boards on which they slept and the blankets which ought to have kept them warm. When they were ordered to leave that particular sector most of the men had dysentery. 'Everyone hasn't eaten anything since the day before yesterday. Daren't for pains. Doctor given us some pills, nothing else out here.' He was helped on with his kit but as soon as they started to leave their dugout, they sank to their knees in mud. After going on for some distance: 'Can't go any farther. Give it up, too beastly weak to pull out feet out of the mud. They are frozen. Icy cold water in our boots. Pitch dark. We lay down in the mud as we are and wait for Lord knows what. My worst day in France. Hope to Lord another shell comes and puts the whole issue of us out before we get any more. Its awful. Can't feel any part of our body and its pouring rain. Everyone in England asleep I expect in beds.' Surely no air Service personnel could have been in closer identification with the troops on the ground than this RFC wireless operator.[8]

A bizarre experience is recalled by Chalke. Working at his set at Bois Grenier, he was nearly deafened by the high pitched signal from a German Telefunken Set. The strength of the signal was ominous, and sure enough it betokened an enemy machine in their vicinity, the signals recognisably directing German artillery fire. Chalke heard signals and near shell bursts – 'O' for *Ober* (over), 'L' for *Links* (left), 'R' for *Rechts* (right), 'K' for *Kurf* (short), then the signal equivalent to 'O.K.'. At that, he was thrown to the floor with the hut shattered around him. The only injury he received was to his ears, wrenched by the headphones as the receiving set to which they were attached was hurled across the room.[9]

As men like Blackshaw and Chalke awaited in tense concentration the results of the firing of the gun batteries to which they were attached, the results were transmitted to them by the crew of artillery cooperation aircraft. If the 'shoot' were of particular importance, the pilot and observer would go in Service transport to the headquarters of the battery concerned the day before the operation to discuss the target and decide upon call signs and recognisable ground signals from the battery. The following day, at a pre-arranged time, the aircraft would overfly the battery at low level before crossing the lines to locate the set target which was very likely to be an enemy gun position. With his wireless aerial wound out and the target found, the pilot or observer would tap out his call sign by Morse code buzzer and the letter 'G' to tell the battery to commence firing. Seeing the gun flash from the pin-point of the battery he would watch for the flash of the explosion, or the dust and debris thrown up by the bursting shell, and would then signal his assessment of where the shell had fallen in relation to a clock code system superimposed on the map showing the target. The target was at the centre of a series of circles, the first two at fifty yards apart, the rest at a hundred so that the angle of error could be indicated by the nearest hour on the clock and the distance from the target by the circles between which the shell had burst. The battery would fire one gun at a time and await the message from the air before the next gun fired. When the pilot, or, in some cases, observer, considered that the target had either received a direct hit or had been well bracketed, he would signal to the battery to continue firing at will.

Along these lines but rather more unusual than the general run of artillery shoots was the

An observer, Lieutenant Burr returns to his hut at No. 13 Squadron's aerodrome at Maroeuil, just north-west of Arras, after completing a shoot with an artillery battery. The pristine condition of his flying kit perhaps indicates that the observer has not been in France for long. (G.B. Burr)

The simple yet effective 'clock code' used by the RFC as from around the time of the Battle of Loos (September 1915) to facilitate the targetting of artillery shellfire on pre-selected enemy positions. Before a 'shoot' took place, the airman would prepare himself with a picture like this of the artillery's target. (Lt W.P. Watt)

The Hun 'plane homeward bound

← Shellholes

Belts of barbed wire →

work of No. 52 Squadron in October 1918. On 9 October, Edgar Thorne actually ranged 25 rounds from a Royal Marine Artillery 15-inch howitzer onto a hostile battery position, observing the dramatic evidence of the destruction achieved by the shelling.[10]

Flying activities as described above were termed N.F. Patrols, i.e. 'neutralisation fire' but in the event of an unanticipated target meriting urgent fire appearing, like a concentration of troops or the movement of enemy transport or guns, a 'Fleeting Target' call (designated LL) was made. Such a call required shelling from any battery within range of the target but as it was likely to have been given at times of advance or retirement and hence great activity on the ground, the crew of an aircraft could not under those circumstances by any means expect response to even the most urgent call. P.B. Townsend and his Canadian observer, Arthur Morris, were in a position on

While carrying out a photographic reconnaissance on 26 January 1918, Lieutenants Carter and Burr of No. 13 Squadron were attacked by five German scouts. After an exchange of fire, the RE8 made its way back to the British lines. One of the photographs taken just at the start of the combat shows not merely the trenches, belts of barbed wire and shell holes but a German two seater which happened to be passing at the time returning to the enemy lines. (G.B. Burr)

4 November 1918 to send from their RE 8 of No. 12 Squadron three LL calls of outstanding targets, one of literally thousands of Germans congregating near a large wood and preparing machine-gun posts on a hillside. There was no response to their calls.[11]

PHOTOGRAPHIC RECONNAISSANCE

Photographic reconnaissance was also conducted from the same types of aircraft from which countless numbers of artillery shoots were observed. The camera was heavy and bulky – about 5 to 6 lb and 18 inches deep and 15 inches long. It was fixed to two cross struts in the body of the aeroplane by the use of rubber foam padding and strong elastic bands so that the lens pointed directly downwards through a hole in the canvas fabric of the fuselage. This was an improvement upon cameras braced to the side of the fuselage. For taking oblique photographs, that is a general view of the landscape at an angle between vertical and horizontal, smaller hand-held cameras were sometimes used. Every effort had to be made to prevent vibration from the engine being transmitted to the camera itself. A 'Bowden' cable from the camera to the pilot's seat enabled him to operate the shutter. Another lead released the exposed photographic plate in such a way that the plate would fall into a box. The box gradually filled as the glass plates were exposed. The arrangement did not always work and then the task was doubled of loading a plate, carried in another box, into the camera, a task made no easier by the likelihood of its having to be done with gloved hands. If the plates were to jam, the whole flight was likely

Near Armentières, snow shows up the trench lines clearly. The parallel lines to the left of the trench line down the centre of the photograph are belts of barbed wire. Note the communication ways running back towards the rearward entrenchments. (Captain C.E. Townley)

to be wasted as a mosaic had to be built up from the photographs taken on the same occasion.

The altitude at which photographic reconnaissance sorties were flown depended upon the purpose for which the photographs were taken, for example 10,000 feet for counter-battery detection. The aircraft had to be flying dead level when the shutter was operated. Further refinement was possible with the taking of stereo photographs from which the height and depth of objects could be deduced. In the squadron's photographic hut the prints were plotted upon Ordnance Survey trench maps and, by interpretation, modifications to old maps were made or new maps would be drawn.[12]

By 1918, the squadron's Intelligence Officer and a sergeant from the photographic section would be in attendance at the briefing of a pilot and observer the day before they engaged upon a photographic reconnaissance sortie. Skill in map reading, relating the map to the ground below and in keeping the aircraft on an even keel, despite wind, turbulence and anti-aircraft fire was certainly necessary but with training, practice and then experience over the lines the task became routine. Always bearing in mind the alternating possibility of clouds making the work difficult and clear days advertising the British presence to the enemy, particularly careful judgement was required in remembering the highest priority in getting the photo-

graphic sequence completed and safely back to the squadron. Enemy interference with Corps Squadron photography could pose the questionable choice of running for home or staying to fight so that the work might be completed. To have to do the whole set of exposures again was an unattractive prospect as a photographic flight could take three hours even under ideal conditions. Instructions differed for Army Squadrons and as Sir Victor Groom recalls 'if enemy aircraft were encountered, our job was to fight and everything else was abandoned.'[13]

In the earlier stages of the war, it might well have been the observer who took the photographs. By 1918, an observer's primary task was to scan the sky for hostile aircraft, warn the pilot on seeing any and operate the Lewis gun to defend the machine. In photographic work he had other tasks. He had to bend downwards within the fuselage and among the bracing wires, take off the top box after all its photographic plates had been exposed and replace it with a full box. He then had to position the empty box to receive the next set of exposed plates. On return to the airfield it was usually the observer who was responsible for handing in the boxes of plates to the Photographic Section while the pilot gave the Intelligence Officer a report on the patrol.

The Photographic Section frequently operated from within a specially adapted and equipped lorry and prints would soon be in the hands of the Intelligence Section who would compare them with photographs taken at an earlier date so that the tell-tale signs of new entrenchments, new gun emplacements, new or widened communication ways could be discerned. This information would be forwarded with the prints to Army HQ there to be re-interpreted and related to the work of squadrons working on adjacent sectors.[14]

OTHER DUTIES

There are some areas of work for the RFC on the Western Front for which it may seem scant, or even, in the case of the pilots ferrying machines out to France, no mention is being made but some attention must be given to

No. 8 Squadron's Photographic Section. The 'furniture' is distinctly makeshift. (P.H.L. Archives)

Lieutenants F.R. McCall and Farrington of No. 13 Squadron, RFC in their RE8 photographed after shooting down a German attacker on 6 January 1918. It appears as if a pet dog has been among the first to congratulate the pilot, a Canadian whose service jacket shows that he has been awarded the MC and whose skill led to his being transferred to a fighter squadron, No. 41, with which he secured many victories, 37 in all, and further honours. (G.B. Bull)

'Special Duties', for example the landing of agents or of carrier pigeons for use by agents and also the more general work of the men in Kite Balloon Sections.[15]

By the very nature of 'Special Duty' operations it will be recognised that references in the official or contemporary personal papers of those engaged are few and at best cryptic. Alan Morton (No. 8 Squadron) has written in his unpublished memoirs of being ordered in 1916 to report to Corps HQ where through a Senior Staff Officer, Colonel Lyon, he was introduced to a Frenchman who had been a peacetime frontier smuggler. The Frenchman was now a spy and was going through Holland to get behind the German lines. He would require pigeons to send back information. In a fortnight, he would be at a location on the now dry St Quentin canal. 'When he got there he would hang out some washing on the edge of a wood and if I flew over and saw the washing and dropped a bomb near it he would expect me at the next full moon, or thereabout. So in a fortnight's time five of us in BE2cs made a reconnaissance over the canal, some 20 miles behind the German lines, saw the washing,

dropped a bomb and started home.' As it happened, the BE2cs were intercepted by Fokker monoplanes and one of them was shot down. The pilot survived. Another was shot down by anti-aircraft fire and its pilot was killed but the purpose of the flight had been fulfilled. As the night for the full moon approached, Morton was sent his basket of carrier pigeons, one of which obligingly laid an egg which the grateful pilot enjoyed for breakfast.

The basket was fitted into the bomb rack and after one scare when he thought he had been caught by a searchlight which proved to be but a reflection of the moon in the Somme: 'I turned off the engine and glided down to 500 feet just over the spot in the St Quentin Canal. I pulled the bomb handle and the basket floated down with its parachute'. Re-starting the engine, he made off for home. Morton learned subsequently that useful information was received from 'his' pigeons. This aspect of his work is concluded by a reference to the earlier landing of an agent in a field well away from the front but one in which some cows had made an unexpected appearance resulting in an unfortunate collision and crash on landing, the pilot being taken prisoner while trying to escape. No detail is given as to the fate of the agent.[16]

It seems likely that the first attempt to land an agent behind the lines was that of Captain T.W. Mulcahy-Morgan of No. 6 Squadron in September 1915 but the BE2c crashed into a tree, seriously injuring both men. Friendly local people removed the pigeons and all other evidence of the real purpose of the landing but there was no hope of the injured men avoiding capture. Within a few days Captain G.L. Cruikshank (No. 3 Squadron) and Lieutenant J.W. Woodhouse (No. 4 Squadron) proved that the difficult job could be carried out. According to the *Official History*: 'These were to the first adventures of a kind that was later to become fairly common.'[17]

The moonlit operations of pilots of Special Duties had in obvious ways striking differences from the long periods of daytime concentration required of kite balloon observers in basket-bound suspension beneath the huge inflated sausage which gave them their opportunity for aerial observation behind the enemy lines and at the same time set up so clear an advertisement of their activities and made it so inviting a target. A kinship of nervous tension there may have been as the Special Duty pilot prepared to land and the kite balloon observer saw the black specks rising over the skyline materialise into hostile aircraft making for his balloon.

Bernard Oliver, as NCO of No. 2 Kite Balloon Section, was based at Locre. In such a section there would be five officers and 93 other ranks. Batmen, winchmen, radio operators, telephonists and motorcyclists, motor drivers, a clerk, cooks, balloon riggers together with a balloon party of 48 were the 'other rank' members of the section under a flight sergeant and two other sergeants. The danger to the party at Locre came from shellfire as well as air attack on the balloon itself. In fact, No. 2 KBS was to move still nearer the front line for the Battle of Messines in June 1917. From this position later in the year strong wind gusted a balloon out of the hands of the party 'walking it up' to its flying position. Serious repercussions upon the Senior NCOs concerned were probably only averted by the worse disaster befalling the party walking up the balloon just to the south of their position. Two men from this handling party were drawn up several hundred feet into the air by the cavortingly free balloon and they fell to their death when unable to cling any longer to the handling ropes.

Oliver himself later became an observer. In his recollections, he lists the equipment which accompanied the two men in the basket; two telephones, two pairs of glasses, two sheath knives, an aneroid barometer, an electric anemometer, an air speed indicator, four sandbags, a flag, a map and a mapboard, a pressure gauge and two parachutes.

Oliver had one discomforting experience when he and the officer in command, each sometimes afflicted by a stammer, found that the tension of the circumstance rendered them quite incapable of using the telephone to report a map reference of a German gun firing on one of the British batteries. Oliver had a still worse crisis in his first flight with Captain G.D. Machin in No. 23 KBS. Their ground position was under steady fire from a large calibre gun imperturbably being observed by Machin. For some reason, the balloon was losing gas and was slowly descending, only being kept aloft by the wind like a kite. From Company HQ they were telephoned to warn them of trouble. From the winch party they were told of very high tension on the cable and when, reluctantly, Machin ordered the balloon to be hauled down, because the shelling was bringing great danger to those on the ground, the winch could not do the work. The party below resorted to the use of a pulley (the 'spider') which fitted round the cable so that the men below could walk the balloon down, but at

No. 2 Kite Balloon Section at Locre in 1916. The balloon is the German designed Drachen type. Note the gas cylinders and, to the right, the motor driven winch on its lorry. (B. Oliver)

Right. Manpower in every sense. Handling parties walking out two kite balloons from their sheds and getting a third into position for its ascent. (B. Oliver)

Left and above. Balloonatic cartoonist G.D. Machin, who was later to become famous as 'Mac', the cartoonist for a national daily newspaper, served with the Army and later the RFC in Flanders as an observer with No. 8 Balloon Company. For some of the time he was a member of No. 23 Kite Balloon Section deployed adjacent to the Ypres Salient and had the unfortunate experience of his balloon being shot down in flames on his second ascent. He drew these impressions of himself and the then Officer Commanding 23 KBS in 1917. (F. Wilkinson)

1,000 feet and now without any lift whatsoever, the balloon collapsed. Machin and Oliver were too low to parachute in the circumstance of rapid descent so they started to climb the rigging to get out of the basket which would feel the worst of the impact. As it happened, the basket fell on a clump of trees through which it descended gently to the ground leaving the crew hanging safely above it. It was from a nearby haven having a nerve-relaxing cigarette that they watched the rescue party peer anxiously into the basket quite evidently expecting fatal casualties.[18]

THE OPERATIONAL UNIT

To return to a consideration of the work and life of the personnel of an aircraft unit in France, the chain of administrative responsibility for the day to day running of a squadron was quite simple. The Officer Commanding exercised a generally overseeing eye upon every aspect and for delegation, he would consider the orders from Wing HQ for patrols or liaison work of some nature with an Army unit and perhaps discuss this with the executive officers concerned, that is his Flight Commanders and Intelligence Officer or for a technical matter his Engineering Officer, and for a movement order, his Transport Officer. He would then delegate the organisation of the necessary steps to be taken to the Recording Officer or appropriate executive officer.

The Recording Officer (an Adjutant in Army parlance) was the administrative hub of every squadron. He would work closely with the Squadron Sergeant Major who would see that whatever was ordered was done efficiently and speedily. From the Orderly Room a clerk prepared typed responses to the correspondence 'returns' requested from Wing HQ. Reports on aircraft serviceability, petrol con-

A kite balloon falls victim to a German fighter in July 1918. The kite balloons were also vulnerable to well-directed shrapnel shelling as such a shell could shred the balloon causing swift loss of its gas, giving less time for parachute evacuation by the observers than under the circumstances of the approach of a German machine. (B. Oliver)

sumption, ammunition requirements and applications for transfer to another unit or for compassionate leave were prepared in addition to the daily Squadron Report which the Recording Officer would draw up from the patrol reports of Flight Commanders and from any personal combat reports filled in by pilots after such engagements.

The Intelligence Officer responsible for gathering information about targets and related details, the Equipment Officer for replacement parts and the stores in Headquarters Flight, the Transport Officer in charge of perhaps seventeen vehicles of different descriptions, a Wireless Officer, an Equipment Officer, all had precisely defined areas of authority, but the Flying Officers also had, by rota, an administrative role to fulfil, that of the Orderly Officer. The Orderly Officer for the day would have his responsibilities assigned to him by the Recording Officer and they might include censoring the outgoing mail, inspecting the men's billets or tents, receiving and checking the delivery of the rations and dealing with complaints about food. While the Orderly Officer was fulfilling these tasks, a more informal supervision was being carried out by the CO who would very probably see patrols off, chatting to the crews beforehand and then be there to see them in. The presence of the Commanding Officer could also be expected anywhere and at any time from a football match and a concert to the workshops and hangars and not just where it would be most tangibly felt (whether he were in or not), the Officers Mess.

The other ranks would be more keenly aware of the disciplinary eye of the squadron Sergeant Major than of their generally more fleeting contact with the CO. It was this most senior NCO who would impose his very considerable authority and personality upon them in their work at all times and not much less in their leisure. He would surely be a figure of impressive bearing radiating a confident and probably aggressive authority with a shrewd awareness of how to get the utmost from every man.

The efficiency of a squadron in the air was of course dependent upon aircrew and machine

A pilot and the Intelligence Officer examining aerial photographs in the office at St Pol. Note the map chest and the strip mosaic of oblique photographs at the top of the picture. (Lord Braybrooke)

performance but in an undeniable even if unquantifiable way it was also dependent upon the tripartite alliance of the Commanding Officer, the Recording Officer and the squadron Sergeant Major.

Within the framework of properly exercised authority and administrative efficiency, several factors influenced service morale and its manifestation in the mutual respect between officers and men. Sound man-management dependent in the most basic analysis upon the way a man was handled by the officer for whom his work was done, like the fitter and rigger for the flying officer, lay at the root of the contentment with which work was carried out. But the roots were nourished or chopped at by the good or poor standards of food and accommodation, the provision or otherwise of recreational facilities and leave and the maintenance of physical wellbeing.

It should not be surprising that officers, who were overwhelmingly from a separated educational and social background, holding dissimilar values and expectations from the other ranks, would follow a different way of life from the men. It was a way of life conforming to service conventions, conventions which were

'I feel it was a great tribute to my fitter and rigger, Mr John J. Williams and Mr J. Clifford that the machine had survived so long.' This tribute was paid by a former Sopwith Dolphin pilot of No. 19 Squadron whose machine (C3833) was worn out after his nine months' tour of duty. Clifford the rigger from Croydon stands behind the fitter Williams from Winsford in Cheshire and each man signed the photograph which they gave to their 19-year old pilot J.A. Aldridge. (Squadron Leader J.A. Aldridge)

themselves a reflection of the 'ordered' society of the period, however much we may judge from a distance that society to have been in a state of fracture. The contrasts are highlit by the separate messing and accommodation facilities and the qualitative differences between them. Sometimes with exaggerated significance, our attention is drawn to the social gulf which brought problems to the sergeant pilot and not just to the sergeant but to the officers serving with him in the same flight. An example might be that of Flight Sergeant H. Bliss Hill of No. 12 Squadron. He slept with the NCOs in hangars, on beds made from the elastic cords used on the undercarriages of the

Two partnerships in flying, observer and pilot, aircrew and 'ack-emmas' (air mechanics). In front of this RE8 of No. 15 Squadron at Vert Galand, Lieutenants Levy and Morrison pose with their fitter and rigger. (Rev. R. Capel Cure)

aircraft but one of his responsibilities lay in taking officers newly arrived at the squadron to show them where the line was and to point out the area for their unit's patrols. To make too much of the awkwardness of the contrasts in accommodation, rank and service experience is however to ignore the necessary stratification of Service society and the social mores of the period.[19] A former fitter, E.L. Bishop, expressed it nicely: 'There was a very good relationship with the officers, mind they always kept their place, we kept them in their place and we kept our's.'[20] What is quite clear from the letters and diaries of officers is a concern for the men and more than that, an appreciation of them. Perhaps the good relationship was founded not least in the mutual realisation of each other's worth, the flying skills and courage of the young aircrew in the forefront of action and the different skills and sheer hard work of the men (frequently a little older) upon whom their lives to a considerable extent were dependent.

When Squadron Commander Geoffrey Bromet was in his first days at Vert Galand in late October 1916 establishing Naval Eight in its new base on the Somme, his diary shows that he blessed the rain and wind, the leaky barn, the mud and many inconveniences because it was going to be 'hard for officers and men alike. It makes the inexperienced ones and those lacking in initiative learn how to shift for themselves; the proud and haughty type to come down to the level of their mates and the good sorts, the cheery sorts, the "always willing to work sorts" shine more than ever and gather more "kudos" than they can ordinarily do.'

In Bromet's diary for December 1916 there is a vignette of the kinship the development of which he had encouraged. Two air mechanics travelled with Petty Officers and Officers the 25 miles to Heilly for the funeral of Flight Sub-Lieutenant Hon. A.C. Corbett who had crashed near there and whose remains were to be buried. 'The funeral was of the simplest. The burial ground was but 300 yards away and it was to here that the two air mechanics wheeled on a stretcher the Union Jack covered remains, escorted on either side by the two Petty Officers (one carrying the Cross) and closely followed by just we five officers. We met the Padre at the graveside and laid our comrade to rest.' Certainly well outside such kinship, as far as Bromet was concerned, were those who either ran the war at a political level or reported on it for their newspapers. A few days after the Corbett funeral, Filson Young of the *Daily Mail* and Philip Gibbs of the *Daily Telegraph* came to enquire about 'heaps of things which did not concern them so I remained mute and got rid of them toute suite. I hate all newspaper sleuth hounds. Politicians and reporters are my pet aversion.'[21]

An example of concern for the welfare of his mechanics is expressed in one of A.B. Fanstone's letters. On 11 July 1916, he wrote that a certain Miss Brown should send no comforts or gifts to him, for he had no need of them but he could recommend very deserving cases such as 'the two mechanics who look after my aeroplane (and on whom in a way my life depends).'[22] An echo of the truthfulness of Fanstone's point is contained in the memoirs of former RNAS pilot E.W. Desbarats who wrote of his 'very competent mechanics as a result of whose thoroughness I did not have a single engine failure.'[23] Lord Balfour has recalled with regret that though his relationship with his mechanics and fitters was good he did not have the intimate knowledge of them nor feel a demanding duty to be concerned for their welfare that he had felt as an Infantry Officer; the business of flying was too major a preoccupation. It might be added that Balfour retrospectively was aware that the closeness of life for the personnel of an infantry company in the front line or reserve trenches or even at rest behind the Western Front could not have a precise parallel in the air services.[24] A soothing story of concern for the men being quickly translated into action is that related by a former air mechanic, H.R. Skerratt. He was in agony with toothache and was spotted by his CO, Major Newall, as he sought relief by putting his face to the hot radiator of a workshop lorry. Newall immediately sent for a motorcycle and side-car and Skerratt was taken to the nearest

Officers (by invitation!) and NCOs of No. 10 Squadron, RAF, enjoy a relaxed evening in the Sergeants Mess at Droglandt, Belgium in August 1918. (Air Chief Marshal Sir Ronald Ivelaw Chapman)

casualty clearing station. Here the agony was intensified but salvation was the reward; a young doctor, without using anaesthetic, took the offending tooth out – bit by bit, nine pieces in all.[25] In a certain sense the CO's action was personally repaid as Skerratt's command of French led to his being asked to secure beer for the squadron. He obtained a lorry, picked a driver who knew his beer and with the CO's several hundred francs, set off to find a brewery. Here the driver tested the beer, approved it, eight barrels were bought, loaded and then the triumphant return made. With beer enough for everyone and a barrel for the Sergeant's Mess (as Skerratt by now had three stripes on his arm) he had become exceptionally popular!

Beer or perhaps wine was the cause of a less than happy experience for another air mechanic, Percy Young, but in deference to the memory of the officer concerned his name and squadron will not be given. Young was taken up by the CO of his squadron for air test of a machine prior to its being used for a night-bombing raid in April 1918. The CO took the opportunity of a hospitality call on another squadron and there he imbibed far too liberally. 'On starting the engine the CO did not give me time to get into the cockpit but took-off whilst I was clinging to the side of the plane. On board was a 56 lb bomb on the undercar-riage [bomb rack] and four 20 lb bombs under the wings. There were no detonators in the bombs as they were fitted just prior to a raid. Whilst in the air, the CO did many foolish manoeuvres. He tried to loop the loop and finally got the plane into a side slip.' The end result of the pilot's intoxication was a crash-landing with injury to both of the crew. 'The CO I never heard of again. He was badly injured. Officers came to see me in the sick bay and said there would be a court of enquiry and said I had better state loss of memory concerning the crash as the FE2b's observer should have been in my place and the CO should not have landed on the other drome.'[26] Young, after recovery, was transferred to another squadron.

Nissen huts provided the most usual form of both accommodation and administration for a squadron though there were interesting variants upon this. Farm buildings frequently enabled helpful adaptation. The barns at Files-camp became good workshops for No. 60 Squadron and hot baths, an improved swimming pool and tennis court were embellishments for this squadron which had its own football and boxing teams and even band.

Leave came for the men rather less frequently than for the officers. In the main it could be expected once within a year but this is a

subject upon which it is impossible to general-
ise. The men would get an allotment of ten
days, nearly three of which were lost in the
travelling. Journeys to Scotland were allowed
an extra day and in W.J. Smyrk's recall, few
men failed to return, something which he
ascribed to the wonderful esprit de corps of his
squadron. Esprit de corps did not necessarily
exclude a front of cynicism and by all accounts
the banner across one end of the canteen at
No. 18 Squadron bearing the legend 'SMILE,
DAMN YOU SMILE' may have disconcerted the
newcomer but not for long. It merely reflected
the serviceman's sardonic sense of humour in
daily circumstances when there was little time
for idle grousing.[27]

Making living accommodation and eating
arrangements for the officers in their Mess

'Décor Chinois': The wall of the Officers' Mess of
No. 211 Squadron based at Petite Synthe in September
1918. The officers seem to have 'commissioned' a
member of the Chinese Labour Corps to give Oriental
artistry to the mural decorations. (C.E. Townley)

Accommodation and ancillary buildings at St Pol. Pools
of water indicate the utility of the raised pathways.
(Lord Braybrooke)

Pilot's Quarters, No. 45 Squadron St Marie Cappel, October 1917. Lieutenant Norman Macmillan, who later became a test pilot for Fairey Aviation and wrote several books on flying, is shown nursing a dog. On the 'sideboard' are two propeller tips made into photograph holders. (Air Vice Marshal R.J. Brownell)

adequate was something which had to be tackled by the poor officer who found himself nominated as Mess President. With adequacy achieved there was breathing space to improve towards 'civilised' standards. No. 11 Squadron at Bertangles provided no real difficulty for J.S. Castle as Mess President of B Flight. The Mess and the living accommodation were in buildings in the town square, all food being delivered by the Army Service Corps – far too much meat incidentally![28] J.W. Baker of No. 4 Squadron, A Flight's Mess President at Chocques near Bethune, faced different circumstances. He was given a bare hut, a Mess waiter and a cook from which to organise a place in which the fourteen officers of his flight could live and feed, but even when shouldering such responsibility he declared that: 'It's going to be some Mess though, when it's furnished and running smoothly.' Baker was merely making arrangements for a flight not, as was far more usually the case, for the officers of the whole squadron but his men wanted things done 'in the most aristocratic way possible, so I have been rushing around buying furniture and crockery, hiring pianos and buying gramo-

phones' and making arrangements for daily supplies of milk and eggs etc. Funds for his purchases came from the Field Cashier but he had still more to see to – the curved roof was to be covered with white cloth and below that there was a black frieze which was gradually being covered with pin-ups (Harrison Fisher's girls) and below them there was green canvas down to the ground.

One of Baker's letters had hurriedly to be finished so that he could see to the table decorations before a dinner being attended by two colonels. Despite his flying work as an observer, the Mess President still had time to furnish and wallpaper his own room nicely when the heavy responsibility of the Christmas 1917 dinner and party fell to him.[29]

The 1914–18 Squadron Mess in one aspect has been historically ill-served by film and novel with regard to its portrayal as the scene of

No. 1 Squadron's Rugby team compiled an impressive record during 1917/18, playing fifteen matches of which they won fourteen and drew one. Back row, left to right: Lieutenants Doré, Lang, Gibbs, Beatty, Collins, le Gallais, Bradford and Williams; middle row: Captain Ferguson, Lieutenant Burnett, Major Pretyman, DSO (Squadron Commander and Captain of the team), Captain Capel and Lieutenant Atkinson; front row: The Mascot 'Pongo' and Lieutenants Collingwood and Willoughby. (Air Vice Marshal A.J. Capel)

frequent drinking beyond reasonable limits and with resultant destructive behaviour contrasting with the other ranks who had neither the money nor the opportunity for such indulgence and who would in any case have had to pay for any damage. The truth of the matter, as with so many legends is best appreciated after a cold shower of logic. Aircrew could not perform their duties and could neither safeguard themselves nor their machines if they were to fly under the influence or after effects of alcohol. In human and material terms there was too much at stake for a CO or his Flight Commanders, never mind the pilot or observer in question, to run such a risk. Of course there were parties, the men were young, their work dangerous, the strain was there for everyone even if some were not aware of it or coped with it better than others. There were reasons for celebrations, like a promotion, a decoration, a victory in the air, there was a need to ease the tension or lift thoughts away from self-injurious depression and accordingly parties were held. Games like Cardinal Puff or High Cockalorum[30] were played and an occasional indoor rugby scrum may not have been much to the benefit of glasses and furniture but with very few exceptions the morning patrol would be on, unless kindly bad weather decreed otherwise. Perhaps on occasion the bad weather was anticipated!

It may seem an eccentric choice to use a

letter from the teetotal A.B. Fanstone to describe a binge in his Squadron Mess (No. 12 Squadron) in August 1916 but one may presume that he had the keenest eye to observe and the clearest head to recall. After champagne

'Short, back and sides' but scarcely matching the barber! No. 32 Squadron barber shop at Vert Galand in 1916. Lieutenant C.L. Bath beneath the towel or sheet seems to be wearing pyjamas and sabots. (Wing Commander G.H. Lewis)

1917 and still playing the game: The serious business of recreation. Behind the row of portable hangars the pilots and observers of No. 8 Squadron make use of their tennis court, Major Ross preparing to smash an ill-judged lob. (W.B. Tisdall)

Right. The fire extinguisher on the left in this photograph of the 'band' of No. 1 Wing, RNAS may be a visual comment on the quality of sound produced by the band. (Lord Braybrooke)

Below. Snowballing at St Pol while a Henri Farman is being refuelled. (Lord Braybrooke)

Below. Pets Corner: A chicken, a fox cub, a rabbit, a Jack Russell terrier, two cats, a puppy and a pig are the pets held here by officers of No. 42 Squadron at the Town aerodrome, Bailleul, in 1917. The white picket fence on the right marks the grave of the squadron piano fatally injured during the course of a party in the mess. (Captain C.E. Townley)

Petite Synthe, 1916: Lieutenant R. Jope Slade, G. . Thorn, St John and T. Ormerod relax in front of the Wardroom. (Squadron Leader C.P.O. Bartlett)

Geoffrey Bromet, the CO of Naval Eight, played both football and rugby for his squadron's teams, selected as they were from across the ranks. Sports days too saw officers and men competing against each other or alongside each other. Concert parties were particularly popular. They gave vent in every sense to talents possessed by many a mechanic which emphasised his usefulness to the squadron, however ironic that may seem of an active service unit. A wireless operator, attached to a squadron based at Bailleul and employed as a stagehand in concert parties there, has admitted that some of the air mechanics had been 'purloined from other squadrons because of their Thespian attributes.' The stagehand's own backroom support was disposed of following an unfortunate rendition of a favourite song 'The Ghost of the Violin' during the singing of which a green light (an aircraft signalling lamp with coloured glass in front) was directed from the wings upon the singer. 'I was the operator, perched on two boxes – when the singer looked his ghostliest, as he warned his audience to "beware and take care!" the lamp, the boxes and the operator collapsed on to the stage amidst hoots of laughter, not shared by the singer.'[32]

The big RFC Depots had long-established concert parties which gave performances at the depot or visited squadron bases for that purpose. Their standard was high, that of the

with dinner, celebrating some honour received in the squadron, there were speeches and 'everyone gets happy and lively and as near drunk as possible – the merriment continues after dinner till say eleven o'clock by which time everyone is rolling about on top of each other wrestling and so on and generally about 4 or 5 a.m. quite drunk and most of the others nearly so, one or two of us (I seem to be the only non drinker here but there are about 2 others out of the 40 who have assumed teetotalism for perhaps purposes of economy) enjoy watching these others rolling and wrestling and spoiling their uniforms and generally making fools of themselves.' To make matters worse in the evening's entertainment being described, the several Scots among the officers had banded together under the leadership of one who was 'huge fat and typical' and were ragging anyone unready to accept a Scottish ancestry. As one of these Scots insisted on practising but perhaps not improving his playing of the bagpipes when everyone was abed, a Caledonian influence was by one means or another forcibly imposed on No. 12 Squadron at this time though whether it were altogether appreciated must remain in some doubt.[31]

The opportunity for the officer to engage in individual or paired sporting pursuits like tennis has been mentioned earlier and an informal binge may have been just what was needed at certain times but, as a regular occurrence, organised recreation and entertainment was part and parcel of maintaining the sense of officer and 'other rank' togetherness in any unit.

Seaplane floats make acceptable canoes for RNAS officers off duty. (Wing Commander G.H. Lewis)

Chorus
  For a batman woke me from my bed
  I'd had a thick night and a very sore head
  And I said to myself, to myself I said
  Oh we haven't got a hope in the morning.

Silent film shows with perhaps a piano accompaniment enlivened evenings in many hangars and H.D. Chalke has recall of a Western film in which an attack by Indians on a waggon train was suddenly given staccato and explosive sound effects by machine-gun fire and a shell burst outside. According to Chalke the real sound effects were greeted with applause!

A word in conclusion must be directed to the general question of maintaining the physical health of squadron personnel and on the provisions for their spiritual welfare. A squadron would not have a Medical Officer but would have attached to its base an RAMC orderly. He

Taking the strain in 1918. No. 216 Squadron sports at Azelot in France. (Major H.A. Buss)

The Propellers, a Concert Party drawn from RNAS HQ in France in 1917. Pierrot costumes were fairly typical for such parties but this group seems very professionally attired. (P.H.L. Archives)

Squadron Concert Parties was more variable. Worsop Hyde (No. 54 Squadron) had embarrassed recall of his performance dressed as a girl in a blond wig singing in a duet 'She'd a hole in her stocking'. Costumes were bought in Dunkirk but there is no mention of the female part in his letters home just that: 'all my time has been spent in rehearsing, learning parts, designing costumes, shopping, painting posters and practising with the orchestra.'[33] No. 54 Squadron actually had their song book privately printed and bound in Cambridge in 1917[34] and there are still attractively amusing verses within 'We haven't got a Hope in the Morning' sung to the tune of 'John Peel':

  We were escorting Twenty Two
  Hadn't a notion what to do
  So we shot down a Hun and an F.E. too
  Cos they hadn't got a hope in the morning.

would attend to minor ailments and injuries and would have the necessary supplies for this. Incidentally, he was not allowed to issue pain-killing drugs. The nearest Army unit would have a Regimental Medical Officer and staff and this was the squadron's first dispenser of advice or aid before Wing or Brigade were to be contacted concerning serious cases. Anxiety neuroses, or the presence of stress related to the performance of flying duties, was but dimly understood. Research was being conducted into this and into physiological aspects of flying but in a basic sense it was well appreciated by the executive officers of a squadron when a pilot or observer had been in France long enough, needed a break or perhaps a transfer to Home Establishment. From reading the contemporary papers or recollections of many flyers, it is noteworthy that aircrew needing a rest frequently had it provided before they had fully realised their need.

In this perhaps the flying personnel were privileged. Though there was no scientifically based awareness of the elements around which flying fatigue developed and a generalised 'he's too old' or 'he's been out long enough' was not the stuff from which a medical research paper could be written, it seems that the Air Services led the way in sympathetic treatment of the man whose reservoir of self-reliance had been called upon too often.

In regard to concern for the spiritual welfare of officers and men in the RFC and its sister service, there really is overwhelming evidence from personal experience material that the formalities of religion made little or no impact on men under active service conditions. A squadron did not have a Padre, though there was a noteworthy exception to this with Padre Keymer attached to No. 40 Squadron. Church parades were not held as a matter of course and so men did not engage collectively, as did the 800 soldiers of a battalion, in a formal act of worship on all Sundays where such a service was practicable. Even allowing for the social attitude of the period when church-going and the expression of a religious faith were common, the Flying Services were simply not military units where religion played any open part except in the brief but moving funerals at which the spirit of the dead was involuntarily committed to the Lord and the thoughts of the pall bearers and witnesses must have been drawn towards the great unanswered questions. This is not written by any means to deny the strength given by prayer, communion, confession or discussion on spiritual matters with a helpful counsellor, a layman or a visiting Padre. Religiously inspired letters from parents or priest at home may certainly have uplifted individuals already confident in their faith or needing reassurance but it does seem that one Commanding Officer, considering in retrospect the question of the interrelationship of the war, the airman and religion, expressed sentiments which may stand for many. He had seen so many men killed, 'all of whom no doubt had families and friends praying for them to no avail, I came to the conclusion that the whole thing was a load of rubbish, despite a fairly strict upbringing as a Christian. I don't think my attitude was unusual: we seemed to be a secular lot, and the only religious observance that I can remember, if it can be called that, was the inevitable party at Christmas.'[35]

7

In Warmer Climes

The Middle East and India. Russia and the Dardanelles

The degree to which the Air Arm influenced British campaigns away from France and Flanders is as open a question as the extent to which the Allied victory on the Western Front was dependent upon the work of the RAF. There are certainly high points of dramatically effective operations, but this chapter does not seek to address a question which draws in so many imponderable and unquantifiable factors. Instead, it attempts to reveal the distinctive elements of personal experience of service in air units where topographical and climatic conditions were so different from those faced just across the Channel. To set against the striking reduction and not infrequent absence of enemy opposition, there were factors which either singly or in association made for characteristic problems in flying in the 'side shows'. For the men there were particular physical discomforts and the possibility of disease, the inadequacy of mapping for many regions, special dangers in a forced landing in remote areas, while the machines themselves, seldom of the latest type, quite apart from the length of supply line, also suffered from the heat and extremes of climate.

EGYPT AND PALESTINE

In Egypt, flying reconnaissance to guard against a Turkish attack on the Suez Canal began as early as the end of November 1914. The RFC establishment in Egypt was streng-

Egypt: Kantara, January 1915. A Maurice Farman Longhorn plays its part as an aerial advance guard for the Suez Canal. (Captain C.R.S. Pitman)

8

No private Photographs of any subject whatever are to be taken within the precincts of the Aerodrome. Private cameras are not to be taken into the air.

Writing and signatures on Daily Flying States must be *legible*.

ACCIDENTS.

1. In the event of an accident no Pupil is to go out to the scene of the accident unless ordered to do so by his instructor.

2. The Pilot must immediately make out a complete list of the damaged parts and report with this to "A" Flight for duty.

The Squadron Telephone number is Abbassia 15.

AERODROME.

1. *No one will cross any part of the Old (Northern) Aerodrome at any hour of the day or night.*

2. Every Pupil will make a sketch of the New (Southern) Aerodrome and hand same to his Instructor within five days of his arrival. This must show clearly the boundaries of the Aerodrome.

3. No Pupil will land outside the boundaries of the Aerodrome without the express permission of his Instructor.

4. Pupils will wear safety helmets and goggles on all Flights. No Pupil will under any circumstances take up a passenger.

CIRCUITS.

1. The RED PENNANT means that right handed circuits will be made around the Aerodrome. The BLUE PENNANT left hand circuits.

2. No Pupil will, on any account, except that of engine failure, change the direction of the circuits e.g. turn right handed when circuits are being flown left handed.

9

3. No turn whatsoever will be made within 300 yards of the Boundary of the new Aerodrome. A right angle turn (90°) is the sharpest turn permitted at any altitude less than 500 feet.

4. Landings and "taking off" will be made in accordance with the "T".

5. A Machine that only just complies with the regulations laid down in paras. 3 and 4 may be described as performing a "Minimum Circuit".

6. No Machine will be navigated so as to in any way interfere with or cross the course of machines performing a "Minimum Circuit".

STARTING.

1. On getting into the machine, the Pilot will :—
1. Shut the door.
2. Put on his belt.
3. Test the controls.
4. Hold the stick full back with right elbow.
5. See that the switch is off and turn on the petrol.
6. Say "Switch off"—"Petrol on".
7. The mechanic will say "Suck in Sir". The Pilot will then open the throttle full, close the Air Flap and reply "Suck in".
8. When ready the mechanic will say "Contact".
9. The Pilot will then :—
   (1) Release the Air Wire.
   (2) Close the throttle.
   (3) Put switch up at "Contact".
   (4) Take hold of the throttle.
   (5) Reply "Contact".

2. *Note.*—Whether the switch is off or on the Pilot must keep his hand clear of the switch, excepting only when actually manipulating it.

Flying Training in Egypt, Abbassia, 1917: 'Thou shalt and Thou shalt not'. Pages from a rule book issued to officer cadets and NCOs undergoing instruction at No. 21 Reserve Squadron. (T.S. Brooks)

thened progressively. Aircraft cooperation was necessary in the Western Desert against the Senussi tribesmen and in the south to frustrate the rebellion of Ali Dinar, Sultan of Darfur, in the Sudan. The Egyptian Expeditionary Force strove to break through the Gaza Beersheba positions which frustrated entry into Palestine until late in 1917 and to fight its way north towards Syria.

Flying training in Egypt played a notable part in preparing pilots for the expanded air commitment in the Middle East. The training of pilots in Egypt by three reserve squadrons had commenced in the summer of 1916 and No. 3 School of Military Aeronautics at Aboukir was formed in November. Sixty pupils per month were to undergo training. The school served more than its 'local' needs. Those who qualified but were not needed for the Middle East establishment were returned to the UK after fifteen hours' solo flying. The climate was markedly more suitable for an uninterrupted seasonal programme of training than the British climate, and the training establishment in Egypt was expanded in 1917 and 1918, despite the fact that by this time Canada and the United States of America had

been drawn into the augmented provision of flying training facilities. Gunnery, aerial fighting tactics, artillery observation, navigation, bomb dropping and armament schools were developed properly to supplement the basic flying training provision in Egypt.

However, it cannot be said that climatic conditions were ideal for flying as the intense heat made the air so bumpy that in Professor A.C. Chibnall's recall of elementary training in November 1917, work was suspended after the early morning period until dusk brought a fall in temperature. 'At this stage we were never in the air for more than half an hour, and as only one lesson a day was possible we pupils were left with much time on our hands. Between 11 a.m. and about 4 p.m. we tried to sleep . . . for want of something to do I'm afraid we wasted many hundreds of hours playing poker.'[1] Stifling hot marquees allotted for recreation were not conducive to reading or indeed any form of relaxation.

Away from either the Nile or the coast, there were few geographical or man-made landmarks for cross-country aerial navigation. On one such flight, a cadet, Miles Thomas, who had just had the thrill of going solo, experiencing

The aftermath of a mid-air collision between two Avro 504 trainers 600 feet over Heliopolis, Egypt. Both the pilots in this crash, Lieutenant P.H. Marchant, RAF, and Flight Cadet Downe, an Australian, were killed. Why the strong Naval presence? (T.S. Brooks)

total self-dependence in the air, was forced down in featureless desert by a broken fuel pipe. He was fortunate to be located and his machine repaired.[2] One test was to fly into the desert and practise gliding down to earth, landing and without delay taking off again: 'bumps'. On such an occasion, the engine of Chibnall's DH6 cut out after landing. He jumped out of the cockpit, having made a slight adjustment to the throttle and went to restart the engine by pulling on one of the propeller blades. 'As the engine was warm she kicked off at once and I stood back a little, feeling rather pleased with myself at my success. Suddenly I noted that the machine was slowly starting to move towards me.' The wheels were un-chocked but the pilot's swift reactions enabled him to get to the cockpit and throttle back.[3]

C.A.L. Meredith was one of the many pilots whose basic flying training was undertaken at Heliopolis and who therefore enjoyed the splendid accommodation of the Heliopolis Palace Hotel. He flew the DH6 from Shallufa on the Suez Canal and remembers that re-cognised dress for flying was shirt, shorts, rope shoes and goggles and that his DH6 was called the 'Dung Hunter' by Australians deriding its slowness.[4]

After the Egyptian Expeditionary Force broke out from the Gaza Strip into Palestine in the spring of 1917, some of the restrictions

The end of a Bristol Fighter on an Egyptian aerodrome. The fate of the crew is unknown. (F.W. Isern-Smith)

upon flying in Palestine may have come as a surprise to the airmen of the RFC. Just before the capture of Jerusalem in December 1917, No. 14 Squadron, based near Latron, was completely water-logged after heavy downfalls of rain and simply could not get its machines off the ground. The CO imaginatively ordered the clearance of rocks from the slope of a hill on the north side of the airfield and then the aircraft were manhandled to the top of the hill. There, men held the struts and these men themselves were held by others behind each wing, the engines were revved up and at a given signal the machines set off down the hill, just managing to lift off before the boggy ground at

A major's car in Palestine. A Crossley Tourer was issued to a squadron for the use of the Commanding Officer. He could on occasion be persuaded to make it available to the officers of his squadron. Behind the wheel of this Tourer is Major Medhurst, the CO of No. 14 Squadron. (Air Chief Marshal Sir Charles Medhurst)

The funeral of a German airman who is being accorded full Military Honours, his pall bearers being British officers, both pilots and observers. The date and place are not known but the front is likely to be Palestine with the funeral party being drawn from No. 14 Squadron. (Squadron Leader G.W. Holderness)

Rail Power: Egypt and the build-up of RFC strength. RE8s are in transit. It is scarcely necessary to draw attention to the removal of the wings but it may be noticed that the engine of the machine on the left has been taken out for this rail journey. (G.D. Breffitt)

Right. Into Palestine: The bombing of Turkish reservoirs. Water can be seen issuing from the rectangular reservoir in the lower centre of the photograph. (F.W. Isern-Smith)

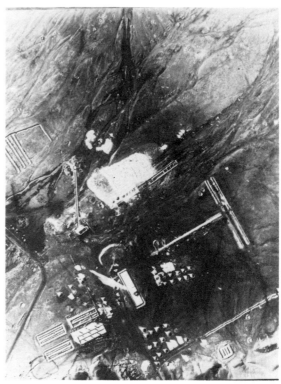

the bottom of the slope. From the air, No. 14 Squadron reported on a Turkish retirement, a retirement in which they played their part with bombing and machine-gunning.[5]

H.G. Penwarden (observer No. 142 Squadron) and his pilot, Lieutenant Garnett, were not in full flying kit as they were returning from a successful bombing raid East of the Dead Sea on 17 July 1918. Their AW FK8 had been damaged by ground-fire. A forced landing was necessary near Arab encampments and the prospect of captivity in Arab or Turkish hands was not to be relished. It proved easy to destroy their machine. The first Arab who arrived to menace the two flyers took the bribe of coins to leave them unmolested but his shouts drew in fellow mounted tribesmen who, having looted the men and burned their aeroplane, drove

Palestine, October 1918. Turkish and German forces retreating to the north provided obvious targets for air attacks. The accuracy of RAF bombing and machine-gunning may be judged from the destruction of this transport column near Damascus. (Squadron Leader H.G. Penwarden)

them as one would drive sheep to their village. Here, they became objects of great interest, drawing visitors from far and wide. After three weeks of tent captivity, horses were brought for them to travel north to a town near Es Salt. In this town they were displayed to the local population and, menacingly, RAF bomb damage was shown to them before they were incarcerated in the local prison. Here, before their eyes, they were sold to the Turkish authorities – the currency being English gold sovereigns. The Turks passed their captives to the Germans in Es Salt and then Penwarden was sent on to captivity in Constantinople by train.[6]

Two years before Penwarden was captured, the RFC had played its part in a minor operation which had been carried out with complete success. A small British military force was sent south from Egypt to the Sudan to deal with the rebellion of Ali Dinar, Sultan of Darfur. There seems just a hint of the explorer and some might think of the imperialist in Lieutenant Thornton's letters relating to this affair. 'I am in Darfur, a country lying between the Sudan and Equatorial Africa. No white man had been here before this expedition since the time of Gordon. So it is mostly unexplored! It was an independent state but the Sultan thought the war gave him a good chance to annoy the British, so became very "uppish". So we are on

an expedition against him and "C" Flight is helping'. This particular observer had had an uncomfortable journey to reach Darfur. It had included an eight day camel-trek. He had never previously been on camel-back and the natives accompanying the camels spoke no English and did not know the area through which they were travelling. At Darfur, Thornton was to do no flying as the weight of a second crew member would have put El Fasher, the objective of operations, beyond range. He mentions, however, that one of the pilots was put out of flying too, in this case because the pilot's eyes became badly affected by the sun.[7]

After the Sultan's army had been in an unsuccessful but gallant charge upon a British defensive square, aerial pursuit harassed the fleeing Dervishes. Sir John Slessor remembers that as one of the pilots flying in protective patrol over the British Column advancing upon El Fasher, he had dropped two 20 lb bombs on the tribesmen in flight. He kept his last bomb for the large white camel which he had been forewarned would carry the Sultan and would have accompanying figures carrying large flags. 'I drew a careful bead and really had rather bad luck. At the time I thought: "That's marvellous, I've done it". I was quite low of course

Egypt: Camel power. Two ships of the desert tow a BE2c to a required location. (Squadron Leader G.W. Holderness)

and it didn't require much skill and what happened actually we heard later, that the bomb landed almost under the camel but fortunately for "Master" the poor camel was between him and the explosion so Ali Dinar got a nasty fall and wasn't hurt. The camel of course was blown to pieces.'[8]

Adaptation in the field was naturally part and parcel of such a technical Service as the RFC but with severe shipping losses in the Mediterranean, a former Senior Equipment Officer at No. 196 Training Squadron, F.N. Trinder, remembers what a struggle it was to keep 70 aircraft serviceable out of about 120 on the station. It could only be done by salvaging parts from even the worst crashes.[9] One successful improvisation was produced by a wireless section which, returning to Heliopolis after undertaking artillery cooperation operations in the Western Desert, engaged in some experiments using a wind-driven propeller to power their Rouzet generator. The generator was intended to re-charge the accumulators which powered the wireless transmitters in the aeroplanes. Trial and experiment were undertaken

Observer pilots a camel in the Sudan. On (or off?) balance, it looks as if Gerard Thornton's camel trek to Darfur is commencing uncomfortably. He shows promise in handling the controls but bumps of one sort or another seem likely to lie ahead. (G. Thornton per Thornton Family.)

Probably 'souvenired' from a captured Turk or German, this photograph was taken behind the Turkish lines in Palestine. The crashed aeroplane is an RE8 from No. 1 Squadron, Australian Flying Corps, and clearly at least one of the crew did not survive. Note that the observer's Lewis gun has already been removed. (T.S. Brooks, 2nd Air Mechanic)

to find the right size of propeller. On one occasion, the Rouzet was mounted on the upper wing of a BE2c and the propeller under test disintegrated in the air causing damage to the aeroplane's engine and tailplane and enforcing an emergency landing. The Wireless Equipment Officer who recorded this information, P.P. Eckersley,[10] had been thrilled when he had an opportunity to go up for a 'joy ride' to see that Egypt from the air was just what he had always pictured it to be: 'Cairo the apex of

The Cheops Pyramid: almost obligatory background for servicemen photographed in Egypt. F.W. Isern-Smith on the left with two friends. (F.W. Isern-Smith)

getting the wireless going and by now two big poles pricked the firmament and we were receiving messages from ships, naval stations etc. all around the place. It's always rather amusing setting up stations in new places, choosing sites, arranging things etc.' His shared tent was by now welcoming with electric lights, Egyptian mats, Persian rugs, drapery over the camp bed, tables and chests of drawers with ornaments or utilities such as ashtrays, metal inlay boxes, pipes, letter-knives, tobacco tins and lots of books. 'In the daytime we take up our rugs with housewifely precision so that dirty boots shall not sully their beauty.'

The degree to which Shepherd's Hotel was ultimately bound up with the life of the RFC officer within reach of Cairo is made clear in Eckersley's diary. 'Shall I ever forget Sammy's farewell dinner. Before supper everyone was inclined to be rowdy but the effect of champagne which flowed like water was something amazing ... I remember Sammy standing up flushed and noisy shouting above the decorous murmur of the crowded restaurant, "Here's to the prettiest girl in the room" ... a poor lonely female was fixed by 20 pairs of laughing eyes which at a given signal were switched round on the poor Miss Haddon sitting with her mother just behind us. Then there were healths [drunk] to Sammy and his engine and people showed more of an inclination to stand up and shout – the scandalised band found itself conducted and accompanied by 20 raucous voices and I noticed neighbouring tables rapidly emptying. The manager of the Hotel was roped in and made to sit patiently while people started to smash glasses. Then slowly things culminated into an inferno – an apple twanged through the air and Dudley Gardener's eye suddenly filled and swelled – Jock Will was trying to make a speech and Sammy was on the table dancing on the liqueur glasses and dessert.' One of the party tried without success to drag a large plant in its huge pot over a glass roof, the piano being rendered less melodious by the addition of glass beads from the chandelier to its internal workings and then: 'finally I got home and was desperately ill but later slept the sleep of the just.'

a triangular green thing called the delta which itself is flanked by a brown flatwash of desert – cutting through the flatwash to the South one sees ... the Nile on and on into the misty unknown.' The brown rolling desert, wind-carved into rounded hillocks and abrupt cliffs, was the new detail outside his earlier imagination. 'Flying out here is different at first ... the air is apt to be bumpy owing to the sudden changes of temperature and also no one judges their landings well at first, why I can't say.' The interest of his wireless work in unfamiliar surroundings was, however, more Eckersley's concern than flying conditions. 'I had been

MESOPOTAMIA

Cairo provided opportunities which were never paralleled in Mesopotamia; indeed, air support work in the land of the Fertile Crescent was infernally difficult for man and machine. Little in the way of relaxed socialising leavened the work of the RFC personnel operating first from Basra then further up the Tigris as the 1915 advance was undertaken. With an Indian Army division besieged in Kut at the end of 1915 after this ill-advised advance, the celebrated aerial exploits of dropping medical supplies, flour in sacks, wireless and engine parts and other supplies in bags and, by parachute, a millstone were carried out. However, the RFC, represented by No. 30 Squadron, had neither the more advanced types of machine nor sufficient aircraft seriously to harass the Turks or aid the British force in Kut – nor, indeed, could the RNAS seaplanes provide more than limited support. From early in the Mesopotamian Campaign, useful reconnaissance had been carried out despite unfavourable ground and climatic conditions. When more machines of a newer type were provided, valuable work was done in preventing German and Turkish overflights of the British preparations and operations. The Turks were vigorously harried in their 1917 retreat as well as the retreat being clearly observed throughout daylight hours. It is entirely appropriate that the *Official History* notes that in all these operations under severe climatic and physical conditions, the air mechanics and transport personnel had worked wonders in keeping the machines serviceable.[11]

Ingenuity had been to the fore among the RFC personnel besieged in Kut. Corporal Candy's diary relates that men were detailed to supervise the pumping of water from the Tigris for drinking purposes while others made bombs and rifle-grenades. A trench mortar was made out of some Gnome engine cylinders. More prosaically, sign boards were made for trench identification, but 'we took over a gas engine and freezing plant to convert to workshop use. It was also connected with a flour grinder which we had put in order.' It was

galling to discover from examination of the fragments of two bombs dropped on them by the Turks that they were bombs the RFC had lost on the retreat from Ctesiphon. Stands were improvised to adapt Maxim machine-guns for anti-aircraft use but no success was achieved against the bombing raids by enemy machines. From the force attempting to relieve Kut, Candy observed: 'Four of our machines came up this afternoon and bombed the enemy boats and aerodrome. About the same time another machine came over and dropped emergency rations of some dates and chocolate.'[12] Further relief supplies were dropped but it was insufficient to avert disaster and Kut fell at the end of April 1916.

If the small 1916 RFC establishment in Mesopotamia were scarcely in a position materially to influence events in that year, expansion of the establishment in 1917/18, hand in hand with overall military reinforcement, played a significant part in the defeat of the Turk. In the successes which followed upon the earlier failure, climatic conditions were again recorded as being exceptionally demanding with temperatures of 50 degrees centigrade in July, 58 degrees within tents. For some men, the humidity as well as the heat of Basra were simply insupportable. These men became incapacitated and a number even died from heatstroke. For the machines, radiator water boiled and timber and fabric shrank. A pilot, 6,000 feet above Basra harbour, actually saw the whole top wing warp into waves and steam scalded his face.[13] Small wonder that Ford trucks and Crossley tenders had to rescue more than the occasional machine when failure of one sort or another enforced an unplanned landing.[14]

In a letter written at the end of June 1918, R.S. Blucke, who had recently transferred to the RAF (No. 63 Squadron) and trained as an observer, complained that not only was the air so hot that it was 'horrible' but that the air in June was now what he called 'thinner' than earlier in the year. 'When gliding down to land the air becomes so thin that it does not give you the same support as when it's denser, of course consequently one seems literally to drop the

Mesopotamia: In field maintenance, Amara, 1917. Block and tackle arrangement for engine removal and replacement, with an RE8 being wheeled into position for this work. (Major General A.H.J. Snelling)

last 500 feet or so.' But even with this problem in landing, Blucke contrasted his acute dislike of Mesopotamia as a soldier with that of his airman's judgement that it was 'quite bearable'. On the subject of hot air of a verbal kind, he wrote that it was absolutely banned and that he personally loathed it but there were a great many who had a predeliction for it and for that reason he judged it would be better if Smith's stopped sending him *The Tatler*.[15]

Ingenuity as described by Corporal Candy was not limited to ground personnel. One of the most striking examples of experimentation towards an increased offensive potential was conducted above the Tigris by Charles Chabot. He mounted five Lewis guns above the wheel

axle of his BE2c and fitted a sort of three-foot long brake lever to a cross tube on the floor of the cockpit with which to activate the triggers. Swooping over the Tigris in full view of sceptical members of the squadron, Chabot had been thrilled by the tremendous noise of the guns, the pattern of the bullets hitting the water and the fact that the aircraft's performance was not affected. Sadly for his hope of more senior endorsement of his inventive capacity, the roar of the guns had so terrified

Mesopotamia, November 1917-January 1918. Lieutenant A.E.L. Skinner (the central figure of the three) and his SPAD S VII of No. 30 Squadron at Faluja. In this machine, he shot down a German AEG two-seater on 31 January 1918. (E.F. Bolton)

The result of a less than satisfactory landing by a BE2c, probably from No. 30 Squadron in Mesopotamia, has drawn the interest of officers and men of the 27th Punjabi Regiment. (Captain C.R.S. Pitman)

cavalry horses watering at the river, that they had fled in all directions to the fury of official-dom which in consequence negated Chabot's 'foolery . . . with a silly contraption'. In such a manner was stifled the first British personal initiative to develop a multi-gun device for the air.[16]

Despite difficult conditions and enemy opposition in the air, albeit limited, the Turks were relentlessly harried by bombing both before the fall of Baghdad in March 1917 and then in the pursuit to utter defeat as they retired along the line of the Diyala, the Tigris or the Euphrates.

The Air Arm was to play its part too in support of the detached force which reached the Caspian, where it came in contact with Bolshevik opposition, and also in Northern Persia and even in operations against dissident tribesmen on the North-West Frontier of India.

NORTHERN PERSIA

In 1918, a British military presence was deemed essential in Persia to combat subver-sion of the Allied cause and the RAF sent a detachment. On landing at Kermanshah, one of the SE5a pilots sent up to Persia from Baghdad, Lieutenant A.A. Cullen, hit an un-marked drainage ditch across the landing field and crashed. A tooth and a propeller were thus the first losses incurred. Cullen travelled by lorry to Hamadan. From here another SE5a failed to take-off in the rarified air at the 6,000-foot altitude of this town. It crashed too, leaving its pilot badly shocked and in no state to renew his attempt to reach Kasvin. Cullen volunteered to take his place but had to travel by night 150 miles in a Ford car to get to Kasvin where a Martinsyde awaited a pilot for a long-distance reconnaissance to search for evidence of any Turkish advance. Cullen's duty was to conduct a 300-mile reconnaissance flight over unknown mountainous country in a machine of a type he had never previously flown. His totally inadequate map was of ap-proximately 31 miles to the inch. A large part of his flight was to be over Kurdish territory where a hostile reception could certainly be expected if difficulties were to force him to land. In fact, he avoided disaster from anti-aircraft fire above Tabriz and effected two rather nervous landings, the second of which resulted in his being surrounded by Tartar horsemen of uncompromisingly unfriendly de-meanour. They searched him, took him pris-oner and gave him an uncomfortable pony ride into Turkish hands. Cullen's lack of full uniform proved dangerous as it was maintained that he was clandestinely stirring up Armenian resistance to their Turkish overlords. Stout defence was made against such a charge and a firing squad was not in the end to be his lot; instead, it was to be Turkish captivity and interrogation by the Germans.[17]

NORTH RUSSIA

A good deal less fortunate still in the conditions of his captivity had been Kenneth van der Spuy, the RAF officer sent to Archangel in 1918 to command a Wing designated to co-operate with anti-revolutionary forces. In April 1919, engine failure led to a forced landing and capture by the Bolsheviks. In his autobio-graphy, Major General van der Spuy provides a stark account of privation within a setting of the prolonged strain of the likelihood of being shot.[18] Even allowing for the practical achievement of the RAF in operating from so remote a region as North Russia and in the Baltic in 1918–19, and acknowledging that 1919 saw some remarkable exploits, like the Kronstedt raid, the squadrons in operation, as with the other British units engaged, were but the most insignificant of pawns on the huge geographical and political chess board of Russia. Corporal Green of the RAF in North Russia was surely exaggerating what might have been accomplished when he used rhyme to announce:[19]

> There's a squadron near the Dvina,
> it's called the RE8
> It might have been a great success
> if it hadn't come too late.

However, he succinctly expressed the futility of the mission in a later couplet:

> They came to bomb the Bolsheviks
> and Vickers guns to fire
> But now they're trying to stop them
> by nailing up barbed wire.

THE NORTH-WEST FRONTIER OF INDIA

From winter snows and summer mosquitoes in North Russia we may come to the North-West Frontier of India where the heat and breathless exhaustion on the ground had to be exchanged for the usual sub zero temperatures encountered in high altitude flying. Aerial operations in India were in regions as geographically remote from the UK as those related above, but they were in areas where there was a long established British military presence. The history of No. 31 Squadron has some vignettes strikingly illustrative of their pioneer air unit work on the North-West Frontier. There was advantage in the fact that tribal chiefs had apparently believed that the BE2cs were only large birds without anyone inside them but in technical terms, engine overheating and the need for longer take-off and landing runs on airfields in the rarified mountain air, were two factors with which the squadron soon became depressingly familiar.

Security of the North-West Frontier was

The North-West Frontier: One of the great birds ready to take to the air. A photograph taken in 1916 of a BE2c of No. 31 Squadron attracts an audience on the airfield at Tank on the North-West Frontier of India. This machine (No. 4535) was still being used in punitive action on the frontier in 1919 by No. 31 Squadron. (S.T. Price)

something over which especial anxieties were held and hence the villages of tribes considered hostile were bombed and files of men and camels on mountain tracks in the vicinity were machine-gunned. 'The tribesman is an adept in the art of concealing himself and it is seldom that a good human target is found for bombs and machine guns. Their flocks and herds, offer however an ideal target, and the strafing of these eventually persuades the bellicose tribesmen to listen to reason, and to return to more peaceable pursuits than raiding and the cutting up of picquets.'[20]

The 'moral' effect of the aeroplane was considerable. Though the Mohmand, Mahsud and Waziri tribesmen proved the renowned accuracy of their marksmanship by hitting low-flying machines, there is an indication of the favourable odds enjoyed by the RAF in the fact that even in 1919, a stealthy approach by tribesmen to a hangar led to its roof being bullet-riddled rather than the structure at ground level because it was reckoned by those who were captured in the raid, that the great birds would rise off their nests in alarm towards the roof and endeavour to escape. There is, however, a sobering reference in No. 31's Squadron History to the cautionary provision of 'gooli chits' against the capture of airmen by tribesmen celebrated for the refinement of the cruel, slow torture by mutilation and then dispatch of their prisoners. 'Gooli chits' were a form of paper receipt offering money in local languages in an attempt to buy the safe and 'intact' return of any grounded airman.

MACEDONIA

In comparison with the limited, negligible or, as in India, non-existent air to air opposition faced by British airmen on some of the distant operations which have been mentioned, there were two where such opposition was a definite if variable factor – Macedonia and Italy.

Patrolling over the Bulgarian positions on the Macedonian front, pilots and observers scanned hill and mountain positions, flat areas covered in long grass with stunted trees and the occasional village presenting an appearance of being deserted, an appearance which in its deception might well prove highly dangerous to British patrols on the ground. Observation from balloon was a key factor in areas of flatter terrain and considerable resources were devoted to achieving aerial superiority over the whole front, one indication of which would be the establishment of air bases on islands which facilitated attacks on Bulgarian communications.

2nd Class Air Mechanic Arthur Perry was with a Kite Balloon Section, No. 26, which was near Janesh in July 1917. A touch of the

Macedonia: Stavros. Flight Lieutenant Jack Alcock with the only Sopwith Triplane to serve in the Eastern Mediterranean, an aeroplane which he flew in combat. In 1919, flying a Vickers Vimy, he completed the first non-stop aerial crossing of the Atlantic, a feat for which he was knighted. (T.W. Walker)

prevailing affliction, malaria, despite the quinine parades, led him to comment acidly in his diary about the splendid feast and panoply for a visit from the French General, Sarrail. 'It does not seem the right thing out here, especially when the great cry coming from home is "economy".' Windy conditions frequently prevented the use of the balloon and grass fires hindered observation. Enemy aerial observation of their unit resulted in shelling which forced them to move to a valley which was 'one mass of ravines and the balloon bed is in one; only mules can use the surrounding paths.' Though recovering from his sickness he was: 'Getting very fed up with unpacking and packing, unserviceable balloons, inflating with air and deflating, then same with gas. Then continually patching and repairing them.' This was despite the fact that he was able to go 'scrumping' in the hills for grapes, pears, figs and blackberries.

In October 1917, torrential rain and wind led at least to the compensatory commencement of the winter rum issue, but a neighbouring section, No. 17, had its balloon brought down in flames by a hostile aircraft on 27 October 1917. This unlucky section was to be visited again on 9 November, Perry recording that No. 17 Section's Commanding Officer was shot in the jaw by machine-gun fire from an enemy aircraft while the officer was observing from the balloon. 'He then jumped from the basket and had not toggled on properly to parachute and crashed to earth. Killed instantly.' The mechanic later in the month wrote of No. 17 Section's revenge on 21 November 1917 over their celebrated opponent, by then known to be von Eschwege: 'The Captain told us that decoy balloon was put up filled with high explosives ... when the hostile plane got quite close to balloon it was exploded by means of electric spark and overturned plane and killed pilot. He was a very daring pilot and had brought down many planes and sausages [colloquialism for balloons].'

In the following year Perry himself was to experience at first hand an attack, not by shelling to which his section had had to become accustomed, but by aeroplane. On hearing a noise early on 16 June and 'looking up see Boche sweeping down to 1,000 feet, he straightens up and fires at balloon, see the trail of tracers showing very good mark; Mr P . . . . comes out of basket and balloon catches fire at top of back, there being no wind the parachute comes down nearly straight and the balloon catching fire very quickly soon descends with an awful roar very quickly, it looked as if it would fall on parachute and the draught of the fire caused parachute to sway very much causing a very bad landing. I was soon on the scene and the fabric was all consumed only the basket ropes and instruments remain scattered about.'[21]

Macedonia, 1917: Undeniably a smart body of men. The Transport Section of No. 26 Kite Balloon Section, RFC. Each man has his swagger cane and 'fashion' dictates that none is without a moustache. For a man to change his appearance by shaving off a moustache or growing one from a clean shaven upper lip required official permission. (W.H. Brand)

Just as an Equipment Officer in Egypt recalled the struggle to maintain effective work there, so does the diary of Wireless Equipment Officer Peter Eckersley, with No. 17 Squadron, record frustrations on the Macedonian Front.[22] Perhaps it ought not to have been a surprise to him that the French had already acquired the only suitable landing ground in Salonika, nor that the Army Command Staff refused to allow the squadron's Commanding Officer to contact RFC HQ in Egypt with details of their problems regarding facilities for both machines and men, but he also had to cope with constant changes of plans regarding the location of wireless stations with the gun batteries to be used in the planning of the 1916 offensive. A period of testing and trials revealed inadequacies in equipment and inexperience in men, his supervisory duties requiring lengthy tedious travel over difficult mountainous terrain. Admitted to hospital with malaria, he perceived that he was getting poorer treatment than that given to patients in an adjacent hospital, the depressing effect of malaria releas-

Macedonia: Balloon biter bitten. A formidable opponent to Allied airmen was the German pilot Rudolf von Eschwege, known to his Bulgarian Allies as 'The Eagle of the Aegean'. Von Eschwege was officially credited with a total of twenty victories which included three kite balloons. He proved a threat in October/November 1917 to No. 17 Balloon Section of the RFC at Orljak and a decoy balloon was especially 'prepared' for him (21 November 1917). In the basket was a dummy observer and 500 lb of explosive. When von Eschwege made his expected attack the explosive was electronically detonated from the ground and the destructive radius of the blast was sufficient to cripple his aircraft, causing it to crash, the pilot being killed. It is likely that the officer (an observer) responsible, is pictured here to the right, looking at the body of his fallen adversary beside the wreckage of the Albatros D.III. (C. King)

Macedonia: Stavros 29 April 1917. Sopwith 1½-Strutter, bombers version, of 'F' Squadron, RNAS (formed in April of that year), preparing to take off for operations on the Doiran/Struma Front. The Commanding Officer's machine with its distinctive markings can be seen taxying out ahead of the other machines. (T.W. Walker)

Macedonia, March 1918: Captain G.E. Gibbs of No. 17 Squadron RFC, a victor in several combats, was probably responsible for the enforced hospitality which these two German airmen are receiving. (Captain B. Foster Hall)

Left. Macedonia, spring 1917: Flight Lieutenant Bradley of 'E' Squadron, RNAS, with the German Friedrichshafen bomber he has shot down. 'E' Squadron was a fighter unit at this period supporting the RFC on the Doiran Front. (T.W. Walker)

ing vitriol from his pen. The Greeks in particular earned his contempt as their 'chatter, extravagant gesture and their dirty, unwashed, low, evil, cunning faces' drove him to distraction. Cooperation with civilians and soldiers of the whole region was something he viewed with little enthusiasm. 'Who talks of a World state of cosmopolitanism? I would rather stick with the narrow minded prejudices of my country than ever call a Greek "Brother". All these Balkan peoples seem compounded of hate, ignorance and cruel stupidity.' Peter Eckersley, however dispirited he might have been by sickness, was it seems more closely aware of some of the difficulties of achieving a united Balkan effort against the Central Powers and their Bulgarian ally than those in Government who credulously

'The Macedonian Front': How near is a 'near miss'? During a bombing raid on ammunition dumps at Cestovo on 26 April 1918, Lieutenant Vaughan MC was grazed by a passing anti-aircraft shell, the marks of which can clearly be seen on the back of his leather flying coat. He suffered temporary paralysis but was otherwise unhurt. (Colonel M. MacEwan)

drew together contrasting threads of arguments convincing themselves that the achievement of overall victory could be secured within this region.

When the stagnation of the Macedonian campaign came to an abrupt end in September 1918, the RAF was involved in an operation which had grim parallels for French and British forces in Northern France in 1940 and for German forces in Normandy in 1944: the bombing and machine-gunning of Bulgarian troops and transport vehicles crowded in the Kosturino defile on the Strumica-Rabrovo road. By later standards, 112 lb and 20 lb bombs may not seem considerable, but the circumstance was such that tremendous destruction was wrought. One of the pilots whose log shows his bombing flights at the time recalled that 'it was sheer murder, the carnage was unbelievable.'[23]

ITALY

Italy was the other front over which British airmen encountered air opposition in significant numbers of enemy machines, during some months of 1917 and 1918. Originally, five squadrons were sent out to assist the Italians after their almost conclusive defeat at Caporetto in October 1917. The front line presented as varied a geographical scene as Macedonia. Airfields had to be found in the regions from the high Asiago plateau to the lower elevation of the Montello and then to the flatlands with their streams, marshes and the pebble-shored, wide river bed of the Piave to enable the multiple tasks to be carried out: air observation of the enemy positions, and denial of such opportunity to the Austro-Hungarians; ranging artillery onto enemy targets; and supporting the Allied counter-attack in June 1918 with contact patrols, and then harassing the enemy with bombing and machine-gunning so severely that their defeat was turned into a rout.

One distinctive element of this aerial work in Italy was that seasoned fighting units were sent out: there was no ad hoc improvisation of learning by trial and error as had largely been the case in the Middle East. Men and machines were combat-proved and support equipment, despite the length of the supply line, was adequately provided. This was all necessary because the Austro-Hungarian Air Service was itself well-experienced and supported by German fighter and bomber assets. The British found themselves first opposing the Austrians in the central position of the line, the Montello, in the renewed trench warfare. As the line stabilised after Caporetto, aerial observation and photo reconnaissance were the main priorities.

At this time, George Pirie's log book re-emphasises the jack of all trades nature of the work of the RE8 of No. 34 Squadron. In January 1918, the log details artillery shoots, some long reconnaissance flights, patrols, a dusk reconnaissance – on which he 'shot a couple [of] Austrians. Put wind up staff car' – a photo reconnaissance during which he was attacked by nine Huns but his Camel escorts brought two down in flames and one out of control, and then a bombing raid in which he led 23 RE8s escorted by eighteen Camels to Pordenone.[24]

Though characteristic of far more than just experience in one of the 'side shows' there is touching evidence from No. 28 Squadron in Italy of the mutual respect established across the ranks. It comes in the form of a letter from the warrant officers, non-commissioned officers and men to the mother of Lieutenant E.G. Chance who had been killed when he crashed his Sopwith Camel: 'Your late son was admired and loved by us all.' The letter is a tiny confirmation of what has been written in a number of sources and must be recognised: the squadron as a 'family'.[25]

It seems clear that there were advantages to serving in Italy. An August 1918 newcomer to No. 28 Squadron enjoyed the plentiful peaches, pears, iced lemon squash and ice cream, and two horses for exercising, a home-made canoe and a swimming pool. The newcomer, E.L. Roberts, wrote home directly for a bathing costume. Again adaptation in so technical a service as the RAF was to the fore as a stream was harnessed to turn an air fan to cool the ante room to the Mess. At this time enemy opposition in the air was far less than it had been hitherto. If a hostile aircraft were seen, 'the blighter puts his nose down and blinds for home or climbs out of our reach.' When he does escort work, Roberts refers to it in a letter home as a 'Cook's tour of Hun aerodromes', or 'Round the Alps with a Camera.' In September, a debating society was started, the young officer rather gleefully reporting to his sister that the first motion on whether the emancipation of women were beneficial to humanity was decided almost unanimously in the negative. By sad irony, in aerial combat soon after this, Lieutenant Roberts suffered a bullet wound through arm and throat but with commendable composure, brought his machine safely to ground.[26]

In May 1918, well before Roberts had arrived in Italy, the British squadrons had shot down 83 enemy aircraft, while 64 successes were recorded in June, but for August and more particularly September, air to air opposition was a good deal less. A Tasmanian Sopwith Camel pilot of No. 45 Squadron, R.J. Brownell, was to have combat experience in January and February. On 30 January he recorded: 'Had a most exciting scrap today. Three of us attacked enemy two seaters. I got down one in flames right away and a second was brought down by Hand. Then the three of us went into the one left. He went right down and the three of us fought him for 10 minutes at a height anything from 20 to 50 feet off the ground. We eventually got him but I was so badly shot about from the ground that I just managed to get back.'[27] The most celebrated of all such combats, but one concerning which there is discrepancy between the British and Austrian reports, was that of Lieutenant A. Jerrard of No. 66 Squadron on 30 March 1918. He achieved three victories against heavy numerical odds before he was shot down fighting in order to let the two other Camels of the flight escape. Jerrard was captured and learned in captivity of having been awarded the Victoria Cross.

Scenically, flying service in Italy provided breath-taking views of the Alps, of the Adriatic and Dalmatian coast and of Venice: 'glittering like a pink opal in the warm early sunlight.' A.F. Wilson of No. 34 Squadron who so described Venice from the air had the opportunity for some degree of tourism too, visiting Verona on Mess business and not missing Vicenza en route. He noticed that Verona had a cleaner, more modern appearance but that there was a 'very fine Piazza Dante and a Torre Lamberti exceedingly graceful especially the lantern above it.' However, more earthly pleasure than Medieval or Renaissance architecture was enjoyed the same week in his Mess: 'We had a binge to celebrate an M.C. Captain Matthias, very well earned. Many were drunk and many were flung into the streams to cool their ardour.'

Not long after this, the Commanding Officer of No. 14 Wing in Italy, Lieutenant Colonel Joubert de la Ferté, came to No. 34 Squadron and gave a lecture on the need for it to smarten

Italy, 1918: No. 28 Squadron's Concert Party, The Sprucers. (F. Brook)

Northern Italy, January 1918, Istranda airfield. Some of No. 45 Squadron's pilots chat with two Italian pilots prior to a patrol from their shared airfield. The pilots have been numbered and are, from left to right, an Italian (8), a Canadian, Lieutenant T.F. Williams (5), an Italian (6), two Englishmen Lieutenants H.J. Watts (4) and H.M. Moody (3), a Tasmanian, Lieutenant R.J. Brownell (1, in the background) and a Scot, Captain N. MacMillan (2). (Air Commodore R.J. Brownell)

itself up. Wilson soberly noted in his diary: 'There was a lot of truth in what he said but we didn't relish his way of saying it. The indications are that his hot air has communicated itself to our new Major Mounsey but we shall see.'[28] There is no further entry to cast light upon this but it is interesting to note that even in a relatively quiet period Wilson did not enjoy a Casualty Clearing Station concert party which ended with a skit on a hospital scene. He considered that behind any such scene was the reality and he did not consider it a fit subject for joking. There was a sad endorsement to his view: within a few days one of their observers was killed in action and then a flying accident occurred which he sensed as he lay in bed. He heard a spluttering engine, then silence followed by the sickening noise of rending wood and another pilot had just been injured in a crash following engine failure. It is in such incidents that we get a valuable reminder that all flying held potential danger in Britain, France or Italy and was in effect, if not in Service designation, 'active service', justifying its 8 shillings a day for officers and 4 shillings for other ranks.

On Colonel Joubert's supervisory visitations to which reference has been made, he used a Sopwith Pup with the gun removed. The alteration in weight distribution made the machine tail heavy but a rigger with No. 28

Squadron, Frank Brook, altered the stagger of the machine, that is re-rigged the wings, and in consequence it behaved perfectly. In a letter written in October 1918, the rigger provided a fine account of the business of moving a squadron to a new location: the hurried packing, the loading of the lorries and trailers with bombs, petrol and stores, and the ground staff personnel travelling in a Crossley tender at the rear of the convoy. A broken fan belt on a lorry delayed progress as did the detours through two cities with narrow, crowded streets in their ancient centres. Their destination was a racecourse on the outskirts of Treviso, Austrian bombing having already damaged one of the grandstands. As it was dusk, the lorry headlights were used to facilitate the erection of hangars but this was quickly disallowed as the Austrians had observation of the area and such illumination was an invitation to shelling or bombing. By the light of two candles and then later by the moon, the hangars were set up but, predictably, bombing interrupted rest after their exertions. The sky became 'alive with searchlights and bursting shells ... we made a dash for the trenches in which we squatted for some time.' Three more raids followed that night, but for the third, not one of the 40 ground personnel stirred from his bed.

Writing two days later on 26 October, Brook described something which from the British point of view well-deserved his concluding exclamation. An enemy machine had dived on a balloon through heavy anti-aircraft fire. As the machine opened fire on the balloon, four observers from the balloon parachuted safely to the ground but the aircraft collided with the balloon cable and its twisted wreckage came crashing down. The pilot, however, 'gently floated down "en parachute", landed safely and was made prisoner!! What a magnificent idea these parachutes are.'

The imminent end to the war was coincident with the almost universal curse, the influenza pandemic. Italy provided no safe refuge. Some wag chalked on the doors of the rooms in the billets occupied by sergeants lying in unfamiliar impotence: 'Ward I', 'Ward II', and so on. Brook ruefully accepted work as a sort of nursing sister. Those not afflicted struggled to keep all the machines serviceable as the Austrian artillery remained very active on their sector. On 27 October all day long, Allied reconnaissance machines sharing the landing ground swooped over the aerodrome sounding a Klaxon horn and dropping weighted messages. The position where the message would land was indicated by the brightly coloured streamers fluttering from the linen envelope with its message and lead weight. A motorcyclist raced off to pick up the message and take it to the wireless station to be wired off to HQ. The drama of the day is brought out vividly in the following letter: 'A big Caproni with a crew of five landed; three of the crew were wounded and the machine was all shot about. Many Italian machines landed, some crashed, others more lucky. We were worked to death, short of hands, our machines had to be kept going, bombing patrols were the orders and we were busy fixing and timing bombs and adjusting gears and so on. Gee it was lively, one pilot landing with a shot thro' his engine, [he had glided motorless from over the lines, only to crash on landing.] A Bristol pilot landed shot thro' the chest and so on.' Peace rumours and prisoners passing through provided excitement which sustained a capacity to accept almost ceaseless work in these last days of the war. Brook, as he wrote of the Armistice, was torn between returning to his safe job at the Bank and the exciting but perhaps soon to be overcrowded and hence underpaid world of civil flying. Confident in the competence he had gathered during his service, he speculated on the future of aviation. Sadly, he concluded that if he were to want a job for a good man with initiative and a chance to use his brains, he would have to look outside the RAF or a Government department.[29]

THE DARDANELLES AND THE AEGEAN

The distinctive nature of flying experience on two further fronts remains to be considered — the Dardanelles area and East Africa. From the start, air support of the 1915 Dardanelles Gallipoli Campaign was innovatively an integral part of all operations but also from the start and to the very end, it was in practical terms limited in resources and hence effectiveness.

The campaign, like a tramp's overcoat, was patched-up imaginatively to do its work, knock the Turks out of the war. At first this was to be done by ships bombarding the forts covering the minefields at the entrance and within the Narrows of the Dardanelles. Pilots of seaplanes from the aircraft carrier HMS *Ark Royal* strove to get necessary height from their machines effectively to observe for the ships' guns and to do the necessary reconnaissance work. When it became clear that a combined operation of military landings against alerted opposition would have to be undertaken, reconnaissance became still more important. The air resources were steadily augmented with further seaplane carriers, an airship, kite balloon ships and land-based aeroplanes operating from several islands, Tenedos, Mitylene, Rabbit Island and, most notably during the campaign itself, from the island of Imbros. They observed mines, enemy vessels, Turkish troop concentrations, trenches, gun positions and supplies in transit, took photographs and bombed, dropped darts on or machine-gunned, identified targets; additionally, dropping propaganda leaflets came within the terms of reference of the land-based machines. Even within the context of the limited effectiveness of machines in such rela-

The Dardanelles, 1915: A Wight pusher seaplane. In a similar machine (No. 172) from HMS *Ark Royal*, Flight Lieutenant Bromet and Lieutenant Commander Williamson made the first aerial reconnaissance of the Cape Helles fortifications on 17 February 1915. They dropped two bombs and their machine received seven hits from rifle or machine-gun fire. (Air Vice Marshal Sir Geoffrey Bromet)

'Bombe Surprise'. Flanked by two more orthodox bombs is a home-made monster, labelled in white paint or chalk '1st Sur-prize'. It looks, and perhaps was, a joke but there is some evidence that No. 3 Wing at Imbros were, around July 1915, actually building this bomb with the intention of dropping it from a Voisin. (R.F. Collins)

tively small numbers, of seaplanes always struggling to find sufficient height for their work, of the great difficulty of observation over the broken terrain of the Anzac sector, there were splendid endeavours and some notable exploits.

Away from the Penisula, boldly sustained attempts were made to destroy the Berlin-Constantinople railway bridge over the river Maritza and there was accurate bombing of a railway junction at Ferejik. During these raids there was a magnificent rescue of a pilot who had had to make an emergency landing. Squadron Commander R. Bell Davies landed his single-seater Nieuport within reach of Flight Sub-Lieutenant G.F. Smylie who was in the act of destroying his machine as Bulgarian troops hurried to capture him and forestall his action. Somehow, Smylie cooped himself under the Nieuport's petrol tank and Bell Davies coaxed the machine into the air again, saving his fellow pilot and in so doing, well-deserving the Victoria Cross which would in due course provide official recognition of his deed. A further celebrated coup, the first in the history of aviation, was the seaplane torpedoing of a Turkish steamer in August 1915, an event repeated on two other vessels. On the third occasion, the seaplane had an engine defect and was taxying within the Narrows when the victim, a tug, was found and attacked. The seaplane, now without its burdensome weapon, was able with further revving to lift from the water for a limping passage to its mother ship. In more general terms there is clear evidence that the bombing of Turkish troops not merely caused considerable casualties but had a discernible effect on morale.[30]

Some of the problems coincident with such a

The first aircraft to launch a torpedo attack was this Short 184 seaplane, No. 842, wearing its early national markings of red and white roundels on the upper wing and the Union Jack either side of the fuselage. Piloted by Flight Commander C.H.K. Edmonds of HMS *Ben My Chree* on 12 August 1915, a large Turkish steamer lying off Bulair was hit and was seen by Edmonds to be settling down by the stern. The full potential of this form of attack was not to be demonstrated until World War Two with Taranto and Pearl Harbor. (P.H.L. Archives)

long supply line for aircraft maintenance in the Eastern Mediterranean are remembered by Leading Mechanic Jefferies[31] who cast and machined new crank-shaft bearings for Commander Samson's BE2a No. 50 when no spares

Technical support but at a distance: Wright seaplanes under maintenance in the seaplane shed at Gibraltar, 1915. (Squadron Leader J.C. Andrews)

were available on the Isle of Tenedos. The extraordinary lengths to which adaptation proved necessary are exemplified most vividly by castor oil against dysentery being drawn on the Doctor's orders from the same drum as that used to lubricate the Gnome engines. Short supply of machines, engines and parts and inadequate quality of some of the seven aircraft types used were constant problems in the 1915 Dardanelles operations. To them may be added the local factors, sand and dust in engines,

The Dardanelles: This particular BE2a (No. 50) was the favourite machine of Commander C.R. Samson, the Officer Commanding No. 3 Wing, RNAS, on the island of Imbros. Talking to Samson who is in the cockpit is one of the officers detached from the seaplane carrier HMS *Ark Royal* to establish a seaplane base at Aliki Bay on the same island. No. 50 had been built before the war, had been flown in Belgium and France in 1914/15 and was used in the Gallipoli Campaign but it was reaching the end of its operational life by the time of the final evacuation in January 1916. It was from this machine that Samson dropped bombs on Turks gathering around the propaganda leaflets he had first released. (Air Vice Marshal Sir Geoffrey Bromet)

The sparse grass and sunbaked rocky surfaces of the Aegean islands offered far from ideal aerodrome sites but from somewhere a steamroller has been acquired (it resembles one which actually saw service in the Gallipoli Campaign), and here an airfield is being prepared on the island of Imbros. A labour force was available in the form of Turkish POWs. (W.M. Garner)

intense heat warping wings, weakening airframes and overheating engines. There were wasted hours in the air flying from island bases to the scene of operations, using up the limited life of airframes and engines and yet the work was done whenever it could be done. For example, 320 flights controlled the fire of bombarding ships between 18 February and 31 December 1915, the majority of these flights being of two and a half hours' duration.[32] According to No. 3 Wing's Commanding Officer, C.R. Samson, 2,600 hours were flown by machines from his unit from 28 March until 29 December. Samson states that on occasion he only had four aircraft in action and on average seven pilots available. His pride in this record is well-founded. 'I think it will be agreed that they, one and all quitted themselves like

The front fuselage of an Avro 504 used as an engine test rig by RNAS mechanics at Imbros. (Major H.A. Buss)

men'.[33] Samson's Standing Orders make clear what a tightly run establishment came under control of this inspiring if irascible officer who required that if an original planned purpose could not be fulfilled on a flight, something else useful must be found. Samson insisted that reports were to be precise and not filled with 'wild statements' and that stunt flying was not for war and was not, he stressed, 'conduct required of an officer.'[34] A particular instruction was given for the unfortunate who had to land in Turkish or Bulgarian lines. 'If you have any bombs or grenades in the aeroplane, and you have time, place them clear of the aeroplane, unwind the fans, and hope they will detonate on being handled.'

For the seaplanes there were special problems: in a rough sea they could not even be put in the water let alone take-off; from flat calm, they frequently could not get off the water. It took one machine 26 minutes to climb to 3,500 feet and another thousand feet proved to be its absolute maximum. The frustrations of sea-

plane work are perfectly illustrated in a seaplane pilot's diary for 26 February 1915. 'Sopwith No. 922 quickly climbed to 1,500 feet and then started to lose petrol through a damaged tank and had to land again. Number 807 went up instead, lost pressure and landed near Tenedos. She was towed back to the ship by HMTDD *Usk*. Number 173 was hoisted out to take her place and failed to leave the water.' When, later in the day, No. 807 did take-off she could not get above 400 feet ... 'We cannot work in any weather other than really fine because being too far away from England, new machines and even spares take six weeks at least to arrive, and it would be stupid policy to break up machines just for the sake of saying that we can fly in more or less rough weather.' When the weather improved, the seaplane pilots were in the air regularly, establishing wireless communication with ships to assist in the ranging of their guns but disciplined concealment of the Turkish troops and their movements on a Peninsula whose terrain crucially assisted such concealment, again limited the effectiveness of seaplane observation. Damaged floats let in water which affected the performance of a machine and Lieutenant Bromet, from whose diary these notes are taken, collected 28 bullet holes in enforced low-flying over a Turkish fort following such damage. The pilot had little sympathy for his damaged machine: 'Served the silly old bitch right for refusing to climb to a safe height.'[35]

There may well have been mixed feelings among the small party of RNAS men from HMS *Ark Royal* which was detailed to survey the island of Imbros for an airfield for land-based machines which were being sent out – these machines, commanded by Samson, soon superseded in effectiveness what the seaplanes had been attempting. This occasioned some jealousy as the seaplane pilots, observers, mechanics and riggers strove manfully to triumph over in-built constraints upon their work.

Wherever the responsibility for such failure lay, a vital line of mines was not observed and serious losses were incurred on 18 March when the British and French warships approached the Turkish shores for close bombardment. The decision for a combined operation followed and the character of the campaign as a prolonged stalemate was ineradicably imprinted by the failure to secure decisive gains at the initial landings: indeed, some would go further and claim that within a fortnight of the landings at Cape Helles and what became known as Anzac Cove, ultimate withdrawal was pre-ordained, the new landing in August at Suvla Bay being merely a reinforcement of failure. The troops were in fact to be evacuated in December and in the second week of the New Year in two separate, dangerous operations carried out with astonishing success dispelling the forebodings of heavy casualties but not the enemy propaganda blow of open British humiliation.

An Avro 504 pilot based at Imbros, H.A. Buss, experienced some of the problems attendant upon reconnaissance work in support of the Gallipoli operations. The strength of the wind, the roughness of the sea and engine failure interfered with wireless-assisted air to sea co-operation. He was in fact to be rescued from the sea in December. The monitor, HMS *Peterborough*, was handily placed when he was

forced by a 'seized ball race and a broken connecting rod' to ditch off Suvla Bay.[36]

No one could have been a more unwelcome guest on the Peninsula at Cape Helles than Flight Lieutenant F.D.S. Bremner and his observer on 8 January 1916, the day before final evacuation of the troops from the very beaches stormed less than nine months previously on 25 April. With his engine damaged in brief combat with an enemy machine, Bremner landed on the tiny airstrip at Cape Helles as he could not have reached the island of Imbros. The machine was man-handled into a sort of dugout for concealment but immediately attracted shellfire. He was not allowed to burn it as this was the sort of evidence of deliberate destruction which might provide clues for the Turks of the imminence of evacuation. Instead, with pick, shovel and sledge hammer the two airmen rendered the machine useless and were then evacuated by lighter with troops also embarking at the conclusion of what has been called the 'Immortal Gamble'.[37]

The machines of the RNAS were never remotely near a position of being able to tip the scales of battle in favour of the Allies. Bromet complained at the end of July that HMS *Ark Royal* had just received a new Short seaplane but without an engine and with only one propeller. At every level and in every aspect, the Dardanelles Gallipoli campaign seemed to have a nail short for its shoe – 'for want of a nail the shoe was lost, for want of a shoe ...' If RNAS personnel in the Eastern Mediterranean were to have felt peculiarly disadvantaged in their task, then they were in close kinship with the soldier but the price the soldier paid in both active service conditions and in the likelihood of dysentery, wound or death was much the higher. On the island of Imbros and on Mudros too airmen lived relatively comfortably in either bell tents or in wooden aeroplane packing cases converted into quite cosy accommodation. Those seaplane mechanics from HMS *Ark Royal* detached after the campaign to a shore base on the island of Mudros much preferred the living conditions ashore. A plentiful supply of figs, nectarines, raisins, currants and eggs was one factor and so was

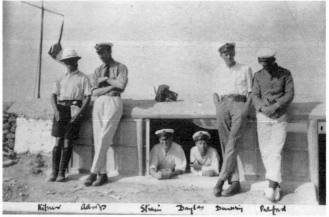

Imbros, August 1915: RNAS Petty Officers and air mechanics at the seaplane base Aliki Bay. As well as seaplanes, this detachment from HMS *Ark Royal* deployed one or two Sopwith Tabloids for scouting duties, No. 1202 being seen in the background next to the Officers' Mess. (Air Vice Marshal Sir Geoffrey Bromet)

Imbros, August 1915: The Signal Station and officers' dugout at Aliki Bay Seaplane Base. Second from the right with hands in pockets is Flight Sub-Lieutenant E.H. Dunning who was to be killed in August 1917 carrying out deck-landing trials with a Sopwith Pup on HMS *Furious*. (Air Vice Marshal Sir Geoffrey Bromet)

having an Army field cooker – using aviation spirit to encourage it to heat more vigorously was tried only once! As if to even the balance of shore and ship delights, those ashore got no bread, their rations being corned beef and large, hard biscuits. It took a good deal of culinary imagination to disguise such food taken on a regular basis.[38]

British raids on the Bulgars from one island air base, Thasos, off the Macedonian coast,

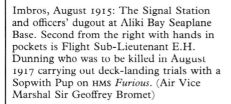

were to lead to the airfield being subjected to a very damaging retaliatory raid. An RNAS anti-aircraft gunner disconsolately described the Thasos squadron's ammunition dump being hit in this August 1917 raid. 'Huge explosions took place one after another as the contents of the dump were reached by the fire and heat and concussion. Bombs of all sizes from 100 lb downwards, hand grenades, petrol bombs, small arms, ammunition and machine-gun ammunition, all were caught; Very lights of all colours soared up, while the screeching and whining of fragments of bombs and stray bullets completed a miniature hell.' A Bessoneau hangar and olive trees also went up in

May 1916: Long Island being shelled. A Turkish shell bursting on the hillside behind the hangar of 'B' Squadron, No. 2 Wing, RNAS on Long Island in the Gulf of Smyrna. Alongside the hangar stands a Nieuport, a Henri Farman and the fuselage of an Avro 504. The RNAS later put dummy aircraft on the aerodrome to draw the enemy's shelling away from real targets. (Admiral Sir Reginald Portal)

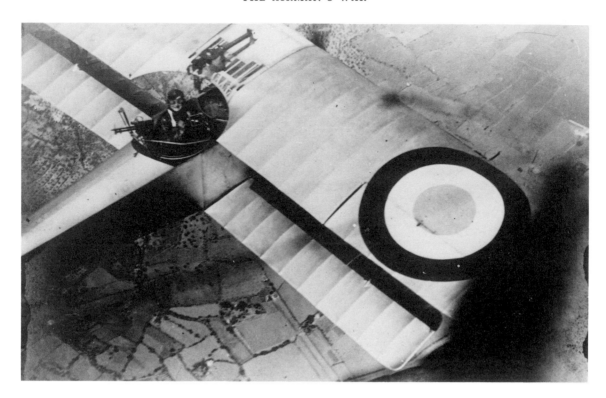

The Aegean area, 1917. This is quite a rare example for World War One of close-up air-to-air photography (No. 2 Wing, RNAS). The observer in this silver-finished Nieuport 12 two-seater is cheerfully pointing his own camera at the photographer. Note the armament of one Lewis gun for the observer and another fitted above the centre section for the use of the pilot. (W.M. Garner)

flames and the raider machine-gunned a party saving two Farmans and 50 cans of petrol from the hangar. This particular anti-aircraft gunner, and one presumes his team, viewed all this from prostrate concealment but their gunnery on the following two days may have caused difficulty to enemy machines attempting to photograph the evidence of the success of their raid.[39]

As a brief tail-piece relating RNAS experience in these Aegean waters, mention can be made of the 1916 aeroplane spotting for the shelling by monitors of Turkish shore positions opposite Long Island in the Gulf of Smyrna and then of the attempts to bomb the German-Turkish ships *Goeben* and *Breslau* in both 1917 and 1918. Reginald Portal as an observer was engaged in the first episode and in a contemporary account he makes clear that Long Island itself was under quite as much bombardment as the monitors themselves were maintaining and in fact one monitor was hit, set afire and abandoned. Shell holes on the Long Island aerodrome interfered with RNAS operations and aeroplanes hidden under trees

were spotted and shelled. Despite the erection of a dummy machine which drew about 200 rounds of 6- or 4.7-inch shells, the 'aerodrome gradually became unusable, the Greek guards chucked their hands in and had to be replaced by Marines (who were nearly as bad) and as all the stores had to be landed in the dark, some 4 miles from camp, it was decided to carry out all flying from [the island of] Thermi'.[40] A defiant note is added by Portal as he dates the evacuation of the island, 28 May 1916, and the fact that 1,000 rounds had hit the island but at a minimal cost: 'one partridge stunned and subsequently eaten in RNAS Mess; one rabbit, hit by 6" — good for nothing but hash.'

As for the battle-cruiser *Goeben* in July 1917 she remained undamaged from a Handley Page's attempt to bomb her as she lay in waters

Torpedo warheads converted to bombs by the naval artificers of HMS *Agamemnon* in order that aerial attack with more powerful 'bombs' could be made upon the German battle-cruiser *Goeben* in the aftermath of her venture out of the Dardanelles in January 1918. The posed nature of the photograph is intriguing as there was a desperate urgency to cause serious damage to *Goeben* in the days when she was lying disabled near Chanak; still, the warhead conversion with the attachment of fins must have been quite an undertaking and one which gave pride to those concerned. (Commander R.H.S. Rodger)

off Constantinople but when, with the light cruiser *Breslau*, she sallied out of the Dardanelles in January 1918 as if to prove that her destructive potential were not securely chained from entry into the Aegean, the two British monitors the German ships destroyed proved but a transient triumph. *Goeben* struck a mine and soon attracted bombing machines from Imbros. In the escaping manoeuvres, *Breslau* was bombed, hit a succession of mines and sank. On striking a second mine, *Goeben* made for the Dardanelles and hit a third before she entered the Narrows. Attempts to bomb her were maintained. She then ran aground near Nagara Point and an observer in one of the DH 4s which attacked her has recall of the failure perhaps even to hit and certainly to damage the battle-cruiser. Aerial photographs, W.J. Kemp remembers, provided depressing proof of the ineffectiveness of the bombing, despite *Goeben*'s considerable bulk as a target. *Goeben* was well armoured and was defended by vigorous anti-aircraft fire, while the bombs being dropped in several days and nights of determined effort were of no great weight (65 or 112 lb) and were not being aimed with any sophisticated sighting.[41] At least two of the bombs were of an exceptional design and this

gives a special interest to the bold but unsuccessful aerial attempt: they were made from the 14-inch warheads of torpedoes from HMS *Agamemnon*. Naval artificers had removed the warheads from torpedoes and attached improvised fins and the missiles were made available to the RNAS seaplanes.[42]

EAST AND SOUTHERN AFRICA

Just over three and a half years earlier than these January 1918 air to sea attacks and the problems they posed for the attacker, another German vessel, the light cruiser *Königsberg*, was the magnet which first drew in aerial support to the Allies in East Africa. *Königsberg*, in late October 1914, lay hidden in the Rufiji river delta where location of her by water was rendered well-nigh impossible by a combination of the maze of channels, islands, shoals and swamps and the overwhelming power of the German ship's guns against any light-draught vessel bold enough to search for her and 'lucky' enough to find her. The *Official History* provides a splendid account of the work to find *Königsberg* by what had been, before RNAS commissioned engagement, a privately-owned and piloted Curtiss flying boat.[43]

The pilot, H.D. Cutler, had remarkable adventures and although he was captured, his flying boat, also seemingly lost, was rescued by the combined efforts of the crew of a tug and a motor boat. *Königsberg* had been located; seaplanes for bombing and heavy-gunned, light-draught vessels for shelling were now an urgent priority but East Africa was a far distant theatre of war. Two Sopwith seaplanes arrived in February 1915, but proved wholly inadequate for their task. In late April, three Short seaplanes were delivered and now *Königsberg* was relocated and photographed. However, in the rarified air of the tropics, seaplanes could not get sufficient height with bombs and an observer and in the scorching heat they suffered warped wood, melted glue, shrivelled rubber and the bottoms of the floats even peeling off.

A Naval officer, B.T. Brewster, received permission to act as an observer in this work while his application to join the RNAS was receiving consideration. He has written that the maximum speed achieved by these Short biplanes was 60 mph and that their ceiling with an observer and a bomb load was a maximum of 1,000 feet, though he does not remember getting over 500 feet over land. 'As soon as we began to fly over the mangrove swamps, we could fall into a succession of air pockets until height was reduced to about 500 feet.'[44]

Two Henri Farmans and two Caudrons arrived in June, a landing field for the aeroplanes having been prepared on Mafia island. Two of the aeroplanes were wrecked in spotting exercises with the monitors preparatory to working together against *Königsberg*. *Königsberg* had a secret land observation post and her counter-shelling of the monitors made the work of the latter difficult and dangerous while the aeroplanes, despite a temporary breakdown of wireless communication with the monitors, were kept in the air observing and assisting where possible in the duel. A further attempt a few days later in July brought about the destruction of the German warship, although one of the aeroplanes was lost to anti-aircraft fire, its pilot and observer escaping

after crashing into the sea near one of the monitors. Flight Lieutenant Cull was the pilot of this aircraft and his report described the aeroplane engine running badly, height being lost rapidly and then 'the engine stopped dead and I started to glide towards the *Mersey* [one of the monitors] as, though the *Severn* [the other monitor] was nearest, I did not want to interfere with her fire. By prolonging the glide as much as possible we managed to reach within about 150 yards of the *Mersey*. On our way down my observer [Flight Sub-Lieutenant Arnold] with great coolness, gave a correction by W.T. to the *Severn* bringing her hits from forward on the *Königsberg* to amidships. He also informed the Monitors we were hit and descending and asked for a boat, after which he wound in his aerial.' The aeroplane somersaulted on touching the water, Arnold being thrown clear but Cull had failed to unstrap his belt and

A Short 807 Folder Seaplane (No. 3098) one of three which arrived at Zanzibar on 12 July 1915, too late to take part in operations against the *Königsberg*. These late arrivals were to remain in East Africa until April 1918. The seaplane is here being manhandled into a hangar, obviously of local construction, at Chukwani Bay on the west coast of Zanzibar. (Lieutenant Colonel F.A. Archdale)

went down with the machine extricating himself only with difficulty. The airmen well deserved the praise they were given in the report of the Senior Officer commanding the Monitor Squadron – Captain Fullerton of HMS *Severn* who considered Cull and Arnold to be 'worthy of the highest praise and reward.'[45]

RNAS service in Southern Africa included more successful armoured car work in German South West Africa in 1915 than had been possible at Cape Helles on the Gallipoli Peninsula. Space to manoeuvre and the flatness of the terrain were to the advantage of the cars which actually were employed in a full engagement and counter-attack as well as on patrol and reconnaissance. Aeroplane observation of the retreating German forces in South West Africa was carried out in Henri Farmans by Kenneth van der Spuy and others of the South African Aviation Corps and by three RNAS officers. After leaving their Walvis Bay base with its newly constructed hangars, the airmen and their machines used forward landing strips on the inhospitable coasts which were continually subjected to dust storms and the extremes of heat by day and cold by night. Van der Spuy crashed into the bush at the end of a landing strip too short for its purpose, sustaining injury to his leg which prevented him from seeing the end of a well-conducted campaign.

One distinctive advantage to the airman in South West Africa, and then in East Africa too after the *Königsberg* affair, was the absence of anti-aircraft fire.[46] In East Africa, some of the RNAS resources concentrated for the destruction of *Königsberg* remained to assist in military operations inland. A base was established at Maktau. Explosives were used to blow up trees and ant hills obstructing the designated landing ground. Aeroplanes were housed in hangars inside a defensive encampment, and enemy snipers had to be prevented from any attack on the machines as they were pushed from the camp through an avenue in the bush to the landing ground for take-off, so each morning the bush had to be flushed-out by an armed party. Generalisation about living and flying conditions is made difficult by the variety of terrain within the very large theatre of operations. Certainly, dense bush made observation exceptionally difficult. Early morning

On Niororo Island off the coast of East Africa, one of the two Sopwith Type 807 seaplanes with a more 'business-like' air than she was able to justify. After a four-day saga of trial and error, one of the seaplanes managed to lift off the water but could not get above 1,500 feet, even with limited fuel and without bombs, so the machines so expensively and laboriously sent out, assembled and tested, proved of no use whatsoever in action against the *Königsberg*. (Lieutenant Colonel F.A. Archdale)

ground mist, heat bumps, the white glare of the sun, seasonal monsoon rain and wind and of course, the almost inevitable lack of spare parts on so extended a supply line were factors throughout the campaign, but the moral effect of the aeroplane and its bombs was naturally considerable among primitive people.

No. 26 Squadron, RFC, arrived early in 1916 but without the propellers for its eight BE2s – of the six spares of a less suitable type, one had been broken – so from the start only five of the aircraft could be used. An airfield was selected at Mbuyuni near Mount Kilimanjaro but other airfields had to be constructed for temporary use as the campaign developed. Supplies were, as ever, a problem, the native bearers for example on having to carry petrol cans over a long distance, frequently emptied the petrol from the cans and refilled them with water near their destination. Disease, of which malaria was the special scourge, rapidly reduced the numbers of fit men but No. 26 Squadron continued to operate in East Africa till June 1918. In the protracted campaign where the enemy earn such credit in their avoidance of defeat until European events overtook them, RNAS and RFC units overcame major obstacles simply in keeping up with the movement of military operations in reconnaissance and bombing work. Railway lines were bombed and retreating enemy columns were located and attacked. If one were to doubt the problem of movement along the ground, the *Official History* records that lions killed and ate three porters en route to one new airfield and one downed pilot spent four days trekking through the jungle. In the course of those days, the pilot lost his revolver, his food, his clothing, and almost his life to a crocodile as he swam across a river. Baboons took more of his clothing as it was hanging out to dry and he had to take 'refuge' for a night up a tree as an alternative to providing a meal for a leopard! Small wonder that this man, Lieutenant G.W.T. Garrood, was suffering from 'fever, shock and exhaustion' when he was found.[47]

Garrood had been more fortunate than an RNAS pilot, Flight Lieutenant E.R. Moon, who fell into captivity after a seaplane re-connaissance of the Rufiji delta was interrupted by mechanical failure and a forced landing. He and his observer had set fire to their machine, had swum a creek and attempted to force their way through the bush. Finding this impossible, they then swam downstream till they came to a derelict house. Here they constructed a raft but failed in their efforts to manoeuvre it against one of the block-ships sunk in the mouth of the channel. When the tide turned they were rushed out to sea, the raft repeatedly capsizing. The observer was drowned despite Moon's efforts to save him and Moon himself, clinging in the final stages of exhaustion to the raft, was washed ashore with the incoming of the tide and taken by German askaris into captivity.

Kenneth van der Spuy has written of other matters which encapsulate aspects of the service of air unit personnel in East Africa, like living in *bandas* quickly constructed from a set of double poles planted in a circle or rectangle between which would be packed long grass, branches and mealie stalks, and the roof covered with palm leaves. Such accommodation proved cool and weatherproof but it was accommodation to be shared with the jigger flea which burrowed under the skin under the toe nails, laid its eggs and caused festering discomfort. The South African has also written of his being responsible for sending a motorcycle dispatch rider on a mission which led to the dispatch rider being chased along a bush-clearing by a rhinoceros. The motorcycle was abandoned to be trampled to pieces by the rhino which remained on the scene and indeed charged again at the dismembered motorbike while the rider cowered in the bush.[48]

With thought of this man and of Garrood and Moon, it is wryly amusing to read of R.L. Lovemore writing that in East Africa during World War One, he had the opportunity of doing a great deal of flying and becoming a 'good pilot with very little personal risk'.[49] It is a comment in retrospect and one with presumably an awareness of enemy air to air opposition and anti-aircraft fire in France. However, no flying was without its basic attendant risks and certainly neither the crocodile nor the lion awaited the grounded airman in Flanders.

Sailing in the Sky

The Royal Naval Air Service in Home Waters

As reference has already been made to the question of Home Defence against attack from the air and the part played by the RNAS in this task, attention can be focussed in this chapter on the two broad areas in which the RNAS was engaged over Home Waters: anti-U-boat patrol and operations with and actually from ships of the Grand Fleet.

Germans subjected to Christmas greetings: An RNAS card for 1917. (Squadron Leader C.P.O. Bartlett)

The facts that the Germans had taken so much of the Belgian coast in 1914 and that in the following year, they made the first of two great efforts to win the war through U-boat depredations were the determinants which dictated that a major concentration of RNAS resources had to be upon anti-U-boat work or, expressed differently, on the protection of the British Mercantile Marine in Home Waters and of Cross-Channel communications. The

"On Christmas Day we sallied forth
To cheer the festive Hun.
A 'U' Boat interfered with us,
And *his* day's work was done!"

"Cheshire."

most outward ramifications of this were that the RNAS units based in the Dunkirk area would have as a principal task the observation of and interference with German naval movements from Ostend, Zeebrugge and the inland port of Bruges. From these ports, German destroyers, mine-layers and U-boats presented a constant danger to communication in the English Channel and assisted in the threat to shipping in the North Sea brought by the longer-range U-boats from their German river bases.

As early as October 1914 aeroplanes and seaplanes from Dunkirk had commenced their work against the U-boat bases which the Germans were developing and which so ominously threatened the English Channel. Dover was in logical consequence developed as the Northern Channel crossing point from which aerial watch-keeping could be conducted. From this time, RNAS seaplanes, aeroplanes and non-rigid Submarine Scout (SS) airships were to become an integral part of the new vital command, the Dover Patrol.

The SS airships engaged upon Dover Patrol duties were based at Capel near Folkestone and Polegate near Eastbourne but further stations were developed to cover the western entrance to the Channel, to attempt to protect St Georges Channel and the East Coast of Britain which of course held the bases of the Grand Fleet and several Home Fleet ports. At Kingsnorth near Ashford in Kent, late in 1915 and into the following year, larger, non-rigid airships, the Coastal or C Class, were developed and introduced. They were able to undertake considerably longer patrols of up to eleven hours and the operations of this class of airship, off Land's End, Pembroke, Norfolk, the Humber, the Firth of Forth and north of Aberdeen, proved invaluable in patrolling busy sea lanes and port entrances.

The work of the Coastal Class airship on anti-submarine patrol in 1917–18 provides some grim examples to illustrate that the long hours of unrelieved and usually unrewarded concentration required in scanning the sea for the slight signs which would betray a U-boat,

A Coastal airship patrols the sea from its base at Mullion, Cornwall. The crew of five was commanded in this case by Lieutenant T.P. York Moore. A patrol would last for around twelve hours at a speed of 50 mph. This airship, C 9, had a total flying time of 3,720 hours, the best record of her class. (Squadron Leader T.P. York Moore)

The car of Submarine Scout Airship *SSZ 30*, the crew preparing for a flight from Polegate, Sussex, probably in March 1918. The three-man crew is from front to rear (i.e. left to right) Wireless Operator, pilot and engineer. Note the camouflage painting on the hangar and wind screens. (A.G. Byron)

could be transformed into minutes of desperate emergency ending on occasion with loss of life for the airship's crew. Four men were drowned in July 1917 when *C 11* from Howden descended out of control upon the Humber: the car submerged and the envelope exploded in flames. There were some survivors from that tragedy but nothing is known from the British side concerning three Coastal airship disasters. *C 17* and *C 27* were shot down by German aircraft and there were no survivors, nor were there any from *C 25*, the fate of which is unknown.

An incident which does convey something of the sense of desperate emergency during technical failure is recorded in a report of troubles affecting *C 33*, operating from Polegate. Descending against all measures being undertaken by the crew, the car's Lewis gun was one of the items discarded when all the ballast had been released. The Lewis gun operated from the top of the envelope and reached through a laddered climbing shaft was the next to go. 'The rating who had been dispatched to the top, instead of bringing the gun down through the climbing shaft, decided to throw it over the side. Unfortunately he did not throw it hard enough and it fell through the side of the starboard lower lobe making a hole 20 feet in diameter. The ship collapsed and fell in a field close to the station.'[1]

Apart from the C Class, there were other advances in non-rigid airship design, the Submarine Scout Pusher (SSP), the Zero (Z) and the North Sea (NS) Class, and throughout the war the airship's usefulness was as an active deterrent to the U-boat having the capacity to call up by wireless naval vessels for depth charge attack and on a small scale late in 1918, actually towing a hydroplane for U-boat detection. Bombs were carried but the airship's slow speed and the swiftness with which a U-boat could dive out of danger meant that bomb and submarine were unlikely to meet. *C 9* (Flight

155

An unnumbered Zero Class Submarine Scout Airship piloted by Lieutenant Harold Ward in flight over the sea. From January 1918 until the Armistice he flew a total of more than 700 hours on airships of this class on convoy escort and anti-submarine patrol in the Channel and around the south-east coast. (H.R.H. Ward)

Commander Struthers) from Mullion may well have bombed a U-boat to destruction in September 1917, but there is no indisputable, unaided sinking of a U-boat by an airship despite the airship reports of sightings, bombs being dropped and then oil being seen on the surface. Even the detection of a submarine was rare. One airship Commander followed an oil slick which seemed to take him in a circular course, only to find that the explanation lay in the oil having come from the drip-tray of his own craft as he was searching.[2] If, however, an accurate sighting were to be quickly reported by wireless to either a shore station or a destroyer with which the airship was in cooperation, then there was some chance of one of the naval vessels destroying the U-boat concerned. However, there was still the question of the Commander of the airship knowing his own location precisely until shore-based directional wireless lifted such a responsibility from him.

Of the free balloon training from Roehampton which was a preliminary to airship handling and navigation experience from Kingsnorth, Sir Victor Goddard has particularly amusing recall. It became established practice to make a landing on the large estates in Essex toward which the prevailing Westerlies wafted the balloon and its basket containing perhaps two young midshipman trainees and the sub-lieutenant or petty officer in command of the balloon. The anticipation was that graciously liberal hospitality would be accorded the visitors who had indeed 'dropped in', but on two occasions wayward handling of the balloon caused problems. The first was when rustic villagers attacked balloon, basket and crew in the belief that what had come from the sky must be connected to the enemy and its Zeppelins. 'Stand back, we're British' was what Goddard remembered a besieged petty officer saying as he tried to spread his arms to keep away from his balloon a menacing mob led by a man with a butcher's cleaver. The sequel to this incident was happier as the RNAS party was able to establish its identity as aerial protectors of the village from airship attack and hence a carousing shoulder-carried welcome transformed a situation being faced with a degree of apprehension. The second incident resulted from misjudging the speed with which a balloon was travelling over the great estate of Theobald's. A trailing rope and anchor (to decelerate passage away from the

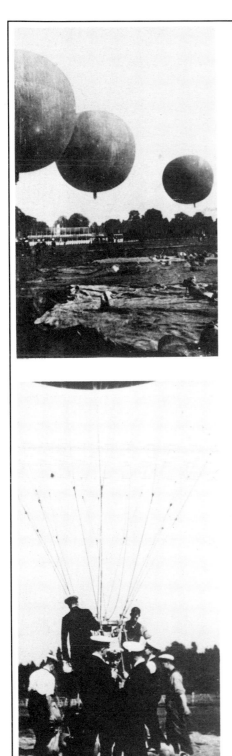

Free ballooning from the RNAS Training Establishment at Wormwood Scrubs, the first stage of the practical education of an Airship pilot. Note the deflated balloons and the ballast bags made ready for taking aboard the basket. During the training, Lieutenant Ward (*above*) made seven free balloon flights, one at night. The maximum height he reached was 6,400 feet and the longest distance covered was 48 miles. (H.R.H. Ward)

An uncertain landing for sailors in the air. F.W. Verry, who served with airships in the war and who had experienced free ballooning, sketches one of numerous close encounters with trees. Note the protesting bird! (H.R.H. Ward)

prospect of tea), uprooted flower beds and a tennis net, and climbed a garden wall, teetering on the top before crashing through a conservatory. The emergency landing precipitated by pulling a rip-cord to evacuate gas from a section of the balloon, deposited the basket and its occupants into the shallow water and deeper mud of an ornamental pool. The bedraggled men who traipsed their sodden path to the main entrance of the great house, learned that they had landed in the estate of a very senior admiral but they were received with every hospitality, the uniforms of the absent admiral being made available to them as their own were sponged clean and dried.[3]

A particular problem encountered in the operations of airships was landing in conditions of gusting wind. Huge screens were in due course erected adjacent to the hangars covering the angle of the prevailing wind. Landing could still be a tricky business, numerous craft being damaged in the process and some men seriously injured and even killed among the ground party whose task was to hold fast the airship's trailing rope and then 'walk' the airship to the hangar. It was a disciplinary offence to let go of this rope, a dilemma requiring instant decision if wind conditions suddenly were to lift the airship to a greater height and threaten a rising daisy chain of desperate figures still clutching the landing rope. In such dangerous conditions the non-rigid airships had a rip-cord which could be operated from the control car and which tore open a panel at the top of the airship, releasing the gas and causing the envelope to collapse. P.E. Maitland, with the larger North Sea craft, has written that they required a landing party of some four hundred men but still, on one particular day in September 1918 at Longside near Peterhead, *NS 10* and then *NS 9* had to be ripped in landing. Repair and re-inflation kept the airships out of action for at least a month, which itself indicates that the emergency action was not taken lightly. After the free ballooning course at Roehampton, Maitland was to be an airship pilot officer from September 1915 until the end of the war. He flew the SS Class at Anglesey and Capel, then the C Class for a week at Kingsnorth before operating from Longside during 1917. From January 1918 until the Armistice, he was in North Sea airships, having one exceptionally fortunate escape when *NS 3* crashed into the Firth of Forth in June. However, in the three years of constant lighter-than-air operational duties, there is just this single entry in his log, made on 27 April 1918, referring to the likelihood of attacking a submarine or even having the presence of one to report. 'Sighted possible submarine. Returned owing to fog.'[4]

Too much should not be deduced from Maitland's lack of opportunity, even over so long a period, to attack a U-boat. Lighter-than-air craft, particularly when they became an

In the swim: Officers from the RNAS Airship station, Luce Bay find that South West Scotland has much to offer. Bathing costumes are clearly 'non issue'. (Air Marshal Sir Thomas Elmhirst)

integral part of convoy protection, provided aerial observation which strengthened this overdue measure necessary to defeat the U-boat. German submarine commanders were well aware that the naval vessels in the convoy which they might have wished to attack, had the inestimable reinforcement of the 'eye in the air', with wireless communication between air and sea. The hours of seemingly fruitless patrol by the full range of aircraft used fulfilled an essential role in the winning of the war.

The protection of merchant shipping is not the whole picture by any means. The safety of troop-ships crossing the English Channel was a vital consideration from the first month of the war. In the spring months of 1918 when the Germans made their tremendous onslaught to secure victory (an onslaught the brunt of which was faced by British and Imperial troops), troop-ship security was of illimitable significance. Operating from Capel, Zero Class airships, usually at between 450 and 1,200 feet, escorted convoy after convoy of troop-ships from Folkestone. An airship log entry on the very day of the opening of the German attack literally records the threat to the Allied lifeline: 'Observed periscope of hostile submarine, three miles S.E. of Dungeness.' In May, seen rather than unseen success could be recorded in the log of this same pilot, Flight Sub-Lieutenant H.R.H. Ward: 'Escorted convoy of eleven ships from Dungeness to Folkestone Gate. Assisted HMS *D48* (*Kangaroo*), *Viking*, *Afridi*, *Leven*, *P39* and *P41* to locate and sink enemy submarine.' In the same month: 'Escorted 20 ships from Varne to S Foreland where I saw periscopes of enemy submarine at 12.45. Attacked same and sent for surface craft who dropped about 12–15 depth charges. Oil and air bubbles rose to surface.' No less important than this was the sighting of oil during a patrol in June, and calling up a patrol boat, the depth charges of which exploded fourteen U-boat-

Not quite as intended! Returning from a three-hour patrol off Dungeness at 10.30 a.m. on 30 October 1918, Lieutenant Ward's Zero Class Submarine Scout airship was unable to cope with sudden turbulence. Instead of landing safely near Folkestone the airship was 'deposited' on adjacent trees and its pilot fell 25 feet to the ground. (H.R.H. Ward)

laid mines. Ward was congratulated in September by the Superintendent of Airships for his fine record of almost 163 hours of patrolling in August, but at the end of October, in *Z 36*, he crashed into trees when waiting to land. His diary records a terrific 'down dunt' causing the accident and the photographs make clear that there is little exaggeration of measurement when he writes: 'Fell from 25′ but was only shaken. Cleared up wreckage. Had a rest. Had a good dinner in Ashford, then went to pictures. Felt much better.'[5]

An airship could not supplement its anti-U-boat work with self-defence against enemy seaplane attack but the RNAS French coast based flying boats, seaplanes and aeroplanes on anti-U-boat patrol were frequently involved in aerial combat in the course of fulfilling their operational duties. An FBA flying boat which shot down a German seaplane on 28 November 1915 gained the first such victory for the Dunkirk Wing. The Germans strengthened their air resources to dispute the aerial command the naval seaplanes were exerting as they patrolled off the Belgian coast but ironically, it

was an accurate shell from a surfaced U-boat which brought down to the water one British seaplane and led to the capture of its pilot by a German torpedo-boat. The crew of two British seaplanes suffered a still more unlikely fate. Following upon engine failure and a forced landing in the North Sea, U-boats twice captured a pilot and an observer for whom rescue by the British or death by drowning or exposure would seem to have been a more likely result. An observer concerned in one of these misadventures, Alick Stevens (later Air Marshal Sir Alick) recalled that his 28 November 1916 dawn anti-submarine patrol from Felixstowe was being conducted between 50 and 60 miles from the coast just outside the mine-swept East Coast shipping lane when lack of engine power forced his Short seaplane down to the water. The pilot, a South African, Llewellyn Davies, attempted to taxi westwards and Stevens fired off Very lights. The engine

A Short 184 seaplane taxying out for an early morning patrol from Dartmouth in February 1918. Note the two bombs carried between the floats. The water seems exceptionally still. (Lieutenant S. King-Smith)

finally packed-up altogether and the seaplane slowly drifted north-eastwards on the calm sea. A U-boat was sighted in the late afternoon. It approached and circled them, and opened fire. Stevens returned fire, observing his bullets striking the gunshield of the U-boat. The firing ceased and the U-boat came still closer, unintelligible shouting being heard by the hapless airmen. Then: 'Vous êtes prisonniers' was heard and they answered it with the briefest of acknowledgements: 'Oui'. A line was tossed to them and they clambered aboard the U-boat, both men being struck about the head with shouts of 'Schweinhund' to match. Directly they were below and suffering more belabouring until an officer commanded it to cease, an alarm call was heard and the U-boat dived, further confirming suspicion that they had been judged a decoy for a British submarine attack upon an unwary U-boat. The German vessel laid her mines and returned to Zeebrugge and Bruges with her unusual catch of airmen who would take no further part in the aerial defence of British shipping.[6]

Practice makes perfect – or nearly so! A near miss from an RNAS seaplane dropping a 230 lb anti-submarine bomb. The target is at the top of the photograph just to the right of centre. (Professor F.A.D. Gauntlett)

The seaplane workhorse of the RNAS was the Short 184 in its various forms. It was a Short seaplane with the old-type Renault engine which let down Jack Bentham and his observer named Wellbourne on an anti-submarine patrol from Newlyn near Penzance in December 1917. The seaplane came down a few miles off the Wolf Rock light-house. Very

Engine power and man power eases this Felixstowe F5 flying boat on its wheeled cradle from the flying boat's shed to the slipway for launching. (Group Captain R.J. Bone)

lights brought no rescue and pilot and observer had to stand on the main floats to save the tail from being smashed by a sea becoming steadily more rough. The tail float however took in water and settled lower and lower as darkness fell. Seasickness, cold and precarious balance made the night seem exceptionally long but at eleven the following morning, rescue came in the shape of a trawler, though the seaplane broke in two and sank when attempts were made to tow it.[7]

As a point of interest, in November 1918 the newly-married Bentham escaped by reason of the Armistice something which would surely have been more dangerous still: he was designated as one of the pilots of 'forty or more flying boats' to be towed to within range of Heligoland. The strongly defended island was to be bombed and then the aircraft were to attempt to return to the South-East coast of England. Peace intervened and neither the German defences nor flying boat endurance was to be tested.

It may be thought that the sedate flying boat would provide no opportunity for high-spirited flying but a wireless operator, 2nd Class Air Mechanic Thorp, enjoyed his flights with a certain Captain Mackworth who, on return from patrolling, would occasionally aim near-vertical dives towards the funnels of vessels in the Channel, carry out dives over Southsea Pier and then pursue a wave and yacht-hopping course up the Solent.[8] Thorp has recall of seaplane floats being made into canoes for recreation but on more sober lines he remembers, with a sense of the narrowness of protection from calamity, the metal gauze which shielded the spark of his wireless transmitter in the F2a. Thorp, as he operated the wireless, was seated upon an 80-gallon tank of petrol with two larger ones behind him, the smell of petrol being a constant factor.

Thorp's F2a carried two pigeons in wicker baskets. They were released from the gun turret when at the furthest point of a patrol in order to give them the exercise of returning to base on their own wing-power. They were not given messages. Ironically, Thorp relates that when his flying boat had to ditch, no one thought of using the pigeons to take a message locating their position for rescue. Apart from the wireless, reliance for communication rested upon the Aldis lamp with its pencil-slim beam clearly visible sixteen miles away even on a bright sunny day.

Anti-submarine work by flying boats based at Calshot involved convoy escort from Southampton to Le Havre. The four man crew of an F2a (first and second pilot, wireless operator and engineer) were trussed up in Sidcot flying suits, thigh-length fleece-lined boots, and flying helmet as well as an inflatable life jacket. Patrols would normally last about five hours or a little longer, seven on one occasion remem-

Final preparations before a Felixstowe F5 flying boat takes off on a patrol which could have lasted up to five hours. (Group Captain R.J. Bone)

An F2a flying boat on the beach at Calshot. Under the wing can be seen one of its 230 lb bombs fitted with a two and a half second delayed action fuse which will give it a depth charge effect when dropped on or near a U-boat. (A.J. Price)

bers A.J. Price.[9] The special rigid, flat, charts and the code book for wireless transmission were weighted with lead for safe disposal against the possibility of capture. Price's most vivid recall is of sighting a U-boat on 6 March 1918. His log merely records: 'Bombed submarine in 15Y Probably sunk (oil observed)'; there is a sketch of three bomb dots across the outline of a U-boat, the central one on the conning tower. He has written of the incident: 'We had just been fitted with new compass bomb-sight which allowed one to bomb from any direction not only up or down wind. (One had to set wind direction and speed in knots, one's own air speed, direction, elevation – all done as early routine and only adjusted if weather report from base required it). So I fused our bombs and we claimed a perfect straddle of the submerging conning tower. We claimed a hit but had no camera and in any case light was bad. We knew there were none of our surface ships within at least half an hour so had little hope of confirmation.' Having circled for a while, they made for home. Despite a fine welcome and the award of a DSC to the first pilot, the Admiralty would not allow a certain hit.

A table of statistics in the *Official History* provides depressing evidence that there were very few U-boat sightings by the airships, flying boats, seaplanes and aeroplanes of the 28 coastal stations, even in 1917, the worst year for merchant ship sinkings. The best results were returned by the flying boats at Felixstowe which eclipse all the others with 44 sightings and 25 bombings. The airships from Mullion produced incomparably the best lighter-than-air figures with 17 sightings and 12 bombings but there is a more even spread among the seaplane stations, Dunkirk leading with 12 sightings and four bombings.[10]

Among several factors which go far to explain the failure to destroy U-boats by bombing, one must certainly be the bombs themselves. This new branch of military science required theoretical and then experimental consideration. In 1915, at the RNAS base at Dundee, Douglas Iron became involved in testing a bomb of unusual design, to be exploded at a pre-arranged depth by a floating bobbin attached to a length of wire. Weather conditions were unpropitious but so that the anxious inventor and his entourage would not be disappointed Iron tried to coax his Wight seaplane, loaded with its special bombs, into a cross-wind take-off from the Tay. The strength of the current of the river was a further element to take into consideration but when it seemed that he was just reaching take-off speed, one of the bombs, with a blinding flash, exploded. Iron's next recollection was of water swirling around in the cockpit. In seconds he realised what had happened. He was still strapped in his seat but freed himself and inflated his life belt. The wrecked machine soon slid below the surface leaving a float, a parting benefaction which enabled the uninjured pilot and his passenger to await rescue with some confidence. In a later recommendation, Flight Lieutenant Iron is noted as having proved himself 'a very capable and zealous officer and a first class seaplane pilot.' He is also noted as taking a 'real interest in his work' so one may presume that he had not been disconcerted by so narrow an escape.[11]

The general nature of seaplane work is made clear in the log of A.C. Kermode.[12] His first Western patrol – on 9 July 1918 – from Cattewater near Plymouth was: 'Very bumpy, rain, hail, strong wind and rough sea. Met convoy.' He bombed an oil patch, photographed a collapsible life boat, sighted a torpedoed ship, released pigeons but there is after all, a more unusual entry in his reporting on the effectiveness of a coastal battery's camouflage.

On the North-East coast the frailities of seaplanes and their engines and the hostility of winter conditions of 1918 give gaunt character to C.N. Bilney's flights from South Shields. On 16 January, he could not get his Short 184 off the sea because of carburettor trouble; four days later a burst radiator frustrated a Tyne-Tees patrol; on 24 January a gust of wind almost brought disaster as he was taking-off. On the following day, the machine was nose heavy and the seaplane scarcely rose for patrolling between Souter Point and Sunderland. On 26 January, the choppy seas and gusty wind prevented take-off for a Farne Islands patrol. Going south on the following day to the Tees,

fog cut off all visibility and he could not even pick up lamp signals for return. Fog prevailed for the remaining days of the month and off Sunderland he could not see the water from 500 feet. It is small wonder that the log has this entry for 3 February: 'Could not find harbour for ten minutes on return and nearly ran into South Pier lighthouse.'[13] Later in the month Bilney bombed an oil patch off Seaham only to learn that the oil was from a sunken steamer.

In 1917, two giant seaplanes arrived at Felixstowe, drawing the attention of everyone to their twin fuselages with a control cabin set between them which was faced with a vast square of triplex glass. As D.P. Capper affirms, the first seaplane rushed fiercely along the estuary in a noble cloud of spray but nothing could persuade her into the air. She was retired to one of the huge hangars, an aspidistra behind her glass as a final affront to her wartime inutility. The sister seaplane was towed on arrival directly to a handy shoal out of the way and there allowed to degenerate into scrap. Apart from his recall of the double-fuselaged phenomena at Felixstowe, Capper paid an attractive tribute to the maintenance crew of his flying boat who, he learned to his embarrassment, even bought furniture cream and metal polish out of their own pocket for that extra shine given to something maintained with pride.[14]

The first posting for the newly-appointed Probationary Flight Sub-Lieutenant T.C. Gordon in February 1918 was to Yarmouth. In training, Gordon had had the unusually wide experience of flying ten different types of aeroplane and four types of seaplane and he also believed he was fortunate in having as a mechanic a fellow Scot, a native of Saltcoats. Gordon, who had a 'nice chat' with him, knew 'how absolutely dependent we are on such fellows, it counts a little to have special care centered on one's machine.' The sentiment was sincerely expressed and undeniably true but his first anti-submarine patrol was short-lived, a big wave sweeping his propeller and engine cowl off and then a week later, engine failure and a gust of wind overturned his Hamble Baby seaplane by which time he was well aware,

Same man, different uniform: from RNAS into RAF. To the left, airship pilot H.R.H. Ward as a flight sub-lieutenant of the RNAS (note the pilot's wings, worn on the sleeve) and then to the right as a lieutenant in the newly formed RAF. (H.R.H. Ward)

protected though he was by strong personal religious belief, that mechanical eccentricities combined with the natural elements would have some say in his fortunes.

Gordon took his work very seriously: 'I feel intensely proud that now I have worked to keep a vigil on the sly and treacherous Hun and it makes me feel that all my training has not been in vain.' Of his crash he wrote with self disgust that it came to 'disperse any pride or self confidence I may have gained. I need to be humbled and know I am not my own governor.'

It may have been difficult for men in the RFC to be other than derisive over what the RNAS felt it was losing as the Service amalgamation of April Fool's Day 1918 approached, but for the aerial sailor the sense of loss was real. Beds not bunks would have to be slept in and trips to the nearest town in the lorry would not be quite the same thing as 'shore leave in the liberty boat.' Naval ranks were to be sluiced away in the flood of change with the current RNAS personnel soon having to accept Army ranks (the present day RAF designations did not come into use until August the next year). The imminent submergence of saltwater stained traditions like 'make and mend', the dog watches and that nice RNAS adaptation, the ship's bell outside the CO's cabin, could scarcely be viewed with anything other than regret for a naval identity was all but disappearing except perhaps within an aircraft carrier.

In an awareness of the aggrieved feelings of many in the RNAS as they awaited the amalgamation, it is quite striking how T.C. Gordon reacted at the time and to note that it was apparently in accord with the spirit of all the Great Yarmouth Air Station officers after they had been addressed by General Sir David Henderson from the Air Ministry on 21 March. Henderson 'explained the intricacies of the new R.A. Force with admirable clearness and tact. He was a particularly sociable and sensible officer and an accomplished gentleman. One feels confidence and pride in these men, knowing the difficulties they have to face.'

Gordon records vividly in his diary the daily life and work of a seaplane station including such incidents as the furore over the theft of aeroplane watches, a station concert party and a deputation by the men complaining to the duty officer of inadequate rations, a complaint considered by Gordon to be fully justified. The incident led him to consider 'the dog-life of these men; some of them magnificent fellows', but he confesses 'Probably I should be much

the better [for] rough experiences, but it is not human to choose the rough when I can get the smooth.' One day in May, while still at Great Yarmouth, an F2a flying boat was lost, a very expensive Rolls-Royce engine ruined through having no water in the radiator and two Short seaplanes were wrecked. 'This is quite a big total of damage for one day and leads me to suspect treachery somewhere in the ranks, but it is quite impossible to fix the blame.' [A Rolls-Royce engine cost £1,430, and a Short 184 well over £4,000.]

In July 1918, after some time at Calshot and then at Lee-on-Solent where he was instructing, Gordon achieved what he had been applying for, a Northern posting, to Houton Bay in the Orkneys. From Houton Bay the Scot was

The establishment of German naval seaplane bases at Zeebrugge and Ostend led to increasing attacks against the British seaplanes and flying boats on anti-submarine and shipping patrols around the south-east coast and the Thames Estuary. The enemy activity reached a peak in July 1918 and following an attack by a German Brandenburg seaplane on an RAF Short 184 in that month, the carrier pigeon depicted in the card was released and returned safely to its Home Station at Westgate on Sea near Margate in spite of its having received an eye injury. (C.P. Bristow)

R.A.F. Pigeon's Gallant Flight.

This R.A.F. Pigeon, though shot through the left eye, brought back to a British Aerodrome a message from a Seaplane Patrol in the North Sea attacked by superior numbers.

regularly engaged upon flying anti-U-boat patrols, experiencing on one occasion the alarm of endeavouring to taxi back to the bay without having taken-off in a flying boat rapidly taking in water from the stern. Weather could be treacherous. In August 1918, one flying boat was sent off in the middle of a snow blizzard and crashed. During that month, Gordon wrote of his determined approach to the German U-boats, – 'merciless beasts beneath the surface of the ocean' – but the bad weather made the flying boat pilot apprehensive about the morale of the men should winter, as might be expected, produce far worse conditions. 'The men were miserable enough in the Summer and they are human beings, after all is said and done . . . it all appears a bad speculation to neglect the social and physical betterment of the airmen.' Indeed, a new CO introduced better working conditions for the men. Almost immediately, morale improved. Gordon had played his part by having improvements made to the hut of men from his flight: 'It is my policy to make the men happy and their quarters comfortable and clean. This alone is the way to win men and derive the most work from them.' Hockey provided much needed organised relaxation too. The serious Scot considered that it was a game in which each player's every stroke or mannerism illustrated his character.

The worst hour of anxiety suffered by Gordon in all his flying experience came in September when one of the petrol pipes to his starboard engine broke in two when his four-man-crewed F3 flying boat was 60 miles out to sea. With a sea swell of about ten feet, it was certainly unsafe to come down on the water. 'The pressure of going through the air at sixty-five knots was the only influence which kept the severed ends of the pipe together'. The engine popped, spluttered and lost revolutions. Petrol was running along the outside of an exhaust pipe inside which the invisible exhaust flames flared. The journey home had to be made over a minefield, so there was no prospect of a ship. Somehow it was managed, the starboard engine cutting out just as the flying boat landed. 'No hour of my life was so crowded with prayer,'

recorded Gordon, though the sincerity of Gordon's life-long faith slipped a little on the very next day when the new CO claimed Gordon's cabin: 'May his fiery head be broken in two with colds, coughs and all sorts of afflictions.'[15]

Throughout 1918 it was not just the flying boats, seaplanes and lighter-than-air craft which were engaged in anti-U-boat work but aeroplanes too were constantly on patrol close inshore of the East Coast shipping lanes. The *Official History*, however, provides evidence that progress in some areas in providing appropriate resources for an amalgamated, expanded flying service had not been great. For example there are details of the exclusive use of a basic trainer, the DH 6, by 32 new flights assigned to anti-U-boat work. The aircraft were operated by men who lived in completely inadequate accommodation and had very few of the essential support resources of proper repair-shop facilities, efficient bombsights and storage housing for bombs. There is furthermore an implication that the flying personnel were of a lower grade.[16]

By whatever means it was achieved, the expansion of aerial anti-submarine patrol work in 1918 over that of 1917 is striking: almost 5 million miles as against one and a half million, although not many more U-boats were actually attacked, 131 as against 106. It seems that aircraft and surface craft in cooperation were responsible for the destruction of six U-boats in 1918. Mention must be made, however, of the splendid achievement of a large American Curtiss flying boat operating from Dunkirk which, under Sopwith Camel escort, bombed and destroyed a U-boat on the surface in September 1917.

Overseas, aerial anti-U-boat patrol work was conducted from Malta, Otranto, Taranto and the Venice Lagoon, and also in the Aegean and Eastern Mediterranean where operations by seaplane carriers, following upon HMS *Ark Royal's* pioneer work in 1915 off the Dardanelles, were of considerable utility. D.R.B. Bentley who had gone out to the Mediterranean as a seaplane pilot with the converted seaplane carrier HMS *Manxman*, was transferred to

The end for a seaplane carrier of distinction, HMS *Ben My Chree*, on 8 January 1917. She was under the command of C.R. Samson and is shown here on fire in Castelorizo harbour off the coast of Asia Minor after having been hit by shellfire from the Turkish mainland. The hangar caught alight and the ship with its Short 184, Sopwith Schneider and Sopwith Baby seaplanes was lost. It was the final episode in a career during which she had been involved in numerous engagements. (Wing Commander H.V. de Leigh)

Calafranca seaplane station in Malta for anti-submarine patrol work and convoy escort. The sixteen officers in his unit found life in Malta very pleasant with 'bathing parties, picnics travelling in flat carts to various parts of the island and visits to the opera house ... but two of us felt that as a major war was in progress, we might be more useful and have a more exciting time elsewhere and so applied for a transfer to No. 6 Wing in Italy and this was granted.'[17]

AT SEA

Attention must now be turned to the experience of those concerned with the development of aviation work with the Grand Fleet and the Harwich Force or the Dover Patrol. In land warfare, the development of reconnaissance roles preceded all others but it can be maintained that the Admiralty was slow to recognise the need to design, build and introduce into service either long-range rigid air ships or purpose-built seaplane or aircraft carriers to provide the Grand Fleet with advance reconnaissance information of the movements of the German High Seas Fleet or detachments of it. The degree to which such stricture can be upheld has to be tempered by an awareness of the immediately pressing need for the RNAS to fulfil its responsibility for Home Defence, a role assigned to it in September 1914, and also to undertake aerial patrolling of the coasts and port entries against U-boat depredations. In mitigation, Naval Intelligence was so quickly able to detect movement of the High Seas Fleet by directional wireless techniques that advanced aerial reconnaissance seemed less important. What of course this meant was that immediately before and during an engagement there was no aerial observation to learn what tactical deployments the German ships were making.

With hindsight, this may all seem frustrating, especially given the fact that practical advances in the appropriate fields had been made before 1914, like the commencement of rigid airship construction at Vickers Works in Barrow, construction which was laid to one side at the outbreak of war in favour of more 'vital' work. There were also successful experiments in launching an aeroplane from a warship. Take-off platforms were built upon the forecastles of HMS *Africa* and HMS *Hermes*, the vessels steaming into the wind, allowing maximum air lift for the machine taking-off.

Although the aircraft had to ditch near its parent vessel for the small hope of a derrick-hoisted rescue before it became waterlogged and sank, in the event of any naval engagement such a reconnaissance patrol was of potentially considerable use. It was, however, some time before this facility was brought into much use, except for the less operationally successful seaplanes with which some ships from light cruiser upward were equipped, like HMS *Doris* in the Eastern Mediterranean in 1915.[18]

The development of the true aircraft carrier with a flight deck for both take-off and landing

Two views of HMS *Ark Royal*, a seaplane carrier converted from a tramp steamer. The hold was made into a single hangar 150 feet long and 45 feet wide with two steam cranes to hoist out the seaplanes (six seaplanes and two land planes were carried for the 1915 Dardanelles Campaign). Note the attendant seagulls in the aerial view. (T. Spurgeon)

is inextricably linked to the names of G.R.A. Holmes and Hugh A. Williamson, the latter having served as a seaplane pilot with HMS *Ark Royal* in the Dardanelles. *Ark Royal* was a converted Blyth-built tramp steamer while the other seaplane carriers early in the war were fitted out from Cross-Channel steamers. HMS *Campania*, a converted Cunard liner, was the first carrier of any description to work with the Grand Fleet. She was joined by HMS *Engadine* which had been involved in the daring seaplane raid on Cuxhaven. In July 1915, *Engadine* cooperated with the carrier, HMS *Riviera*, in a clever but optimistic plan foiled by the fragility of her aircraft. Some of the carriers' seaplanes were to reconnoitre the islands of Borkum and Juist and the naval base estuary of the Ems, while others were to attack the Zeppelins which would be drawn out by the British incursion. G.E. Livock had an alarming experience on this raid. His engine faltered on the way to his target, the Nordeich wireless station. On his precipitated return, he sighted four Zeppelins. In facing such opposition the odds against his spluttering-engined Short seaplane with its four 16 lb bombs and the pilot's revolver and Very pistol did not seem encouraging. He headed for the British naval flotilla now firing upon the Zeppelins and was perhaps fortunate to land safely. However, the whole experience had done nothing for his composure and he taxied up to HMS *Riviera* too fast, crashed into her side and shattered his propeller. As for the

whole enterprise, its failure, together with the indifferent performance produced by the seaplanes of HMS *Campania*, were not the sort of evidence to give the British Commander-in-Chief, Sir John Jellicoe, great confidence in the utility of seaplane carriers in the North Sea.

Quite apart from Zeppelins, mines, German surface vessels or U-boats, a major problem in raids on the German coast was roughness of the sea preventing seaplane take-off. Group Captain Livock has written of early 1915 intended raids from both HMS *Riviera* and HMS *Ben My Chree* when sea conditions made it quite impossible to take-off. There were unforeseen factors too: on one occasion, using detachable wheels for a seaplane take-off from the short wooden platform on *Ben My Chree*'s foredeck, things went extraordinarily and unpleasantly wrong. 'When the pilot turned the handle inside the cockpit to start the engine, there was an explosion and the engine ran backwards for some time. The starting handle, revolving at tremendous speed inside the cockpit, broke the pilot's wrist and knocked most of the instruments off the dashboard.'[19]

The potential of aircraft in spotting for naval shelling of accessible shore targets like those offered in occupied Belgium seemed much more evident than in naval engagements or in German coast operations as described above. On numerous occasions the RNAS, quite apart from the regular duties of reconnaissance, photographic work and bombing, assisted

Routine reconnaissance a month after the Zeebrugge Raid of 23 April 1918. A photograph taken by No. 202 Squadron on 30 May showing the block-ships HMS *Thetis* (at the top), HMS *Iphigenia* (middle) and HMS *Intrepid* (bottom) but not the Mole which is beyond the frame to the left and the top. Note that the tide is out. (Lord Braybrooke)

monitors in shelling the Belgian coast. Lawrence Pendred's log for May 1918 shows that enemy motor lighters as well as aircraft could be kept clear of the monitors by RNAS patrols but air cover for naval vessels could not be provided well out into the North Sea except by large rigid airships working with the Grand Fleet or Harwich Force.[20]

In the absence of such airships it was as well that the kite balloon did offer possibilities. In trials from HMS *Engadine*, the balloon and its basket remained stable even as the carrier manoeuvred at a speed of 22 knots in a heavy sea. As a result of these trials, HMS *Campania*, undergoing reconstruction, was now to be fitted to carry a kite balloon.

In September 1915 a carrier was added to the vigorously led Harwich Force. This converted Isle of Man passenger steamer, renamed HMS *Vindex*, took part in the March 1916 raid on the German airship base thought to be at Hoyer. The seaplanes were unable to effect any serious bomb damage. Three of them were forced down by engine failure, their crews falling into German hands, and one returning pilot reported the disarming information that the airship sheds were actually at nearby Tondern. Nevertheless, a glimpse for the imaginative was being offered of the direction in which progress might be made – a carrier with a deck not merely for take-off but for landing.

Long before that development, the single full Battle Fleet action took place, that of Jutland, and who can tell what difference to the outcome of the battle the presence of a British capacity for aerial reconnaissance would have made. All commentaries upon the battle make a good deal of the fact that HMS *Campania*, with ten seaplanes aboard her on 30 May and her balloon too, did not take part at Jutland, leaving Scapa late through a chain of circumstances. In the belief that she was too late to reach her allotted station and that without escort she was in danger from U-boat attack, Sir John Jellicoe ordered her back to base.

As a result of *Campania*'s delay, the battle-cruisers from Rosyth were alone in having aerial support, that of HMS *Engadine*, carrying four seaplanes in all. One of the seaplanes, a

Short, enabled the pilot, Flight Lieutenant F.J. Rutland, and his observer, Assistant Paymaster G.S. Trewin, to carry out the sole British aerial reconnaissance conducted during the battle. In carrying it out, the seaplane came under fire but it was a mechanical defect which forced it to come down on the water. The offending petrol pipe was repaired on the spot before wireless instruction from HMS *Engadine* ordered the seaplane back to its carrier. *Engadine*, keeping well to the disengaged side of Beatty's battle-cruisers took no further part in the action other than in standing by and even towing the stricken HMS *Warrior*, taking off the crew of the armoured cruiser when she had to be abandoned. The fact that Rutland's information about the change of course of the enemy's first-sighted scouting group was not successfully relayed to the battle-cruiser flagship, HMS *Lion*, is but one example in the sad catalogue of British failures in communication during the ensuing hours. Too much should not be made of this, however, as signals of the change of course did get through from the British cruiser which had in fact first come upon the German units.

Nevertheless it is tempting to speculate what would have resulted from the presence of the British Air Arm in a battle where the vital element was the German need to escape being overwhelmed and whose tactics were therefore to conceal their evasions until such time as it was judged direly necessary that a bold bid to break through or behind the main British Battle Fleet had to be made. The fact that bad weather conditions prevented the departure on time of the German airships can scarcely match what had been lost to the British, because *Campania*'s seaplanes, flying so much lower than vulnerable airships, could well have made up much of the ground lost by British failure in the gathering and passing on of intelligence. The lessons were not lost on the Admiralty and the 'next generation' of carriers were designed to steam at speeds as great or greater than the Battle Fleet and to operate independently.

Disappointingly, the provisions for aerial reconnaissance were no better in August when a second Jutland might well have developed from movements of the opposing Battle Fleets. In October 1916, however, particularly bold aerial reconnaissance of the Schillig roads was carried out by seaplanes from the carrier HMS *Vindex*.

Sir David Beatty, recently appointed Commander-in-Chief of the Grand Fleet, wrote to the Admiralty in January 1917 of the great possibilities which the Air Arm offered, not least to the Grand Fleet itself. In particular he stressed that there were not enough aircraft carriers. In reply he was informed that the RNAS was fulfilling a bombing role over Alsace Lorraine and a vital support role in the operations of the BEF but that before the end of the year, a new aircraft carrier, *Argus*, would be ready: 'All machines to fly from the ship's deck. It is further hoped that Reconnaissance machines will be able to alight on the ship, experiments now being carried out at Fort Victoria being most promising. In this case aeroplanes would be used for Reconnaissance.'[21]

It is quite clear in Garth Trace's letters from the carrier HMS *Pegasus* (in service with the Grand Fleet in the second half of 1917 and in 1918), that no matter what exciting experimentation was taking place, not all RNAS men were coping comfortably with the North Sea at wave level. Trace wrote humorously to his cousin Hilda of his qualms and on other matters too but a touch enigmatically on a 'stunt' in which he had been involved. 'The complete mariner has been on board two days without being seasick. However, as the ship is still in dock, the trick is really not as difficult as it would at first appear. We sail on Friday when will commence a life of appalling misery, as this ship is very bad in rough weather, having a roll of 45°, causing us to walk carefully down the centre of the deck and to part our hair in the middle for fear of setting up a roll.' In a later missive: 'My cabin is right forward in the worst place in the ship for rolling and whenever I go to it I am reminded of that song. "The great big world keeps turning".' Some months later Trace was to write: 'I am steadily going daft, so is everyone on board. The Paymaster thinks he is a Pansy and the Flight Commander is up on

deck pretending to be a coffee pot. Very sad is it not but it's the nautical life you know. Which reminds me; we got back yesterday from a small stunt, it was rough, yes, I was – ever so – 3 times. I thought you would like to know. It was very amusing though, the whole thing, we were all quite the complete intrepid heroes until some ass fired off a machine-gun when we were not ready, we nearly died of heart failure. I am now the proud possessor of a large revolver, hair-raising looking instrument of death. The only person it is ever likely to hurt will be myself I expect, the damned thing goes off if you look at it ... I am at present very bored with life in general, the aspect is so dammed monotonous, that is what gives me the pip. However, I suppose we are helping to win the war, What! What!'[22]

In 1916 and 1917, experiments had been carried out to test the viability of close cooperation of Coastal Class airships with vessels of both the Harwich Force and the Grand Fleet. The problems of refuelling and airship crew exchange had been managed in trials under fair weather conditions. In July 1917, however, there had been a costly failure in gusts of wind off Peterhead. *C 15* was further and further damaged till she was completely destroyed in an attempt to attach her to HMS *Phaeton* and then to tow her while she was being refuelled by the light cruiser.

In fact, the Coastal Class airships had too short a range to be used effectively with the Fleet, even the North Sea Class brought in to supplement them proving insufficiently equipped for such work. There was a need for much larger rigid airships of which only a very few were completed for operational use during the last year of the war. The answer in both the short and the long term lay with the aircraft carrier.[23]

The evolution of the carrier does not concern us here; what does is the experimental work to land on the flight deck of a carrier.[25] In July 1917, the widely experienced E.H. Dunning was appointed to the command of five Sopwith Pups with HMS *Furious*, an aircraft carrier which had been converted from a ship originally being built as a special heavy-gunned

cruiser. Take-off, with the carrier in Scapa Flow, proved relatively simple. The carrier was aligned into the wind and a Pup, held by steel wire with a quick release arrangement and with its tail supported, was revved up on deck and then released. An adjacent field provided a landing ground. Rafts were used to return the aircraft to the carrier but Sir William Dickson has spoken of pilots touching the deck with their wheels in unofficial dummy landing exercises.[26]

The first successful landing on a ship was effected on HMS *Furious* by Dunning when the carrier was steaming into the wind. On 2 August, his approach, just above stalling speed, enabled him to position the aircraft within reach of a waiting deck party of fellow officers and the aircraft was held and secured. A second landing was made on 7 August but on that same day a third effort ended in tragedy. Three times Dunning seemed to hover above the deck before opening up the engine to rise again, then the aircraft sank towards the deck but, before it could be arrested, a gust of wind threw it heavily onto its starboard wheel and the aircraft slewed round to starboard. Dunning attempted

HMS *Furious* on to which the first ever deck landing was made on 2 August 1917 by Squadron Commander Dunning who was so tragically drowned a few days later making a further attempt to repeat his achievement. HMS *Furious* is shown here in 1918 with alterations which increased her flight deck to 300 feet and enabled her to carry sixteen aircraft. (Commander G.F. Evans)

to open out the engine to take-off, failed and crashed into the sea. Knocked unconscious, he drowned.

After this tragedy and the question it gave rise to concerning the need for a carrier to have a full-length deck for landing, which *Furious* did not at that stage possess, successful experiments were conducted at taking-off from a platform constructed upon a gun turret turned into the wind, a technique which allowed a ship to steer a course independent from that required by the aircraft taking-off. The celebrated Jutland pilot, F.J. Rutland, proved the practicability of this method from HMS *Repulse* on 1 October 1917. Thereafter, numerous large ships in service and similar vessels under construction were equipped with turret platforms. One of HMS *Renown's* Naval officers, G.F. Evans could not recall any occasion which

warranted their Sopwith Pups and Camels being flown off while at sea, simply in harbour. In taking-off, an aircraft's wheels ran along guide troughs in the platform from 'A' turret to the foc'sle head. It became known as the 'scenic railway'. When a machine ran straight off the ramp into the sea, the demise of the scenic railway went generally unregretted.[26]

The use of lighters on which to tow aircraft to increase the range of aerial operations produced one spectacular success in an unlikely way as it was achieved by a land-based aeroplane and not a seaplane – the only occasion during the war when such a machine was used in this manner on active service. On 10 August 1918, the destroyer HMS *Redoubt* of the Harwich Force towed a lighter carrying a Sopwith Camel to take part in a coastal motorboat and lighter-carried flying boat operation in the Heligoland Bight. The main purpose of the operation was not realised but Lieutenant Culley in the Camel took off to engage a patrolling Zeppelin. It took him an hour to get to 18,000 feet and despite his machine failing fully to respond to the controls at this height, he managed to get within about 300 feet of *L53*'s

A Sopwith $1\frac{1}{2}$-Strutter flown by Lieutenant W.F. Dickson taking off from the 'B' turret platform of the battleship HMS *Revenge*. The mounting of the platform over the guns can clearly be seen, the turret having been swung into the mean wind direction with the ship steaming ahead. Note the passenger attempting to keep some weight on the tail by sitting half out of the cockpit. (Marshal of the RAF Sir William Dickson)

height. As they approached each other, the Camel pilot stalled his machine to direct his aim along the huge underside of the Zeppelin. One of his Lewis guns jammed but he used the full drum of the other. He dived away and saw the little burst of flickering flame which soon led to an all-consuming blaze. Culley's report of the action succinctly stated: 'Fired 7 rounds from No. 1 gun, which jammed, and a double charge from No. 2. Zeppelin burst into flames and was destroyed.' The success of his exploit was capped by his own escape from injury, German captivity or Dutch internment. He was rapidly running out of petrol and clouds hid the friendly destroyers. He knew that the Dutch coast was outside his range but a fishing boat he had glimpsed might at least rescue him from drowning. He dived down towards the

A pilot whose Sopwith Pup has taken off from the gun turret platform of HMS *Renown* now awaits rescue by a steam pinnace from that battleship. This would be the end result of any such flight unless land lay within range. This photograph probably documents a ditching trial in the Firth of Forth in 1918. (Commander G.F. Evans)

fishing boat which was Dutch and, as one of Culley's fellow officers later related, 'suddenly he saw two destroyers come out from under the edge of the cloud. And then he saw the whole flotilla. Looping and rolling over the fleet to relieve his pent-up feelings, he picked up his destroyer with the lighter, fired a light as a signal, and landed in front of her. He was picked up, the Camel was hoisted on the lighter, and the flotilla started back for Harwich.'[27]

In March 1918, destroyers towing flying boats on lighters had enabled the aircraft to undertake reconnaissance of the German coast and then fly back to their British base. Their reconnaissances were repeated.

To return to the question of carrier flight decks, a design compromise was reached, HMS *Furious* being reconstructed with an after flightdeck while changes were made to HMS *Argus* to give her a flying deck absolutely unobstructed by any funnel or bridgehouse. It was from the flight deck of HMS *Furious* rather than from the towing of lighters carrying a flying boat or another type of aircraft that saw a revolutionary and successful operation midway through the final year of the war.

On 19 July, *Furious*, under light cruiser escort, approached the coast of Schleswig Holstein for the launching of a Sopwith Camel raid on the German airship base at Tondern. Captain W.F. Dickson was one of the seven pilots. He has recalled that at an earlier date, while *Furious* was being refitted, he had benefitted from an advanced flying course at Redcar. On rejoining the carrier, he was one of the pilots who managed to effect a landing on the new after-deck, his personal experience confirming what became the official judgement that the air turbulence from the funnel gases made the whole design unsuitable. In after-dinner gesticulatory description of the landing to the Admiral in Command, Dickson was to have the embarrassment of sending his glass of port flying too, staining the tablecloth.

Sopwith Camels on HMS *Furious* a few weeks before the Tondern raid. The Lewis gun fitted on each aeroplane's centre section identifies these machines as 2F.1 Camels, the 'Ship's' Camel actually used in the Tondern raid and in a number of successful operations from gun platforms and lighters in 1918. (Marshal of the RAF Sir William Dickson)

Before the Tondern raid, bombing practice in the Firth of Forth from Turnhouse aerodrome gave the pilots useful training for their raid. They were expected to try to return from their raid to ditch sufficiently near to destroyers to be picked up: as a poor alternative they were instructed to land in Denmark. Dickson was in the first flight and the two giant hangars themselves were found, though not without difficulty. Two 50 lb bombs were carried by each machine. Choosing the larger hangar which happened to have Zeppelins *L54* and *L60* within it, the Camels dived upon it and released their bombs at what was of course a very large target.

A huge conflagration was the result. The other hangar, as it happened without Zeppelins, was seriously damaged by the second flight.[28] Seven Camels had embarked upon the raid. One machine with engine trouble ditched early, the pilot being picked up. Of the remaining six pilots, two, Dickson and Captain Smart, were able to return sufficiently near to the naval force to be picked up, one was drowned and three were interned in Denmark. None of the machines was recovered but the loss of seven Camels had been a small price to pay for such success. It had been an unique raid of its type in World War One and though continued air/sea cooperation in operations off the Belgian coast, the Tondern Raid can still fittingly conclude testimony of 'Sailing in the Sky' during the war and also provide the broadest of hints about the future of naval aviation.

Carrying the War to Germany

Longer Range Bombing

In considering the impact upon the enemy of the service of the British soldier, sailor, airman and industrial worker during World War One, there must be an awareness that the work of each was essential and that it was inter-related to the service of the others. The German homeland suffered by the defeat of the German army in France and Belgium, by the strangulation exerted by the naval blockade and by the unflagging British war industrial production sustained of course by the United States. Their concerted influence steadily bore down upon Germans and Germany. Opportunity however came to the airman alone to bring the war directly into Germany. In the understandably emotive thinking of the time, this was the chance to wreak vengeance upon the enemy for all the sufferings, indignities and costs of a war brought about by German aggression. It was in such terms that strategic bombing was conceived in Britain, though the 'material' and the 'morale sapping' rationale was added in varying measure to the reprisal argument for air raids over German territory.

Strategic bombing is being considered here separately, as a new departure in air operations but in fact it can also be seen as a natural extension of the tactical bombing conducted from 1915. From the bombing of roads, bridges, railways, troop concentrations, ammunition dumps, etc., it was logical to reach out to the major centres of communication and locations of war materials under factory production.

From the early days of the war, the Royal Naval Air Service showed a readiness to engage upon longer-range bombing. It is, some would judge, though not Neville Jones in his stimulating book *The Origins of Strategic Bombing*,[1] just as understandable that the RFC, a Corps of the Army, should seek primarily to serve the Army. Whatever may be the case – and the debate continues[2] – the Navy was more advanced in its requirement of machines designed to have a bomb-carrying capacity, more ready to work on the development of bombing techniques, more open to providing training in night navigation, and more forward thinking in the way it pushed ahead the development and production of sophisticated instrumentation towards the goal of effective, long-range day and night bombing. Accordingly, it may be claimed for the RNAS that the true origins of the concept of strategic bombing lay with the junior branch of the Senior Service.

In the early summer of 1916, the Admiralty, cooperating with French bombing plans, authorised the re-establishment of No. 3 Naval Wing – disestablished after serving in the Dardanelles – operating from Ochey near Nancy and Luxeuil not far from Belfort. From these airfields, once enough single-seat Sopwith $1\frac{1}{2}$-Strutters and some French supplied Breguet Michelins were concentrated there, raids were launched in October and during the next few months across the Rhine upon Oberndorf and Rottweil and in the Saar region upon Volklingen, Thyssen and other towns. Whenever possible the bombers flew in a defensive 'V' formation and were additionally protected by two-seat fighter escort. The targets were chemical works, iron foundries and munition factories. The success of the raids forced the Germans to allocate ill-afforded anti-aircraft guns and numbers of air detachments to home defence. These resources were in fact a less serious counter to the raids than two other agencies. First, the weather that winter of 1916/17 produced heavy, low cloud and such low overnight temperatures that the

oil froze in the bombers' engines, calling forth all sorts of experimental endeavour to keep No. 3 Wing's machines in operational readiness. In addition, the Ochey/Luxeuil operational area Westwards had the characteristic regional problem of much autumnal fog so that flying conditions were frequently impossible. The second, still more damning difficulty, was that Army needs drew away pilots and machines for work in other sectors. This was compounded by Army disapproval of independent RNAS work of the nature of this strategic bombing. It was predominantly because of this disapproval that the Wing was closed down at the end of March 1917 just after a single Handley Page O/100 aircraft had demonstrated its ability to carry a far higher bomb load for effective night bombing.[3]

The concept of strategic bombing had not been still-born. Economic intelligence was

Longer range bombing: Within the patchwork of untorn, green fields lies a German military target, a rail supply route (see the white smoke of a steam train) or an ammunition or fuel dump (centre top). The bombs just released are clear but those released earlier have altered their profile as they nose downwards and are just visible in the light area just below the centre of the photograph. (Captain C.E. Townley)

being made available to high French and British authorities informing them that Germany was heavily dependent for her vital steel production upon areas of Lorraine and centres in occupied territories which were within reach of bombing. The seed took some time to germinate in the infertile soil of what seemed the more immediate and therefore prior need of the Army engaged in answering the massive daily demands of the Western Front. It has to be accepted that the most powerful influence upon germination was the motive of retaliation for the Gotha raids on London in June and July 1917. (The process by which resentment was translated into retaliation is well described in Neville Jones's book.) At the beginning of October 1917, the 41st Wing was established with a day-bombing squadron of DH4s, No. 55 Squadron, RFC, and two squadrons for night-bombing, one with FE2bs, No. 100 Squadron, RFC, and one with Handley Pages, No. 16 Naval Squadron. The squadrons operated from Ochey.

The 41st Wing cooperated initially with the French priority of targets, which were the railways serving the iron foundries of Lorraine and Luxembourg. In several ways the work of the 41st Wing had limitations upon its effectiveness; for example, the wing had no meteorological service. There were cartographical and navigational instrumentation deficiencies too, though some of these drawbacks were removed as the wing was up-graded to the status of a Brigade – VIII Brigade – on 1 February and further squadrons were added to its strength. To reach a target like Cologne, the DH4s had to make a flight of two and a half hours. The return journey against the prevailing wind would have taken longer but for the fact that the aircraft were now lighter after dropping their bombs and using so much fuel. The bombers flew in formation on the day-time raids but night bombing was carried out by a succession of single aircraft flying at irregular intervals. Accurate assessment of the material and moral effect of the raids is of course difficult – all that need be reaffirmed here is that the work of British, Allied and enemy pilots engaged on long-range bombing in World War One was sufficiently influential to convince policy makers of the potential unstoppability of the bomber in its role of bringing destruction, panic and collapse of will in the civilian population. It was a dangerous delusion which was drawn from a selective interpretation of what had been achieved.

In June 1918, VIII Brigade was still further expanded as an 'Independent Force' with a declared aim of bringing down 'the German army in Germany, its Government and the crippling of its sources of supply'.[4] To do this,

Bombing Mannheim, 16 September 1918. This photograph was taken on a bombing raid over Germany. It shows one of No. 110 Squadron's DH9As at a lower altitude. DH4s from No. 55 Squadron were also involved in this raid. (Sir Robin Rowell)

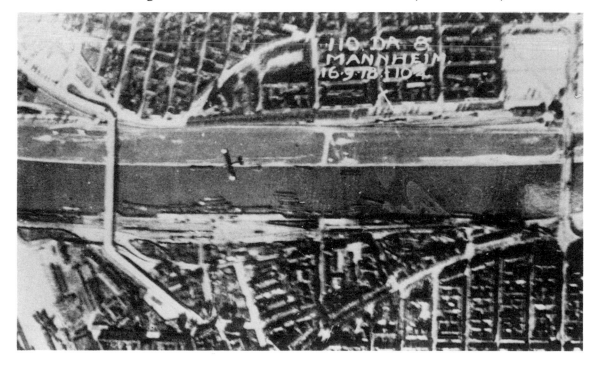

the commander of the new force, Major General Sir Hugh Trenchard, judged that German aerodromes from which counter-operations could be mounted and German railways and blast furnaces must be attacked. Trenchard may have been unduly cautious in placing German aerodromes so high on his list of priorities. The fact that through a combination of pressures Germany was exhausted and beaten in 1918 not, as was anticipated by Trenchard and many others, in 1919, makes assessment of this difficult too. Those who recall from personal experience the operations of the Independent Force cannot provide conclusive evidence for this debate. They can, however, make clear emphatically today that long-range bombing raids, especially if by night, provided flying service of a very particular character, strikingly different from short-range tactical operational duties.

A DH4 pilot, A.S. Keep, was part of a formation from No. 55 Squadron bombing Cologne by daylight on 18 May 1918. His diary marked it as: 'The record raid of the war.' Six DH4s left their aerodrome at 6.20 a.m, climbed to 11,000 feet and were untroubled by anti-aircraft fire on their 175 mile flight, reaching their target in about two and a half hours. Keep's machine began to lose its place in the formation as air got into a fuel pipe and enemy fighters were able to close on him. Cologne was partially obscured by mist and clouds but his 112 lb bombs were dropped and observed to have detonated. Photographs were taken before leaving the target area but the enemy fighters attacked and damaged his machine. Keep's observer, Patey, fired on one of the aircraft and forced it out of action. The remaining scouts did not press the engagement and the British machine, rapidly losing height, made for France. 'Saw three Huns approaching us from Treves ... put nose down slightly to increase speed and outdistance the Huns. While watching them we were suddenly dived on by two Albatri who had been about 4,000 feet above us out of sight. The first fired as he dived past and hit us through the right hand tank. The second came under the tail and got in a good burst taking away variable incidence wires, part of

the undercarriage, longeron, main spar of tail and several other minor hits. Jammed on full left bank and rudder and swung round on him and so out-manoeuvred him bringing him alongside about 50 yards away. Patey was waiting for him and got in a splendid burst with his last drum. The Hun turned over and went down out of control.' The other scout was left behind as the DH4 crossed the lines and a safe landing was achieved despite the damage to the aircraft.[5]

Keep's final raid was on a munition works at Oberndorf. The pilot's log book reads simply: 'Pollack killed, self wounded', but a personal diary provides the detailed story. After bombing their target, they were attacked by nine enemy aircraft. One of the British machines was shot down in flames and the German aircraft got right in among the bombers no longer protected by their formation. Keep was wounded in the right upper arm but Pollack, his observer, shot down the aircraft responsible. Suffering from loss of blood, Keep endeavoured to catch up to the realigning formation but three enemy aircraft were in pursuit. The observer again shot down one assailant whom the French later reported had crashed just within the German lines. Immediately following this incident, an anti-aircraft shell burst just below their machine, hitting the aircraft heavily and wounding the observer. With fuel supply lines shot through, Keep still managed to glide down to land very fortunately at a French hospital. It was not soon enough to save Pollack who died from loss of blood.

According to Sir Hugh Walmsley, who, as Lieutenant Walmsley, had also been a DH4 pilot in No. 55 Squadron before it was posted south to the 41st Wing, bomb-aiming was far from scientific before the new sighting devices were fully in use. 'The leader sighted the bomb and as he was going to release his bomb, his observer fired a green Very light which attracted the other pilots in the formation – he was the only one who aimed the bomb and all the rest of the formation released their bombs when they saw their leader's going down.' By chance, a pep talk by Trenchard was the preliminary to Hugh Walmsley's first raid, the

objective being the Zeppelin shed at Gontrode: 'I would like you Gentlemen to know that I have no intention of withdrawing any squadrons from France [for the defence of London] because in my opinion it does politicians good to be bombed occasionally.' Small wonder that with such talk Trenchard was worshipped and respected by the men in his force. 'He put the fear of God into all of us but he was a terrific leader and we would have done anything for him.'

By his experienced flight commander, Captain Stevens, Walmsley was assured that all he need be concerned about was to 'formate on the chap in front'. In the event, the first Walmsley knew that he was being attacked was hearing the noise of the enemy machine-gun: 'I saw a chap flying just underneath me, he was known to the Squadron I heard afterwards as "Cucumber Bill" but he was painted yellow and then just in a flash I observed an aeroplane painted red and another painted blue.' Wisely and with self-discipline the young pilot did not react to the alarming kaleidoscope of visual impressions tempting him out of his formation and he survived an experience which proved

Independent Force: Outside the camouflaged hangars at Tantonville H.S.P. Walmsley and Captain Ward MC sit in their DH4 of No. 55 Squadron. As a team they flew together from September 1917 to July 1918 and usually in this machine. (Air Marshal Sir Hugh Walmsley)

fatal for a number of inexperienced pilots caught in the same situation.

When No. 55 Squadron moved south to Ochey, Walmsley found the anti-aircraft fire particularly unpleasant. 'Just when one was feeling drowsy with lack of oxygen there would be a 'Woomph' of the first shell, a 'sighter'. If one were the leader of a formation, the immediate reaction was to 'crab' to left or right, keeping in level flight and then skid off to right or left and so avoid any grouping of shells based on the sighter.' The combustibility of the extra petrol tanks fitted to the DH4 to increase its range became a worrying thought to pilot and observer caught by anti-aircraft fire – the pilot actually sat above his tank.

The aircrew's dependence upon fitters and riggers is nicely acknowledged by Walmsley whose fitter, named Laidlaw, and rigger, called Taylor, were the recipients of weekly food parcels from the pilot's mother. 'They looked after my aeroplane as if it were their own child. There was no such thing as working hours, if there was anything to do they did it. They used to work like blazes day and night. I had the greatest respect for them.'

In May 1918, Flight Commander Walmsley lost a particular friend in a raid on Saarbrücken during which the raiders were attacked by sixteen enemy aircraft. The diary entry reads: 'Poor old Sammy shot down in flames.' Having seen this happen from his position in the second flight, Sir Hugh remembers that it triggered off a period of venom against the enemy which achieved physical expression as he pulled the bomb release.[6]

The pilot and observer in a DH4 were separated by the petrol tank making communication difficult, and Walmsley used a mirror in his centre section and sign language when attempts to signal by pulling on a string proved unsatisfactory. In similar vein, Roy Shillinglaw remembered the surmountings of small problems like night map-reading in an FE2b by a flash-light connected by a loose flex to its battery strapped to his belt. Shillinglaw has also described the work in the roomier but still open cockpit of the Handley Pages using the drift indicator to calculate drift angle, the change of direction and the wind speed and make adjustment to the course he had worked out in the mapping room.[7] Navigation on the return flight was easier as the beacons, or lighthouses as they were called, provided reference points and if the airfield landing lights were not on, they could be requested by the use of a powerful Klaxon horn.

With regard to enemy searchlights, Shillinglaw has written that there was competition in No. 100 Squadron's Mess for the long tapered-necked Crème de Menthe bottles which, on being thrown at a cluster of searchlights, made a screaming noise in descent not dissimilar to a falling bomb and could lead to the dousing of the lights.

An observer's duties in a Handley Page extended beyond navigation and gunnery to bomb-aiming and release. He had also to check the fuel consumption dials, engine temperatures and rev counters, operate the Aldis signalling lamp if necessary, and fire the Very pistols and the Michelin flare used in exceptional need for a forced landing at night. He sat alongside the pilot who was fully occupied controlling the heavy, cumbersome bomber which might have been flying at no more than 70 mph. There was a rear gunner who was totally out of communication with the rest of the crew in the front cockpits, but had two separate Lewis guns firing upwards laterally and to the rear for company.

The fact that in No. 100 Squadron the airmen knew of the reprisal nature of their work

Near Bruges in occupied Belgium, the remains of the Handley Page bomber which did not return are being surveyed by German troops. It seems that some items have been collected for salvage. The Lewis guns, ammunition drums and flare cartridges are in the foreground while in the centre some of the fabric of the machine has been draped over the body of one of the aircrew (see the sad evidence of an outstretched hand). (Sir Frederick Russell)

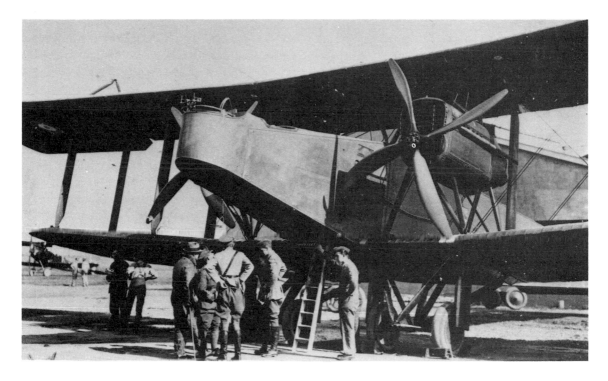

and of Trenchard's attempt to bomb Germany out of the war is nicely confirmed in a letter from Shillinglaw's pilot from Colorado, Lieutenant J.H.L. Gower, on 12 October 1918: 'For every town the Huns burn in France, we have got to demolish one in Germany. And believe me we have a bomb which can lay everything flat within a mile radius. So with four well placed bombs on Cologne we could absolutely demolish the town. It does seem a crime doesn't it, but we are hoping that if we successfully finish one Hun town they will be ready to quit.'[8] Gower did not develop his point about the morality of bombing civilian targets but other pilots sometimes recorded similar sentiments. Gower's optimism about the results of a single bomb may stem from the fact that a 3,000 lb bomb was under discussion and rumours of this may have reached him.

Some crew members combatted the cold at high altitude by wearing an electrically-heated waistcoat or gloves but movement frequently caused a break in the wiring and they proved more of a hazard than a protection. Stevenson Jones, an observer with No. 55 Squadron, scorned the 'costly rubbish' he was given to try

The RAF's main heavy bomber of the war, the Handley Page O/400. It was used by five squadrons of the Independent Force and by three other squadrons on the Western Front. This H/P was retained in England for armament trials at Orfordness. Dwarfed by the machine is the Commanding Officer at Orfordness, the tall Colonel Sheckleton, with his back to the camera. He is playing host to Winston Churchill, dressed in a Sidcot flying suit but wearing a Homburg. (C.H. Shelton)

out, flying helmets which did not turn with one's head, anti-frostbite cream which did not work as well as boracic ointment and in particular, the tangle of electric leads to clothing being heated, and the pipe to an oxygen mask which was 'quite futile'.[9] Such flying aids as were tried, were as limited in their issue as in their effectiveness. This observer also stoutly ignored the advice given to take tea and well-margarined bread before taking off. 'If you were empty the body reacted to the rarified air of high altitude, one broke wind lustily and all was well.' Stevenson Jones carried Huntley and Palmer's Ginger Breads for the descent from considerable heights to avoid the feeling of deflation and then on landing he got rid of the inevitable headache with a wash, shave, sponge down with warm water, a meal in the Mess and then by walking, walking and walking before supper and bed.

Physical inability to cope with high altitude flying affected the commencement of Alan Perry-Keene's active service but his experience was on the DH9 with its disappointing performance. It was with justified apprehension that Perry-Keene, on arrival at No. 98 Squadron, was told to try one out. 'Just the same as a DH4, old boy and you're on a show this evening.' That evening he went on his first 'show'. He had never previously flown in formation, never dropped a bomb, fired a gun in the air or been over 5,000 feet; moreover the DH9 was not 'just the same as a DH4' and that day he had made his initial flight in it and had been unaccompanied. Perry-Keene had but three raids in a DH9. On the third he blacked out when at a ceiling far above his previous experience. His NCO observer brought the machine down to lower altitude, using dual

control from the rear cockpit and the pilot recovered sufficiently to make a rough-landing with no disastrous results to the crew. A conversion course enabled Perry-Keene to be posted to the Independent Force to fly Handley Pages at their much lower operational ceiling but at No. 115 Squadron's aerodrome at Roville aux Chênes near Nancy, he and 2nd Lt Hill, his observer, witnessed a costly tragedy when their aircraft with its sixteen 112 lb bombs aboard was having the release mechanism for the 20 lb Cooper bombs tested. The safety device preventing the bombs becoming live before dropping some distance, failed. The bombs exploded, killing and injuring a large number of ground staff besides destroying the

Bombing up: Final preparations for a raid by a night flying squadron of FE2bs. It seems that the sergeant who will be responsible for the fusing of the bombs is explaining some detail to one of the airmen. (F. Wilkinson)

costly Handley Page, wrecking an adjacent aircraft and damaging others.[10]

Less tragic in their result were some of the dangerous incidents described in the entertainingly written history of No. 16 Naval Squadron (No. 216 Squadron, RAF) which formed part of VIII Brigade and then the Independent Force. There are some splendid stories of damaged aircraft returning from raids, one hitting the spire of Ochey church leading to the squadron acquiring a reputation for 'running down' churches rather than bombing them; then of a crash landing in which the shocked pilot and observer were 'not unanimous' in whether responsibility lay with anti-aircraft fire damage to the undercarriage or a slight misjudgement on landing. This history also pays a deserved tribute to the gunlayers who attempted to defend the aerodrome at Ochey from enemy air attacks from their cylindrical gun-pits. Boredom, tiredness and intense cold must have been in predominance but when the airfield was under machine-gun and bombing attack from the air, the men manning the guns must have felt very vulnerable.

It was No. 16 Naval Squadron which made an experimental attempt with incendiary bombs and cans of petrol to set alight the part of the Black Forest near Offenburg. French reconnaissance aircraft reported that the fire was still alight two days later. This target was not pointlessly vengeful, because wood was important in the aircraft industry in particular.[11]

With regard to General Trenchard's insistence upon enemy airfields becoming a priority target, there is a log entry of one pilot revealing an intriguing response. It must be stated that this reference is from the coast (No. 214 Squadron) and not in the sector of the Independent Force. It is from Handley Page pilot H.R.W. Ellison for 1 July 1918. After raiding three German aerodromes: 'A splendid trip after eternal Bruges Docks and enjoyed it greatly. These 'dromes had landing "tees" on and so gave them a little hate and woke them up a bit.' Ellison's log is a particularly interesting one and not merely for its vivid detail of anti-aircraft fire and on several occasions diving to

Far too large to be accommodated in internal bomb racks, this 1,660 lb bomb had to be slung externally beneath the fuselage of this Handley Page O/400 bomber of No. 214 Squadron, RAF. A bomb of this weight was first dropped on the ammunition dump at Middlekerque on the night of 24 June 1918 by an HP O/400 of this squadron flown by Captain Ellison. (H.R.W. Ellison)

machine-gun and extinguish searchlights. What is quite striking is the sense of enjoyment and also a sense of humour. For instance, he wrote on 24 March 1918: 'Owing to a misunderstanding left before signal had been given and took up ladder and electrician by mistake. The ladder fell off undercarriage and has since been found on the road near 'drome. Got somewhat "strafed" for leaving before signal had been given. (This flight made immediately after day in Boulogne!!!).' He writes of the return from an attempted raid on Douai railway junction on 12 April 1918: 'Became very misty, could not see sky or land. One compass dud and other quite hors de combat. Quite

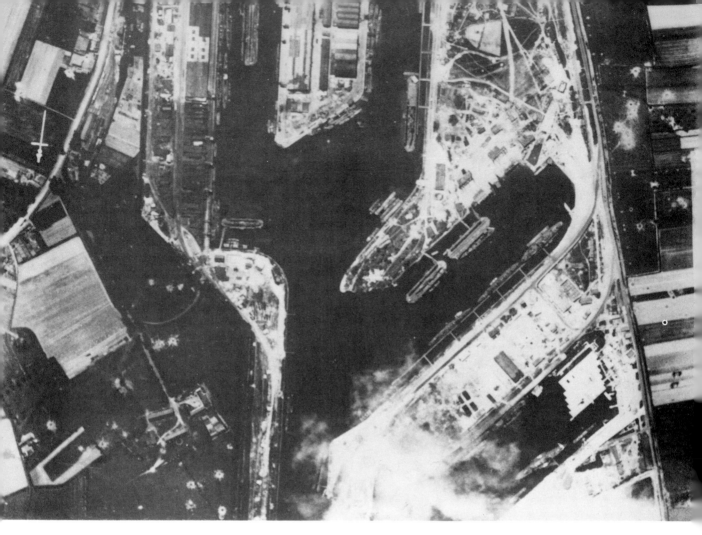

Handley Page pilot, Lieutenant H.R.W. Ellison's log book details the raid on 24 July 1918 when, despite anti-aircraft fire, searchlights and even, uncommonly, a night flying German scout, he dropped the RAF's first 'blockbuster' the 1,660 lb bomb. Note the letters G/L (gun-layer) for his rear gunner, an abbreviation indicating that Ellison had been in the RNAS. (H.R.W. Ellison)

lost!!! and language awful.' Somehow on this moonless night he brought the Handley Page down for a successful landing between trees, slept in the machine and despite a hilly slope to his 'landing strip' he managed to take off and return to his base the following morning.

Recording the bombing of Courtrai the humour again appears but also what some may consider a sad disregard of cultural values. 'A very soft trip and an easy place to find. Played with the Huns by not dropping for some time to make them think I could not find the place. Dropped two 250 lb bombs in centre of town and blew a cathedral up. Confirmed by photograph.' Two more entries must suffice to document a man for whom the personal nature of the log was paramount: 'Took up the Padre for a joy ride and did a few things until he wondered where he was' and then: 'Went over channel and nearly to Margate. Went wild when I saw Margate and nearly jumped over side.'[12]

Of all the raids carried out by the Independent Force, the daylight attack of Thionville railway station by Nos 55 and 99 Squadrons on 16 July 1918 was perhaps the most successful. A munition train was hit and the resultant explosion set stationary ammunition trucks alight. A horse transport train was also wrecked as were locomotives, trucks and various ancillary buildings or railway facilities. This destruction was wrought by but 37 bombs, only seven of which were of the heavy weight of 230 lb. Against such success may be measured a raid on 31 July in which only two of the seven DH9s which approached the revised target of Saarbrücken escaped becoming the prey of German fighters which had first forced the diversion of the raid from Mainz and then harried the bombers on their alternative target and homeward flight. As a result of losses in this raid, No. 99 Squadron was unable for some time to resume offensive operations until its replacement pilots had been trained in the necessary art of formation flying. Men who flew in these DH9 machines knew just how

Pilots and observers of No. 217 Squadron in front of a DH4 bomber with 230 lb bombs well to the fore. This photograph may have been taken at the time of the Armistice. (R.N. Bell)

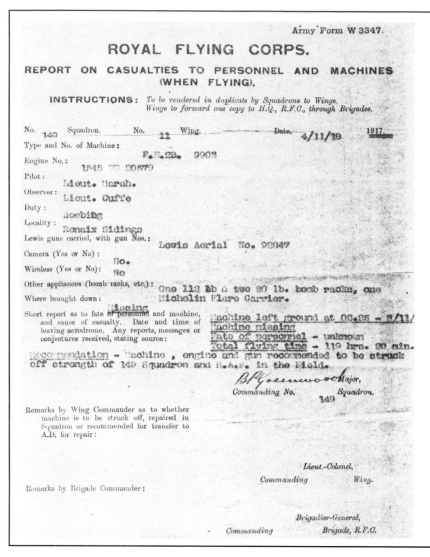

Army Form W 3347.

ROYAL FLYING CORPS.

REPORT ON CASUALTIES TO PERSONNEL AND MACHINES (WHEN FLYING).

INSTRUCTIONS: *To be rendered in duplicate by Squadrons to Wings.*
Wings to forward one copy to H.Q., R.F.C., through Brigades.

No. 149 Squadron.   No. 11 Wing.   Date. 4/11/18   1917.

Type and No. of Machine: F.E.2B. 9905

Engine No.: 1545 WD 20579

Pilot: Lieut. Marsh.

Observer: Lieut. Cuffe

Duty: Bombing

Locality: Ronaix Sidings

Lewis guns carried, with gun Nos.: Lewis Aerial No. 92947

Camera (Yes or No): No.

Wireless (Yes or No): No

Other appliances (bomb racks, etc.): One 112 lb & two 20 lb. bomb racks, one

Where brought down: Michelin Flare Carrier. Missing

Short report as to fate of personnel and machine, and cause of casualty. Date and time of leaving aerodrome. Any reports, messages or conjectures received, stating source:

Machine left ground at 09.25 — 4/11/
Machine missing
Fate of personnel — unknown
Total flying time — 112 hrs. 30 min.

Recommendation — Machine, engine and gun recommended to be struck off strength of 149 Squadron and R.A.F. in the Field.

B.F. Greenwood Major,
Commanding No. 149 Squadron.

Remarks by Wing Commander as to whether machine is to be struck off, repaired in Squadron or recommended for transfer to A.D. for repair:

Lieut.-Colonel,
Commanding Wing.

Remarks by Brigade Commander:

Brigadier-General,
Commanding Brigade, R.F.C.

Lost but later found: Lieutenant Frank Marsh, piloting a veteran FE 2b in the night bombing role at the end of the war was posted missing but he and his observer, Lieutenant Cuffe, turned up over 24 hours later having got lost in the mist and making a forced landing within the Allied lines. Note that Major Greenwood of No. 149 Squadron is showing a concern for economy by continuing to use his stock of official RFC stationery, though this report dates from the last month of the war. (F. Marsh)

unreliable and underpowered they were. Much more of course was possible with the twin engined Handley Pages. Even so, one may well pause to reflect upon what was required in terms of nerve and capabilities beyond trained expertise in bringing these large machines through a searchlight barrier and its attendant anti-aircraft fire and then making an attack from 200 feet as was achieved by one pilot in a raid on Mannheim on 25 August. It is scarcely surprising that one observer of No. 100 Squadron, Roy Shillinglaw, recalls being bathed in perspiration after getting clear of a target, no matter how low the temperature.[13]

In October, three Handley Pages each dropped a 1,650 lb bomb on Kaiserslautern. The pace at which technology triumphed over formidable obstacles is clearly indicated by the development of the four-engined Handley Page V/1500, three of which, with their crew of six, were ready to bomb Berlin from Norfolk with 30 250 lb bombs, this enterprise being just forestalled by the Armistice.

1918: The Western Front

Staving off Disasters – Achieving Victory

When fate forced upon, as much as gave, the Germans the opportunity in the spring of 1918 to mount a series of offensives larger in scale and different in nature from anything they had previously essayed in the West since the first days of the war, the role of the British Air Arm in support of the BEF assumed an importance which it would be difficult to exaggerate. When, where and in what strength was the initial attack to be made, in what direction would lie the thrust of the attack, where would supplementary or indeed superior attacks be made and what picture would emerge of the strategy behind the achievement of tactical successes? Though there were other sources of information, no agency could answer these questions with the speed and certainty, while at the same time doing so much to hinder German progress as could the airmen of the RFC and the RNAS on the eve of their amalgamation as the Royal Air Force.

Preparing to answer the first and funda-mental question related to the expected Ger-man attack – when, where and in what strength – the air units were simply ordered to intensify the long-established policy of maintaining the offensive in the air, but now over a newly-extended British line. Photo reconnaissance progressively revealed the signs of railway and road construction, train movements, ammu-nition dumps, new airfields and related evidence from which could be deduced that an attack in huge strength would have to be faced in the St Quentin area, behind which lay Amiens. A new battle of the Somme would have to be fought with the 1916 roles of attacker and defender reversed. While the Ger-mans did much to hide the strength of their developing build-up, the RFC observed its accretion and assisted in the registration of British artillery on detected gun positions, ammunition dumps, communication routes and then by day and night bombed and machine-gunned to cause destruction and erode morale. German . aerodromes were singled out for attention, a top level instruction detailing that: 'The effect on morale of a suc-cession of bombing attacks on hutments or billets at short intervals is much greater than that of the same number of raids spread out over a longer interval.'[1]

There were not the resources fully to con-centrate a programme of bombing and to avoid spasmodic and hence less effective air attack. Indeed, it was judged expedient to maintain the longer range bombing by those squadrons sent south to the Independent Force specifi-cally for this purpose but much was done even though in retrospect it may appear to have the aspect of the little Dutch boy attempting to plug the hole in the dyke.

A notebook of statistics compiled by Cap-tain S. Wood, a Staff Officer at RFC HQ, shows clearly that the bomb-dropping tonnage climbed steadily in the second and third week of March and that in the fortnight before 21 March over 1,500 photographs were being taken on each day that flying was possible (on each of two days over 2,500 were taken). There is a similar picture from the figures of hostile batteries destroyed through aircraft coopera-tion, over a hundred on 17 March.[2]

Concerning aerial interference with the Ger-man build-up, Flight Lieutenant C.R. Watkins (DH4 of No. 5 Naval) wrote a contemporary account of the raid on Busigny aerodrome on 18 March. He felt the four tremors through his machine as his sixteen bombs were released in groups of four. 'I turn my head to watch my neighbour's bombs falling, my own being hidden by my wings. I can follow the little shining shapes down and down and then after losing sight of them for some seconds, am rewarded by the sight of many little balls of smoke, each with a tiny heart of rose coloured flame, which mysteriously appears among the cluster of pygmy hangars, 16,000 feet below.' Watkins goes on to describe the German response, flights of machines climbing up to oppose them: 50–60 fighters, including those of Jagdeschwader No. 1 commanded by Richthofen. His DH4 was attacked by two scarlet triplanes. 'Tracer bullets whine to and fro like luminous shuttlecocks and I shrink into myself instinctively trying to reduce the gigantic target which I feel my back must present.' He sees holes multiplying in his wings and a cut flying wire curls up like a watch spring. The escorting Camels and SE5s were late and for some time the eight DHs were unsupported though they still managed to account for three hostile aircraft.[3]

In this period, organisational changes permitted the widening of the responsibilities of the officer in command of a squadron. As supplies permitted, a fighter squadron's establishment was increased to 24 machines (27 pilots), usually operating in three sub-formations of five aircraft each under a Flight Commander, but additionally the Commanding Officer had a further machine added to his strength, one for his own use. Clearly his role of administrative authority was thus being optionally extended to that of exercising leadership in the air though not every Squadron Commander would have the time or would feel that his responsibilities were being best fulfilled by regularly flying over the lines.

In the initial attack on 21 March, the Germans had 730 machines available as against the British total of 579; in single-seater fighters German superiority stood at 326 to 261. Numerically outmatched, the British air resources strove to fulfil their expanded role, that is, tactical bombing and troop harassment, together with the task of taking on the enemy's air strength so that the basic responsibilities of reconnaissance and artillery cooperation could be maintained as critical days, weeks and months tested the capacities of men and machines. It was a battle to be waged at every level

Spring 1918 and German infantry enjoy a close look at an aerial adversary, a Sopwith Camel of No. 54 Squadron forced down near Crépy. (M. Bier, Leutnant, 111 Reserve Infantry Regiment)

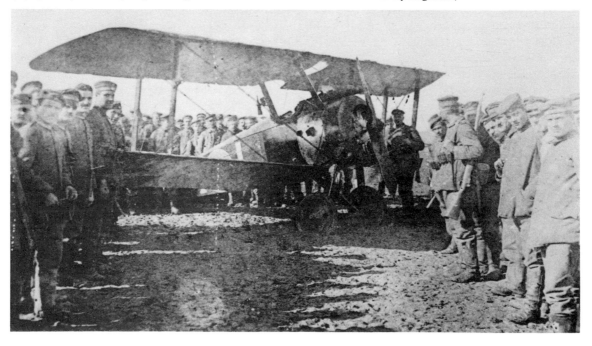

throughout the whole Service and not merely by the squadrons at the Front and at the depots in France, but in Britain, where aircraft design, factory production, aircrew recruitment and training were the forges which produced the weapons without which the battle could not have been fought.

In the early hours of 21 March, the final petals were blasted rather than plucked from any fading flower of uncertainty. A bombardment of hitherto unmatched, scientifically purposeful ferocity heralded and shrouded, in combination with ground mist, the advance of the storm troopers trained in infiltration tactics. Defensive coordination had been considerably neutralised, strong points by-passed, communications cut, units of troops and artillery batteries isolated and forced into surrender as successive waves of attacking troops took advantage of the confusion spread by the dislocation of command.

"ALL RISKS TO BE TAKEN" – SALMOND

For the RFC squadrons in the eye of the storm, one element in their work had been permanently destroyed, the stability engendered by operating from a fixed base. Apart from those men with 1914 experience, a new warfare was to be encountered, one which would very largely dominate their experience until the Armistice, warfare from what had to be almost a mobile base, at first in retirement and then, from the summer months, in the advance. If this brought, as it did, much less opportunity for the flying personnel to rest and enjoy a few hours of respite in the relatively comfortable fixed accommodation and recreational facilities of a 'permanent' base, how much more was the working day of ground support staff drastically changed by a need for a constant readiness to move all that was essential to the maintenance of aircraft which had to be kept operational in all circumstances. As a result of the loss of ground on the first day of the onslaught, all the squadrons on the 5th Army front had to withdraw from their airfields as did five squadrons on that part of the 3rd Army front which had been attacked.

RFC HQ-made decisions about the withdrawal of particular squadrons sent our officers by car to search for new sites. One such officer, W.C. Balmford, was given a stack of red flags and the map locations to which squadrons had to retire. His instructions were to place these flags on awkward spots on the newly designated airfields.[4] RFC HQ also ordered the marking out and clearance of obstructions on the new airfields by men from the nearest available Aircraft Park, and the resupplying of a squadron in precipitate retirement to a new base. Petrol, oil, bombs and ammunition were dumped at the selected field ready for use by the pilots whose aircraft gave them a mobility denied to the squadron's lorry and tender transport in slow movement on congested roads. Depots and stores were themselves not immune from the need to evacuate. The huge depot at Candas with all its air of ordered permanency, was hurriedly emptied of most of its holdings (some being left for approved 'looting' by certain squadrons needing stores and within reach of Candas). In a few days and nights of ceaseless work from 25 March a veritable aircraft 'Aladdin's Cave' of neatly piled stores of every description disappeared, though in point of fact neither Candas nor the other major depot vacated, Fienvillers, was to be captured. Naturally, during the days of retreat, much valuable material was lost like, for example, machines which were damaged and awaiting the repair for which neither facilities nor time were available. A sledge hammer was used by RFC Wireless Operator Reginald Smart to smash up a new wireless set when German troops suddenly appeared a few hundred yards from his listening station at St Leger Croiselles. He returned to his base, No. 12 Squadron at Boiry St Martin, but even in the imminent danger he was expected to go by lorry to the out stations later in the day to retrieve the Army watches deemed to be of such pre-eminent concern to Stores![5]

No. 84 Squadron (SE5a) was forced to withdraw first from Flez and then Champien and then Vert Galand though, on 21 March, the squadron claimed the unusual bag of an Albatros scout shot down by the rifles of two of

A South African who served with distinction in No. 84 Squadron, Hugh Saunders (on the right) was credited with sixteen victories and was awarded the MC, and the DFC and Bar. His friend Cecil Thompson is to the left. (Air Chief Marshal Sir Hugh Saunders)

Allies in the air. From No. 84 Squadron, RAF. Left to right, Lieutenant Simpson and Captain Highwood from Britain, then, the celebrated Captain Beauchamp Proctor from South Africa and Lieutenant Baldwin of the United States Air Service, one of several US officers attached to British squadrons for active service experience. (Air Chief Marshal Sir Hugh Saunders)

their motorcyclists. Sir Hugh Saunders provides a succinct account of No. 84 Squadron's almost ceaseless low-flying activity over a three-week period. 'We worked in pairs, leaving the aerodrome at fifteen minute intervals throughout the day. Every aeroplane carried bombs and a full supply of ammunition which was loosed off on the most convenient hostile troops. Pilots and mechanics fully realised the serious situation and all worked themselves to a standstill. Columns of infantry, guns, ammunition wagons etc. provided excellent targets and the casualties inflicted by low-flying aircraft must have been very heavy.' Saunders describes the method of single aircraft attack used by his squadron, diving, but not too steeply on the target, opening fire from 500 feet continuing till 50 feet from the target and then to zoom away in a climbing turn. The fact that not one pilot was lost to this squadron by ground fire during the March offensive may seem to justify this method rather than the

seemingly attractive but demanding method of a converging attack by two aeroplanes.[6]

Mention might deservedly be made of two quite remarkable aerial feats in these critical days, first that of Captain J.L. Trollope, a Camel pilot of No. 43 Squadron who shot down six enemy aircraft on 24 March and then that of Second Lieutenant A.A. McLeod, a Canadian pilot of an Armstrong Whitworth FK8 of No. 2 Squadron whose skill had to be matched by great fortitude. The Armstrong Whitworth was attacked on 27 March by eight Fokker Triplanes, the observer, Lieutenant A.W. Hammond, firing successfully at three of them. In the combat, McLeod suffered severe wounds and his machine caught fire. Somehow, he climbed out of the burning cockpit to stand on the bottom wing and from this position piloted the aircraft in a steep side-slip to keep the flames to one side and enable Hammond, though he also was badly wounded, to maintain fire upon their assailants. The mach-

Above. A German anti-aircraft detachment awaiting the approach of enemy aeroplanes. The machine-gun (left) will be used against any low flying aircraft but the main function of this look-out post is to use the range finder (right) to calculate the height and speed of aircraft moving towards them from the west and then to use the field telephone (centre) to provide this information to a larger calibre anti-aircraft battery on the Eastward slopes of this ridge. (M. Bier, Leutnant, 111 Reserve Infantry Regiment)

Below. A German anti-aircraft gun and its crew. Note the soldier at the breech, casually balancing a shell (in its case). The British airman's slang word for shellfire directed against them was 'Archie' after a Music Hall song, 'Archibald certainly not!', but it was the German equivalent slang which lasted into World War Two 'Flak', the initial letters of the German words for anti-aircraft gun. (M. Bier, 2nd Leutnant, 111 Reserve Infantry Regiment)

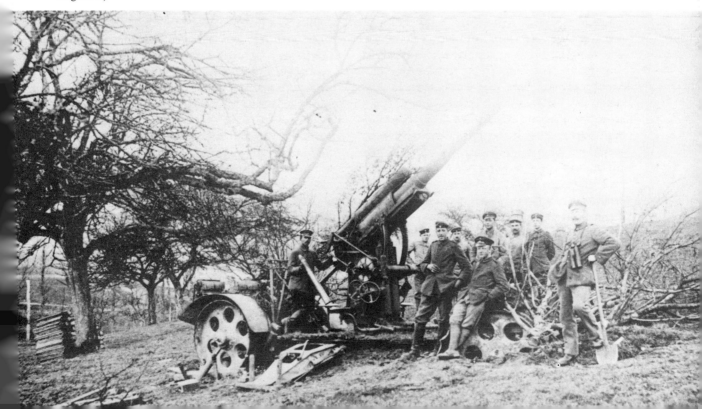

ine crashed in no-man's-land and McLeod dragged his observer clear even though they were now under ground machine-gun fire. McLeod was awarded the Victoria Cross but did not recover from his wounds, succumbing in Canada just before the Armistice.

When aerial observation on 21 March was possible through the early morning fog and the swirling clouds of smoke, earth and debris of shell explosions, aircraft observers sent wireless messages regarding troop concentrations and other targets, and written messages to that effect were dropped in weighted streamers. All too frequently there was no response. Artillery batteries were on the move or they had no aerial up or they were fulfilling Divisional orders, quite apart from which there was so much confusion and movement on the ground and so little communication by field telephone that in this scarcely 'ordered' retirement it was small wonder that one vital casualty was aircraft-cooperation in artillery registration. Even the 'zone' calls, signalled in emergency by aircraft observers spotting a new target and calling for fire from any battery which could register upon it, were going unanswered.

It was not just on the ground that ineffectiveness held sway because significant targets for tactical bombing like the bridges over the St Quentin Canal were attacked from the orthodox day-bombing height of 15,000 feet, far too high for any chance of success. However, in something of a departure from the general nature of the 'Offensive Patrol', British fighters were now engaged upon ground-attack duties often from exceptionally low level. The German soldier quoted in his Regimental History as having seen his Company Commander hit by the wheels of an aircraft while he himself just flung himself aside from the wheels of another may well have been embroidering some detail on a frightening experience but an effort should be made to imagine the skill and presence of mind required in the fulfilment of Major General Salmond's orders to 9th Wing and three squadrons stationed in its vicinity. On a day of crisis, 25 March, pilots working on a line just west of Bapaume were instructed to 'bomb and shoot up everything they can see on the enemy side of this line. Very low flying is essential. All risks to be taken. Urgent.'[7]

On 9 April, a new direction was given to the axis of the German offensive. This time the drive was against British positions further to the north between La Bassée and Armentières, the Battles of the Lys, which posed a potential threat to the Channel ports and the very maintenance of a British Expeditionary Force on the Continent. This was a danger even more critical than that of a decisive defeat on the Somme which would of course have split the BEF from the army of her French ally, leaving the latter, still sorely weakened by the aftermath of defeat and mutiny in the previous year, without the security of contact with an unbroken ally.

Further south, just six days before the new threat arose, 9th Wing received orders that their offensive patrolling was to consist of not less than two squadrons continuously flying over their part of the line near Bray sur Somme. This attempt still further to seek out and destroy enemy aircraft had arisen from the new German tactics of appearing high above the Somme battlefield in mass formations. The German approach was really a subtle concentration of their resources upon a selected sector at a particular time, obviously related to military operations on the ground. Le Blanc Smith of No. 73 Squadron was once to lead three squadrons in the British attempt to maintain a 'Cordon Sanitaire' over their sector and remembers 'what a thrilling sight it was to look back and see all 53 machines echeloned upwards and outwards above me but the idea was not very successful as our opponents seldom let us make contact and after a time the plan was dropped.'[8] In any case, the need to cooperate still more closely with the Army was to maintain the low-level flying character of operations during this Spring Offensive.

Reconnaissance had revealed the transport movements indicating that a new major offensive was being prepared but dry weather enabled the German preparations to be accelerated at a faster rate than defensive measures could be undertaken. There had been some reinforcement of RAF resources but growing awareness that the danger on the

Somme was over could only with caution be assimilated and squadrons in consequence released for transfer northwards. Again, morning fog aided the enemy on the initial day, flying not being possible till the afternoon by which time a situation as serious as on 21 March had developed. Major Chris Draper, No. 208 Squadron Commander at La Gorgue had the chastening decision to take of setting his sixteen fogbound Camels alight when he received information that the appearance of German infantry was imminent, the airfield having been under shell fire for some hours.[9]

Indifferent weather hampered flying operations during the afternoon of 9 April and on the following day too but reconnaissance, maintaining contact with British troops and making low-level attacks on the advancing Germans were carried out by squadrons also having to cope with evacuation from their airfields and the inevitable toll from ground-fire. Improved weather coincided with the culmination of the crisis on 12 April, the RAF on that day playing a sterling part in the stemming of the attack, flying more hours, dropping more bombs and taking more photographs than the British air Services had previously achieved on any one day. RAF balloon observers too gave information swiftly utilised by British artillery as were the wireless calls being made by aircraft observers.

Remaining in the air for long hours under abnormally bad weather conditions, often in darkness or mist, the work of RE8s of No. 4 Squadron on 9 April can be deduced from the Military Cross citation of an observer,

A pilot and no mean artist, Robert Best sketches himself and his observer, Captain F.G. White from No. 53 Squadron. Best was wounded in the back by machine-gun fire on 11 April 1918, the third day of the Battle of the Lys. White, observing for another pilot, was reported missing in action ten days after the wounding of his former pilot. (R.D. Best)

Canadian-born J.W. Baker. Engaged in low-flying reconnaissance and contact patrols under heavy machine-gun, rifle and anti-aircraft fire, he had 'remained over the enemy lines taking notes until quite dark, when he returned with his machine riddled with bullets. On every flight he obtained most important information, which was dropped at headquarters, and throughout the period his work has been magnificent.' His log-book record of the battle relates the landing after dark that first night at the 'retreat aerodrome – Trezennes near Aire.' On 11 April, his dawn contact patrol was made at a height of 300 feet in mist and on the fateful following day there is evidence, however tenuous, that the front was regaining some stability and that he himself had played a part in this: 'Sent two SOS calls on enemy attacks which were repulsed.'[10]

Though Baker was able to record a second SOS call having received an effective artillery response, nothing could minimise the fact that the RAF was engaged in a fighting retirement where, as on 21 March, steely resolve in all units and all ranks was needed to reduce the significance of those sectors or incidents where events had been giving the appearance of a disorganised rout.

A Bristol Fighter pilot of No. 20 Squadron wrote: 'I had to map the position of the enemy advance along miles of front for 2nd Army HQ. We flew low enough to see blood on the faces of the wounded. At the big locomotive repair depot at Hazebrouck we saw engines being blown up. The situation was chaotic. On the evening of 12 April, St Marie Cappel was being shelled and we were ordered to fly to an aerodrome further West. We all took off individually in the gathering dusk. It was too dark to read a map and we had no night-flying lights.' However, the observer H.G. Crowe, had had infantry service in this area which he judged helped him to find Boisdinghem, the only Bristol Fighter to land there that night.[11]

In retrospect, 12 April may well have been the day on which it can be judged that the BEF and the RAF together ensured that no vital strategic loss was to be conceded in the Battles of the Lys but German thrusts did secure still more ground though to no seemingly coordinated purpose. Villers Bretonneux on the Somme was taken on 24 April though swiftly recaptured. Kemmel Hill flanking the Ypres Salient was lost at the same time. In four weeks, a thousand British aircraft had been lost through enemy action and from other causes. Nothing could show more clearly the dependence on aircraft production in Britain because the figure falls not far short of the number of

Vintage quality! Lieutenants Sammy Hughes and Freddy Peacock, the pilot and observer of an Armstrong Whitworth FK8 of No. 10 Squadron, with their combined age in the region of 70 years claimed to be the oldest crew flying together on the Western Front. In May 1918 they shot down an attacking Fokker Triplane, the wing tip of which they have kept as a souvenir. (Air Chief Marshal Sir Ronald Ivelaw Chapman)

aircraft available to the RFC in France on 21 March, the day the German offensives commenced.

Another matter to which only brief reference can be made here was the serious damage done by the German bombing of British airfields and depots like those at Blarges and at Saigneville during the early months of 1918. Many British airfields were to suffer shelling and bombing in 1918. No. 214 Squadron was on the receiving end of one such raid in June and H.R.W. Ellison annotated his blotched log book: 'Ink splashes result of "Hun" bombing raids wrecking my cabin and breaking an ink pot' but two German raids in the month of August wrought damage on an unusual scale.[12] Number 2 Base Mechanical Transport Depot at Calais was hit and motor vehicle spare parts in enormous number and of every description were destroyed. This was a very serious loss indeed but in some senses the raid of 24 August 1918 on the airfield at Bertangles was still worse. Several squadrons were based there but No. 48 Squadron was the unlucky one. A direct hit on a hangar which contained six Bristol Fighters fully laden with petrol, ammunition and 25 lb bombs resulted in an explosion of flames which

Sopwith Camels and pilots of 'A' Flight of No. 213 Squadron at Bergues in May 1918. Note the fuselage marking on the nearer Camel. Left to right, Lieutenant Taylor with his fug boots and Naval uniform; Lieutenant Gray, Captain Horstmann (RNAS uniform) and Lieutenants Pinder, Talbot (RAF uniform) and Hancock (and fug boots). (W.E. Gray)

acted as a focal point for further bombing. Another hangar holding machines was hit. Between the two roaring infernos of flame and explosions lay a hangar designated for entertainment and being used for a concert party at that moment. No one was hurt from fragments of the bombs so far dropped as the men were protected by a four-foot sandbag wall around the hangar but as the audience of more than two hundred officers and men, many of them visitors to the squadron, poured out, a second German aircraft was approaching. 'This coupled with the intense heat of the burning hangars on either side caused a complete panic.' In such a manner has the squadron's Commanding Officer, Major Keith Park, described what happened. Two bombs caused casualties to men in the stampeding crowd. Park, his Equipment Officer and some Australian soldiers who were bivouaced on the edge of the airfield, managed to drag seven burning machines clear of the hangars but more bombs were dropped. More casualties were suffered and more damage was caused to ancillary buildings. From No. 48 Squadron and from the visitors, at least eight were killed and about 28 wounded. All the squadron's transport was destroyed and the Bristol Fighters 'rescued' had been rendered virtually unserviceable by fire and other damage. That the experience proved to have lasting effect is made clear in Major Park's account in his post-war Staff College essay. 'The effect on everyone's nerves was very marked for some months later . . . the efficiency of the other ranks fell as also did that of my officers.'[13] In tape-recorded recollections, Park rather attractively associated himself with the initial panic but had been brought up sharply by the realisation that this was 'my unit I was running away from.' It was clear to the interviewer that the decoration Sir Keith Park received for his work on that night was for actions he considered to be in a sense more praiseworthy than his work in the air for which he had already been honoured.

Though the German bombers were no longer crossing the English Channel they were still vulnerable in their shorter flights to and from targets in Belgium and France. They suffered losses from both anti-aircraft fire and from the Camels of the only operational night fighting squadron in France, No. 151, from June to the end of the war. The squadron's first confirmed success was by A.B. Yuille on 25 July. His log book states that he 'attacked New-type Gotha at Etaples 12.45 a.m. Brought down near Robecq. 3 prisoners, Capt. Von Schepke, Lt Schweider and Lt Schwabe.' In the demanding sphere of nocturnal combats, No 151 Squadron shot down at least 21 enemy aircraft and suffered no losses. Yuille himself had further success on 10 August: '5 Engined machine in flames at Talmas'. He had shot down a huge Staaken R XIV Giant bomber with its crew of seven. Sufficient of both of his conquests was undestroyed in their crash for valuably detailed illustrated reports to be made as a result.[14]

As the land and aerial battles of the Lys were

being fought, a Rhodesian, piloting a Sopwith Camel, fell victim on 20 April to the renowned von Richthofen the day before the latter was killed under circumstances which still occasion debate. The Rhodesian, D.G. Lewis, was with two flights of No 3 Squadron on an offensive patrol led by Captain D.J. Bell. One of the flights has been lost in thick cloud but Bell took the remaining flight on a collision course against about fifteen brightly-coloured Fokker Triplanes. Richthofen's was red, some were blue and some of draughtboard design. Lewis has written: 'We met head-on firing our Vickers and Spandau machine-guns at each other.' He himself was firing on a blue Triplane in the swirling combat which ensued when Richthofen got on his tail. He could not be shaken off. 'Struts splintered before my eyes, wires severed by bullets danced wildly in the air, the compass before my face was shattered and the liquid poured over me and my goggles went over the side. I think the elastic where it joined the frame had been severed by a bullet. I had one bullet through my right sleeve and one through my trousers at the knee. Then I heard the roar of flames, smelled petrol and then realised I was afire.' There was slender hope of avoiding a crash but sufficient fabric remained on the elevators to enable the pilot to flatten out the Camel before impact after a nose dive which had doused the flames. Lewis was thrown out of the cockpit, his fate being to be taken prisoner, stunned and with minor burns but lucky to be alive![15]

To escape unscathed from a machine well on fire required a refusal to panic and the intervention of that indefinable, invaluable element, good fortune. Did one stay or did one jump to a quicker death? Fear of being burned alive lay within the anxieties of many. On 8 August 1918 when Bryan Sharwood Smith (No. 48 Squadron) momentarily lost control of his Bristol Fighter in combat and flames flickered along the right-hand side of the fuselage, his 'instantaneous reaction was to switch off the engine and pull up the trimming control for landing, both quite pointless, for we were well alight.' In fact, it was 'the imminence of death' which led to a different reaction, that of throwing the Bristol into a vertical side-slip as McLeod, the Canadian, had done under still worse circumstances for his machine. After Sharwood Smith's crash-landing he found that his bulky leather flying clothing had prevented the flames from doing more than scorch his cheeks.[16] Hugo Ibbotson (No. 70 Squadron) encountered flames in a different manner and in his case the bulkiness of the flying clothing proved a menace. In a crash behind German lines as troops came up to take him prisoner, he was using a small demolition charge looking like a rolling pin to ignite his petrol-soaked Camel when the resultant explosion of flames engulfed him. He made desperate but for some time unavailing efforts to loosen the thin leather waist belt over which the coat bulged

A French decoration for a British pilot. In July 1918 Frank Ransley was at home after recently having served as a Flight Commander in No. 48 Squadron. He must have been pleased to receive this notification from his old CO Major Keith Park. Park of course was to play a key role in the 1940 Battle of Britain. (F.C. Ransley)

until he had to draw off his burning gauntlets to use fingers from which strips of charred skin were hanging.[17]

Grim documentation of this nature should not remove from our consideration the intoxicated exhilaration felt by many aircrew actually in combat and sometimes in writing about it. Victor Groom wrote home in the early Summer of 1918: 'You go absolutely mad when in a scrap. I mean this quite literally. You see Hun machines around you and you dive and fire, then pull out. Probably some Huns are diving on you. The Huns use a bullet which leaves a trail of smoke, the effect being like a ray of sunshine coming through a cloud. It is very strange altogether – you hear the cack, cack, cack of bullets whistling by and all the time you are either diving, climbing or twisting about. I can remember now that I was shouting out at the top of my voice . . . When a scrap starts you simply say a prayer, open up the engine and go right into it and practically go mad and you

```
To,- Capt. F.C. Ransley,
     "Perrysfield",
          Conisboro' Avenue,
          . Caversham,
               Reading, Berks.
     - - - - - - - - -

Dear Ransley,

          You will be very pleased to hear that you are being
awarded CROIX de GUERRE avec ETOILE.

          Attached French Army letter will be of interest to you.

          The actual medal I am keeping until you write
acknowledging receipt of this letter and telling me to what address
you wish the medal sent.

          All the old members of the Squadron send you
hearty congratulations.



In the Field,                    Yours sincerely,
17-7-18.
KRP/GLC.
```

Closer than Allies. These three American Navy pilots, left to right, Lieutenants 'Shortie' Smith, D.S. Ingalls and K.A. McLeish, are on voluntary attachment to No. 213 Squadron, RAF in the spring of 1918 at Bergues (the CO's office is to the rear – note the horticultural enterprise). Ingalls's attachment was made official following his success as a Camel pilot. He shot down eight enemy aircraft, the top score for a US Navy pilot. At his retirement from the US Navy he had attained the rank of Rear Admiral. (W.E. Gray)

don't become sane until you are out of the machine on your own aerodrome.'[18] In such a manner an unharmed pilot might well describe his early victories but time would test and influence him – months of fiercely contested warfare remained.

Frustrated in their strategic purpose on both the Somme and the Lys, the Germans returned in May to the Aisne for a further extension of their offensive, then in June to the river Matz and in July to the Marne. On each of these sectors RAF squadrons were heavily engaged in support of the British and French military units ensuring that no more than tactical losses should be sustained. The first perceptible turning of the tide might be the date deliberately chosen for its significance to the American soldiers sharing the responsibility of the attack with Australian and British troops in a battle the planning and conduct of which owed much to an Australian General, Sir John Monash. In this battle of Le Hamel on 4 July, the RAF fulfilled three special roles, in addition to artillery cooperation and the normal infantry co-operation in an attack: first, in night-flying to

drown the noise of the tanks moving up to their assembly points; then in the pioneer parachute-dropping of ammunition to troops in the developing advance; and finally, working closely with the tanks in the battle.

Le Hamel on 4 July seems to have been the last flight in the war for Hugh Pryce, an RE8 pilot of No. 9 Squadron whose log has this last entry after listing practice ammunition drops on the previous two days. 'From 3.30 a.m. operating from No. 3 Australian Squadron's aerodrome. Dropped 6,000 rounds ammunition to troops during great Hamel show (Australian). 10 a.m. over Hamel Wood attacked by 3 Huns and chased 5 miles to 100 ft. Leader shot down in 1st burst. 10 shots and confirmed. I got hit in knee, two bits going in and several scratches. Landed safely. Went to hospital 2 p.m.[19]

Advantage was taken of the successful inter-arm cooperation at Le Hamel in planning the major counter stroke of 8 August in front of Amiens. From that date to the signing of the Armistice in the November of that year the RAF proved its capacity to play an integral role in the wresting of ground from the enemy in an unbroken series of victories over a foe certainly being beaten but never routed and scarcely ever failing to put up stern resistance. Infantry training out of the line had done much to prepare the BEF for the 'new' warfare and for the RAF, in addition to the maintenance of the work which had supported the BEF in the past, there were new responsibilities of assisting in the softening-up of objectives before and during infantry assault, attempting constantly to cut German rearward communications and exercising a protective supportive cover for the Allied troops in their advance frequently dropping ammunition to them by parachute and getting information to a wireless Central Information Bureau for speedily appropriate relay.[20]

The ceaseless work of so many men both in the air and among ground staff personnel inevitably included certain special cases where great deeds were performed regardless of cost. The cost had been high and in terms of those whose career had already made them honoured in the Service and publicised in the Press for a Domestic Front needful of heroes, the losses in the month before the great August counter-attack of Major J.T.B. McCudden vc (killed in a flying accident) and Major Edward Mannock (who died in the flames of his crash caused by machine-gun fire from the ground) were severe blows. McCudden, who had risen from the ranks, had 57 enemy planes to his credit and Mannock, who was to be awarded a posthumous Victoria Cross, had taught and inspired so much in others by his gifts of personality, leadership and quality of mind as well as by his combat record of 73 victories which left him as the highest scoring British or Commonwealth pilot.

In the first days of the August offensive there was an example of conduct worthy of these two men shown by the pilot and observer of a No. 8 Squadron Armstrong Whitworth FK8, Captain F.M.F. West and Lieutenant J.A.G. Haslam, each of whom has given the author an account of the experience. On 8 August, they were sent from Vignacourt on a tank contact patrol but also to find the precise location of the German Reserve. They came under heavy machine-gun fire from the ground, their FK8 being so seriously hit that they only just kept sufficient height to reach and crash-land at their fog-bound aerodrome, whose position had been indicated by rockets fired from the ground. Their relatively slight injuries were dressed at a casualty clearing station and they insisted on returning to their squadron from which a further tank contact patrol the following morning had a similar result. Again they were forced to return in a damaged condition,

Flying his usual SE5a (B6496), Hugh Saunders the Senior Flight Commander of No. 84 Squadron records his varied action in the summer of 1918. (Air Chief Marshal Sir Hugh Saunders)

Date and Hour.	Wind Direction and Velocity.	Machine Type and No.	Passenger.	Time.	Height.	Course.	Remarks.
17.7.18	Fair	B6496	—	2.0	14.000	No EA Seen	
18.7.18	"	B6496	-	2.10	15.000	" " "	
19.7.18	"	B6496	-	2.5	8.000	4 LVG Seen two engaged no result	
18.7.18	"	B6496	-	1.45	8.000	Reconn and Bombed Hit by archie	
20.7.18	"	B6496	"	2.5	17.000	Escort to Oniecourt on way back	
21.7.18	"	B6496	"	1.55	1.000	Scraped 7 Fokker Bipes Crashed One.	
22.7.18	"	B6496	"	2.5	12.000	Shot down EA Balloon in Flame	
22.7.18	"	B6496	"	2.15	10.000	No EA seen	
24.7.18	"	B6496	"	2.10	14.000	EA two Seater chased east	
24.7.18	"	B6496	"	1.35	17.000	had scrap. Caught in Storm Squadron had terrible time landed all over the place	
25.7.18	"	B6496	"	2.5	12.000	Chased three twoseaters	
26.7.18	Major Douglas MC went to Wing to take Command was appointed Acting CO 84 Squadron While he was away						
29.7.18	"	B6496	"	2.5	15.000	Shot down EA two Seater (crashed)	
29.7.18	"	B6496	"	15	2000	Test OK	
31.7.18	"	B6496	"	15	1000	Gun flip on new target OK	
1.8.18	"	B6496	"	1.50	14000	Chased two Seater came home "dud"	
1.8.18	"	B6496	"	10	1.000	Engine test	
				26.45		Total to date 314 hrs 45	
In France				277.25			

Captain F.M.F. West leaning on the propeller of an Armstrong Whitworth FK8 of No. 8 Squadron in the summer of 1918. His companion, almost certainly his observer, may have been his usual observer J.A.G. Haslam. It was in this particular machine (C8594) that the West/Haslam reconnaissances were carried out in the first days of the August Offensive. (Air Commodore F.M.F. West VC)

effecting a satisfactory landing beside a tank and later making their way to an Australian Divisional HQ where the pilot provided a full report.

West has spoken of concern at not being able to report with certainty the location of the Reserve and on 10 August a further attempt was made. They flew further east and came under concentrated anti-aircraft and machine-gun fire. They saw a railway junction and large numbers of troops and in West's view confirmation that this was the Reserve concentration seemed to lie in the fact that he saw armoured cars for which he had specifically been told to search. They knew the importance of getting this information back to the British lines as quickly as possible but they were intercepted by seven German fighters. 'We were heavily attacked and one of them got quite close to me

and an explosive bullet virtually severed my leg, my left leg. I was fortunate enough not to faint and to carry on flying until we reached our lines and somehow managed to land reasonably safely.' In fact, his left leg was jamming the rudder. It had to be moved out of the way and then: 'I twisted my pants as tight as I could and made some sort of tourniquet which reduced a little bit the amount of blood which was coming out of my wound [he was wearing shorts].' The tourniquet was held in place by his left hand while he piloted the FK8 with his right foot and right hand. His injury had not left him numbed (he had been hit in the right heel too): 'it was very painful and that kept me going.'

Haslam too had been slightly wounded, in the left leg, but he fired at the German aircraft which had attacked them from under their tail and caused sufficient damage as it appeared below and to his right that it ceased its attack, the other machine also breaking off the engagement. Haslam believes that West must have lost and then regained consciousness; certainly the pilot managed to avoid a 'tangle of telephone wires,' landing in a field, the undercarriage collapsing from damage caused in the combat. Canadian troops extricated West from the aircraft and while on a stretcher, he gave their officer information on the location of the German Reserve, details which he repeated to his squadron's Recording Officer who had hurried over to where he lay at a Field Ambulance station awaiting surgery.[21/22]

While West and Haslam's No. 8 Squadron was working exclusively with the tanks in the great counter-stroke from Amiens, other squadrons were concerned with assisting their progress by, for example, dropping 40 lb phosphorus bombs with contact fuses to emit smoke which screened the armoured vehicles' approach to enemy strongpoints. Then there was too the attacking of German troops on all escape routes and their bridges leading back from the battlefront which encountered stiff aerial opposition interfering with all attempts to bomb the Somme bridges. The *Jagdeschwader Richthofen*, now under the command of Hermann Goring, was itself reduced to a quarter of its strength in almost constant day-long combat which may seem to bear some resemblance to the struggle by attrition which was at last being transformed on the ground. It was not just the sheer courage and perhaps impetuous tactics of the outnumbered German flying service which brought heavy casualties to the British airmen, it was their possession from the early summer of 1918 of a new engine which gave their machines a superior performance. On 8 August, in a day of great military victory for the Allies, 45 RAF aeroplanes were lost and a further 52 were so wrecked or damaged that they had to be written off the strength of their squadrons. The bombing of the bridges, vigorously pressed as it was, did not secure the desired results nor could it be claimed that railway station bombing critically reduced rail transportation. Furthermore, the difficulty of maintaining protection of the bombers by the escorting fighters was a prime cause of the heavy losses incurred among the DH4s and DH9s. As far as the RAF was concerned, victory at Amiens had been dearly bought but in the following weeks as the Germans were forced back from the Somme, then the Scarpe and the Hindenburg Line itself was broken in a

series of battles, the RAF was finally to take the measure of its opponent. In aerial combats which on occasion drew in 100 machines, the balance of success was perceived at the time and still more clearly in retrospect to have become decisively weighted in favour of the British and the three Australian squadrons on the Western Front.

After a period of more cautious deployment of fighters at the beginning of September to allow the squadrons some opportunity for recuperation, the final week of that month showed the III Brigade Commander, Brigadier General C.H.A. Longcroft, requiring two or more squadrons to work together on Offensive Patrols with an SE5a or a Dolphin squadron above one or more Camel squadrons, the flight formations of each of these squadrons themselves to be flying at varying heights. The leader of the lowest squadron was in command of the patrol and it was the responsibility of the squadron flying above to keep in touch with the one underneath. The object of the patrol, initiated by the lowest squadron, was to find and attack enemy formations in the air and in the absence of such, bomb and machine-gun enemy aerodromes. The Camels were to release their bombs over enemy territory in the event of aerial combat being imminent, but as has already been mentioned, the Germans often refused to rise to the bait.[23]

The scale of combat which could develop as a result of the increase of aerial activity on escorted bombing raids at this time has led Sir Donald Hardman to compare 30 October 1918 with 15 September 1940 during the Battle of Britain and produce the surprising statistics of 67 German and 41 RAF aircraft lost in the earlier encounter and 60 German and 26 RAF in the latter. Hardman was leading twelve Sopwith Dolphins of No. 19 Squadron which had been detailed to escort No. 98 Squadron's DH 9s to bomb Mons. Between 30 and 40 Fokker D.VIIs attacked the DH 9s which 'put their noses down for home and we had a running fight back to the lines. All the aircraft in A Flight were shot or forced down early on and I got back with only two other aircraft in my Flight. I remember glancing back when we

T.C. Traill in his heavy flying kit with a non-issue flying helmet, photographed in England before being posted to No. 20 Squadron in France where he served from April 1918 to the end of the war as a pilot of Bristol Fighters. (Air Vice Marshal T.C. Traill)

got to no man's land and seeing the line of the Mons-Condé Canal strewn with burning aircraft. It was the only time that I remember running out of ammunition but I was lucky enough to shoot down two aircraft.'[24]

In August, the Bristol Fighters of No. 20 Squadron had been moved down to Vignacourt on the Somme replacing Major Keith Park's bombed No. 48 Squadron. From this airfield No. 151 Squadron's Camels were having night-flying successes over Gothas and T.C. Traill of No. 20 Squadron had a mascot tied to the bottom of the interplane struts of his

Bristol Fighter to bring him good fortune too. It was a figure of Bairnsfather's Old Bill, one of several thrown into the stalls by Beatrice Lillie during the revue *Cheep* which Traill had seen on his recent leave. No. 20 Squadron engaged the German single-seaters, bombed Busigny sidings and, when it moved with the advance, its aeroplanes became pack horses: 'Camp kit, beds, valises, bedding were tied round the undercarriage axle and to the interplane struts, suitcases in the observer's cockpit and coats and clothes stuffed down the fuselage among the bracing wires. Bennett and I had a little chest of drawers that must have been nearly the last straw.' The chest was placed on Bennett, Traill's observer, in his cockpit the last thing before take-off, after Traill's small puppy Pop (from Poperinghe where he had been picked up) had been inserted by his feet.

On 20 September, Traill led a Flight of seven Bristol Fighters against twelve enemy aircraft, a combat joined by other machines. It was a long fight and only two or three of his flight returned directly to the aerodrome at Suzanne. Most of the others rang in to report their safe arrival at other aerodromes. Several victories had been earned not least as a result of the cooperation of the SE5a's of No. 84 Squadron and Traill flew over to thank their CO, Major Sholto Douglas, 'a smart, dapper young man.'

Further combat brought more successes for No. 20 Squadron but Traill, who had earlier had an observer with him killed in action and then in September one wounded, was to have a particularly alarming experience on 23 October from which yet again his observer was not to come unharmed. His log book tersely states, within details of a bombing raid on Aulnoye Junction, that on the way back, his observer, a very unmechanical but excellent machine-gunner, L.W. Burbidge, had shot down one of the enemy aircraft harassing them, that four others were accounted for and that 'Goodearle hit us. He was killed. We crashed with Burbidge on right wing. He broke his nose, self OK.' What had happened was that at the very moment Traill was feeling under his seat for streamers to give to Burbidge to attach to his guns in their individual way as a victory sign, they had been hit by another aircraft of their flight. The other machine spun to the earth very fast, 'like an Ash key in Winter.' Damaged and with all aileron control lost, Traill's Bristol began a slow steep spiral to the left. Traill shouted to Burbidge to get out onto the wing where the observer's weight and drag would compensate for the loss of lift from the other wing which, deprived of the rear outer interplane strut, had warped out of shape. Burbidge's mechanical ignorance was shown first by his shouted query as to which wing and then when he had intrepidly clambered out and along the wing, by edging his way back once Traill had signalled that he had regained some control! The observer of course had to crawl back again clinging on to the bracing wires against the slipstream, the pilot only regaining control when the ground was perilously near. On landing, the parados of an old trench was hit and the machine turned over hard. Traill was temporarily trapped and soaked in petrol from a fractured fuel tank while Burbidge's determined grasp of the streamlined strut caused it to impact against his face, leaving him with a severely damaged nose.[25/26]

To return to the matter of aircraft working with tanks, the experimentation work conducted to secure efficient cooperation is detailed in an almost contemporary account by Major T.L. Leigh Mallory, in command of No. 8 Squadron which had been attached to the Tank Corps from 1 July. Wireless telephony and telegraphy, the showing of marked discs from the aircraft and the firing of Very lights or smoke bombs to indicate to the tanks the objective for which they were to make, all these means were tried in experiment or in action, but message dropping at Tank Battalion stations, for all its related problems, proved the most effective means of collaboration. This meant of course that an intermediate agency, the Battalion HQ was being used and pilots had to overfly it to drop their information but wireless developments were not yet sufficiently far advanced for the next leap forward, an efficient, direct, two-way contact by wireless.[27]

Anti-tank gun location and destruction were soon given a high priority in No. 8 Squadron's work something in which they were to be assisted by No. 73 Squadron, then commanded by Major Le Blanc Smith who had made the light-hearted point that in one attack co-operation was assured by reason of the fact that the Divisional General, the Tank Battalion Colonel and the Tank Section Major were all brothers (the Raikes family) and that the youngest of the three had been a close school friend of Le Blanc Smith himself.[28]

An example of the valuable work done by the airmen in neutralising anti-tank guns may be taken from the Leigh Mallory report referring to Captain S. Toomer and his observer, Lieutenant Shirlaw, on 23 August: '3.10 p.m. anti-tank gun located firing in the open in G23 at one of our tanks at about 1,500 yards range. Capt. Toomer dived on this gun, machine-gunning it, and dropped 6 25 lb bombs, 3 of which fell to the left of it and 3 to the right. The gun appeared to be damaged and the crew deserted it and fled down the road Eastwards. Lt Shirlaw fired 500 rounds into them with his double Lewis gun and appeared to do good execution.'[29] In September, this sort of support was rendered still more immediate by the throwing of a flare out of the back of a tank when the tank commander believed he was about to reach a particularly exposed spot or come within near range of an anti-tank gun which had already knocked out some tanks.

For the breaking of the famed Hindenburg Line on 27–29 September, No. 8 Squadron actually used an advance aerodrome at Mory as a refuelling depot thus enabling their aircraft to complete a full period over the tank operations in the forefront of the advance but even in the last weeks of the war the weather would have its say as No. 8 Squadron tried to carry out its work. A new observer, Lt Stephen Horscroft, who had on 13 October assisted in the provision of valuable reconnaissance reports to assist in the crossing of the Selle, wrote on 23 October: 'Got hopelessly lost in mist at 150 feet as soon as we took off. After firing umpteen lights found the drome and landed.' However, visibility improved later in the day and from his Armstrong Whitworth, Horscroft

The grave of Sergeant F.W. Shuffle-Botham marked with a cross made from the propeller of one of the DH4s of his squadron. As observer to Lieutenant Padmore on 28 September 1918 on a bombing raid along the Belgian coast, the men had the misfortune to fly into the trajectory of a 15-inch shell. (G.J. White)

Opposite. The Armistice, but a little early! No. 10 Squadron indulge themselves with flares on the evening of 10 November. (Air Chief Marshal Sir Ronald Ivelaw Chapman)

had duly: 'Pinpointed tanks and dropped a message.'[30]

Flying conditions continued to be indifferent but the victory scale of the Allied advance was undeniable. A few days earlier, on 17 October, Lawrence Pendred and his observer, Lt N. Jenkins in a DH 4 of No. 202 Squadron had out-stripped the advance on the Belgian coast. 'Crossed coast at Middlekerke and circled round Slype gradually getting lower as we met no trouble. Saw no activity and all guns gone. Went up to Ostende and flew over town and coastal batteries at 1,000 ft. Everything seemed dead and gave no signs of Hun occupation. Went to Ghistelles and had good look at aerodrome. Nothing happened to us so we

decided to land and say Cheer-Oh to the Belgians. Like an ass I wiped my undercarriage off on landing and so we were stuck for good. We found that the majority of Huns had left the aerodrome an hour before but that there were still some machine-gunners in the neighbourhood. We got a splendid reception from the Belgians who had not seen anyone but Hun aviators for four years.' Two days later the unofficial British liberators were themselves relieved by a not too pleased CO and a crash party.[31]

On 9 November, Stephen Horscroft from No. 8, the Tank Squadron, noted: 'Fritz going back fast so went up with Toomer to harass the Hun. Caught him on a road in the forest. Dropped our bombs and fired 1,000 rounds into him. Utter confusion. Gee it was great to see him run.' The retreat was so unchecked now that on 10 November Horscroft relates that the weather was lovely but very little flying 'cos Fritz is going back and we're out of touch.'

The Armistice was celebrated early by No. 8 for at midnight when the news came of the signing: 'We all got up, fired lights then pinched gallons of petrol and oil and made a bnfire. Kept this up till 9 a.m. Everybody mad as hatters.' The celebration continued throughout the Eleventh with photographs being taken, bonfires everywhere and 'A' Flight managing to set light to the village pond and then dancing round it far into the night, oblivious of the sharp white frost.[32] An Armstrong Whitworth of No. 10 Squadron had actually been on patrol from 10.30 a.m. until 11.15 a.m. on 11 November, the pilot, Captain Ronald Ivelaw Chapman, later recording in his log the electric moments of suspense shared by many on the ground and at sea but

Opposite. 11 November 1918 at RAF Sedgeford. It looks as if more anxiety about the future is being felt by the officers than any desire to celebrate the present. (Captain F.C. Ransley)

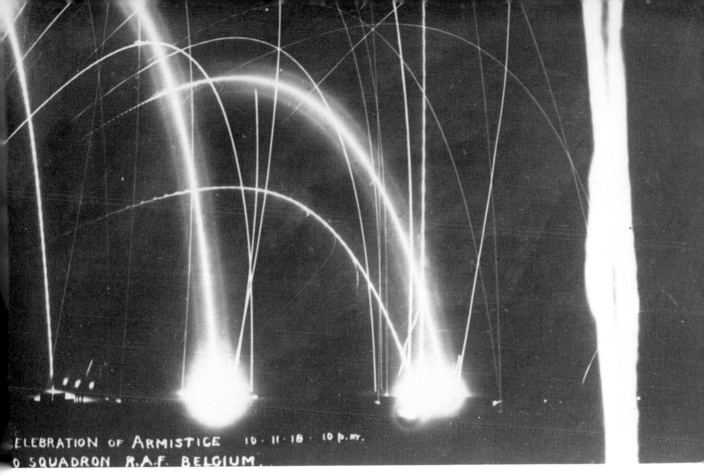

CELEBRATION OF ARMISTICE   10·11·18·   10 p.m.
0 SQUADRON R.A.F. BELGIUM.

by very few in the air: 'Saw the last few minutes of the war'.[33] More symbolic was the action of a Bristol Fighter pilot, Bryan Sharwood Smith of No. 48 Squadron. As the minute hand of his cockpit watch touched the hour, he contentedly fired eleven single shots on his front gun, treated himself and anyone who might have been watching to a valedictory loop and returned home.[34]

The historic significance of these minutes was something concerning which the least imaginative must have been aware but it was not just what was over, what had been achieved, lost and endured which was uppermost in the minds of so many but also what would the future hold. For the 'hostilities only' men, how soon would demobilisation come, what earlier employment prospect was still in view or what new avenue might be attempted? For the officers and men of the RAF, how secure was their future in an establishment certain to be reduced and in fact if some were to have their way disbanded as a separate entity? Would civilian flying hold opportunities for enough of the many likely to be tempted by the expected birth and expansion of commercial flying? The answers to such anxieties lie outside the framework of this book but there was within the Service at all levels a clear understanding that the Air Arm had made its mark. A pride in this was felt individually and was matched by some expectation that it would be recognised by soldiers and sailors and indeed by the nation and by its policy makers.

End Notes

Preface and Acknowledgements

1 The receipt of flying pay by qualified pilots and observers can in no way be seen as a comparable inducement to join.

Introduction

1. Bruce, J.M. *The Aeroplanes of the Royal Flying Corps*. Putnam, London, 1982, p. 353.
2. Neville Jones in his book, *The Origins of Strategic Bombing* (William Kimber, London, 1973), strongly asserts such a charge against the RFC but Dr Malcolm Smith has recently rebutted the assertion with the compelling argument that the demand for tactical support had to claim primacy (see his essay in *Home Fires and Foreign Fields*, edit. P.H. Liddle, Brasseys, London, 1985). Malcolm Cooper in an article in *Cross and Cockade International 1986* further attacks the Jones thesis but on technological grounds.

Chapter 1

1. Vol. 1, p. 187.
2. Brig. General Sir Robert Pigot: Typescript recollections. P.H.L. Archives.
3. Wing Commander J.N. Fletcher: Tape-recorded recollections. P.H.L. Archives.
4. Wing Commander T.E. Guttery: Typescript recollections. P.H.L. Archives.
5. W.J. Smyrk: Typescript recollections. P.H.L. Archives.
6. *Chasing the Wind*. Major General K. van der Spuy. Books of Africa, Capetown, 1966, p. 25.
7. Group Captain R.J. Bone: Typescript recollections. P.H.L. Archives.
8. Air Vice Marshal S.F. Vincent: Letter 17 March 1914, from A.V. Roe himself. P.H.L. Archives.
9. Roskill, Capt. S.W., edit. *Documents relating to the Royal Naval Air Service*, Vol. 1, p. 59. Navy Records Society, London and Colchester, 1969.
10. Mead, Peter. *The Eye in the Air*, p. 46. HMSO London, 1983.
11. Air Vice Marshal Sir Geoffrey Bromet: Diary. P.H.L. Archives.
12. Air Vice Marshal O.G.W.G. Lywood: Diary. P.H.L. Archives.

13. In fact there had been two RFC fatalities on take-off from Dover.
14. Lieutenants Waterfall and Bayley. The information in these paragraphs is drawn from Wing Commander T.E. Guttery's unpublished memoirs. P.H.L. Archives.
15. H. Jameson: Letter 4 November 1914. P.H.L. Archives.
16. Major L.G. Hawker VC: Letters. P.H.L. Archives.
17. D. Corbett Wilson: 1914 Letters. P.H.L. Archives. In these September 1914 references he could scarcely have written of two men who were to be more significant in the history of British air power. Captain Dowding later achieved fame as the C-in-C Fighter Command during the Battle of Britain.
18. Air Vice Marshal Sir Geoffrey Bromet: Map and tape-recorded recollections. P.H.L. Archives.

Chapter 2

1. Cole, C. and Cheesman, E.F. *The Air Defence of Britain 1914–18*. Putnam, London, 1984.
2. See Gibson, Mary, *Warneford V.C.*, published by The Fleet Air Arm Museum. Yeovilton, 1979.
3. Squadron Leader H.A. Buss: Log. P.H.L. Archives.
4. Wing Commander E.B. Beauman: Tape-recorded recollections. P.H.L. Archives.
5. M.R.A.F. Sir John Slessor – Tape-recorded recollections. P.H.L. Archives. Sir John added that after the war he entertained the Zeppelin Captain to lunch at the RAF club in London and the German told him that with the Zeppelin engines off, the buzz of the BE 2C had easily been heard and escape had been ordered immediately.
6. Report of Lt. W. Leefe Robinson quoted in the *Official History of the War in the Air*, Vol. III, p. 225.
7. Not all the victories were for Home Defence aircraft. There are only two further known air-to-air victories over German airships, both achieved by French pilots.

8. Professor G.C. Cheshire: Manuscript recollection. P.H.L. Archives.
9. Squadron Leader G.T. Stoneham: Log and letters July 1917. P.H.L. Archives.
10. Wing Commander A.B. Fanstone: Letters January and February 1918. P.H.L. Archives.
11. A.H. Bird: Log. P.H.L. Archives.

Chapter 3

1. J. McCudden. *Five years in the Royal Flying Corps*. The Aeroplane and General Publishing Company, London, 1918, p. 76.
2. Air Vice Marshal A.J. Capel: Log. P.H.L. Archives.
3. Air Vice Marshal A.J. Capel: Log. P.H.L. Archives.
4. Major E.W. Furse and Flight Sergeant W. Burns of No. 3 Squadron.
5. Air Vice Marshal C. de Crespigny: Letters 6 October 1915, 28 October 1915. P.H.L. Archives. It is worth noting that Major L.G. Hawker's letters reveal the same sensitivity for those whose 'ground happens to be chosen as a battle', 25 October 1914. P.H.L. Archives. With regard to Darley and Slade, they were taken prisoner, Darley later effecting a successful escape.
6. Illingworth, Captain A.E., and Robeson MC, Major V.A.H. *A History of No. 24 Squadron, Royal Air Force*. Privately published. No date. p. 19.
7. Major L.G. Hawker: Letters. P.H.L. Archives.
8. Hawker, T.M. *Hawker V.C.* The Mitre Press. London, 1965, p. 88.
9. *Ibid*, p. 120.
10. *Official History*. Vol. II. p. 161.
11. Revell, A. *British Fighter Units on the Western Front 1914–16*. Osprey. London, 1978. p. 16.
12. *Official History*. Vol. II Appendix VIII, pp. 471–2.
13. Letter dated 28 August 1916 from the papers of Air Vice Marshal H.V.C. de Crespigny. De Crespigny, at the age of 19, had become the youngest Major in the RFC. P.H.L. Archives.
14. Boyle, A. *Trenchard, Man of Vision*. Collins. London, 1962, p. 181.
15. The highest scoring American serving with the British, W. Lambert, in his autobiography *Combat Report* (William Kimber, 1973) actually states that reading of Ball in a Toronto newspaper inspired him to join the RFC.
16. Major T.L.W. Stallibrass: Log. P.H.L. Archives.
17. Wing Commander J. Duncan: Log. P.H.L. Archives.
18. Lieutenant J.L. Horridge: Letters. P.H.L. Archives.
19. Papers of J.S. Castle: Report written 24 August 1918 by Air Mechanic Ernest Coleman during his internment at the Hague, Holland, to which as a long term POW he, like Castle, had been transferred. The nacelle to which Coleman referred was the body of a pusher type. Its equivalent in a tractor where the crew sat behind the engine was the fuselage. P.H.L. Archives.
20. C.L. Roberts: Typescript recollections. P.H.L. Archives.

Chapter 4

1. In a tape-recorded interview with the author, Marshal of the RAF Sir Arthur Harris said of his work at the time: 'I came to the conclusion though I didn't like to say it at the time, that we were just flying about waiting to be shot at.' P.H.L. Archives.
2. Wing Commander A.B. Fanstone: Letter. P.H.L. Archives.
3. Lord Balfour of Inchrye: Tape-recorded recollections. P.H.L. Archives.
4. E. Pierce: Typescript recollections. P.H.L. Archives. 'Cardinal Puff' was a drinking game in the Mess in which a set sequence of word and gesture had to be followed precisely, an error resulting in the culprit having to take a drink and repeat the set sequence until it was correct, each further error requiring a further drink.
5. Rev. G. Worsop Hyde: Log 1917. P.H.L. Archives.
6. Hints for Observers: See papers of W.G.D. MacLennan: P.H.L. Archives.
7. Air Marshal Sir Victor Groom: Manuscript recollections. P.H.L. Archives.
8. Major M. le Blanc Smith: Typescript recollections. P.H.L. Archives.
9. Privately published commemorative booklet: Hugh Welch. P.H.L. Archives. It was of course normal practice for the CO to write to the next of kin of those lost in his squadron.
10. Rev. G. Worsop Hyde: Log and typescript recollections. P.H.L. Archives.
11. R. Smith: Typescript recollections. P.H.L. Archives.
12. Wing Commander A.B. Fanstone: Letter 29 April 1917. P.H.L. Archives.
13. Wing Commander Sir Archibald James: Typescript recollections. P.H.L. Archives.
14. Brig. B.U.S. Cripps: Log and diary, summer and autumn 1917. P.H.L. Archives.
15. Air Vice Marshal Sir Geoffrey R. Bromet: Tape-recorded recollections. P.H.L. Archives.
16. Dr E. Davidson: Typescript recollections. P.H.L. Archives.
17. Papers of Wing Commander A.B. Fanstone. P.H.L. Archives.
18. The story is well laid out by Mike O'Connor in an article on Fullard in *Cross and Cockade, Great*

Britain, The Journal of the Society of World War One Aero Historians, Vol. 13, No. 2, 1982, pp. 63–69.

19. Public Record Office – Air – 2387/228/11/41 XC 026968.
20. All the material on Air Commodore P.F. Fullard is taken from his Log, diary, letters, related papers and manuscript and tape-recorded recollections. P.H.L. Archives.
21. *The Eye in the Air*. Mead, Peter. pp. 92–94.

Chapter 5
1. Air Vice Marshal S.F. Vincent: Manuscript recollections. P.H.L. Archives.
2. Squadron Leader J.A. Aldridge: Typescript recollections. P.H.L. Archives.
3. Dr Eardley Davidson: Typescript recollections. P.H.L. Archives.
4. The only realistic shortening of this period was in the case of Army Officers applying for transfer to the RFC as for them the two months at the Cadet Wing would not be a requirement.
5. *Official History* Vol. V, pp. 430–1.
6. A. McL. Mooney: Manuscript recollections. P.H.L. Archives.
7. The Immelmann turn, credited to the German fighter pilot of that name, is a useful manoeuvre in both defence and attack for regaining altitude. It consists of a dive upon an opponent followed by a climbing half-loop and a half-roll off the top, the aircraft then being at the same height and facing the same direction as at the start of the manoeuvre.
8. G.F. Court: Log. P.H.L. Archives.
9. Sir Austin Bradford Hill: Typescript recollections.
10. Sir Charles Illingworth: Typescript recollections. P.H.L. Archives.
11. *Oliver* by Peggy Hamilton. Privately published 1972, Christchurch, New Zealand, p. 83. P.H.L. Archives.
12. *Experience in Early Flying* (Part I) J.T.P. Jeyes, Private publication N.D. P.H.L. Archives.
13. R.M. Morris: Typescript recollections. P.H.L. Archives.
14. G.N. Trace: Letter 19 March 1917. P.H.L. Archives.
15. A.J. Price: Typescript recollections.
16. C.E. Smith: Cadet Lecture notes. P.H.L. Archives.
17. In the typescript recollection of C.L. Roberts there is a beautifully written and hilariously funny account of Roberts's first flight. P.H.L. Archives.
18. F. Adkin. *From the Ground Up*, Airlife, Shrewsbury 1983, p. 32.
19. Sir John Dean: Typescript recollections. P.H.L. Archives.

20. R.S. Smart: Typescript recollections. P.H.L. Archives.
21. J.E. More: Letter 17 July 1915. P.H.L. Archives.
22. F. Thorp: Typescript recollection. P.H.L. Archives.
23. G.H. Price. Typescript recollections. P.H.L. Archives.
24. F. Brook: Typescript recollections. P.H.L. Archives.
25. Dr H.D. Chalke: Typescript recollections. P.H.L. Archives.
26. Published by Jarrolds, London 1968.
27. The RNAS research establishment work was conducted from the Isle of Grain.
28. Sir Vernon Brown: Typescript and tape-recorded recollections. P.H.L. Archives.
29. Lord Braybrooke (H.S. Neville): Typescript recollections. P.H.L. Archives.
30. O.B.W. Wills: 1917–18 letters. P.H.L. Archives. The friend who died was 'Toddie' Jones (Lt B.H.M. Jones, killed 14.4.18), the younger brother of the Commanding Officer, Major B.M. Jones.
31. See 'Orfordness 1916–19', an article by Squadron Leader F.D. Holder in *Cross and Cockade* Vol. 8, No. 2, 1977.
32. For Brown see Note 28; for Rowell see Sir Robin Rowell: Tape-recorded recollections. P.H.L. Archives.
33. *opus cit.* Arrow Book Edition, P. 305.
34. Or indeed men in France at Base Depots.
35. Daisy Howe (Mrs D. Morgan Davies): Manuscript recollections. P.H.L. Archives.
36. Miss J. Lambert: Tape-recorded recollections.
37. 'Whispers from Wye' by David G. Collyer, article in *Cross and Cockade*, Vol. 15, No. 1, 1984.

Chapter 6
1. C.I. Methuen: Manuscript recollections. P.H.L. Archives.
2. W.J. Smyrk: Typescript and tape-recorded recollections. P.H.L. Archives. In *From the Ground Up: A history of RAF Ground Crew* by F. Adkin, (Air Life, England, 1983) there is a good chapter which deals among other things with the problems of rain, mud and freezing temperatures upon aeroplanes, engines and those who maintained them.
3. Percy Young: Typescript recollections. P.H.L. Archives.
4. T.O. Wilkins: Diary. P.H.L. Archives.
5. F.E. Waring: Letter, 24 February 1917. P.H.L. Archives.
6. E.H. B**Room**: Manuscript and tape-recorded recollections. P.H.L. Archives.

7. Air Vice Marshal Sir Victor Tait: Tape-recorded recollections. P.H.L. Archives.
8. D.W. Blackshaw: Diary. P.H.L. Archives.
9. Dr H.D. Chalke: Typescript recollections. P.H.L. Archives.
10. E.P. Thorne: typescript recollections and log. P.H.L. Archives.
11. Squadron Leader P.B. Townsend: Typescript recollections and log. P.H.L. Archives.
12. The Rev. Dr J. Kennedy: Typescript recollections. P.H.L. Archives.
13. Air Marshal Sir Victor Groom: Manuscript recollections. P.H.L. Archives.
14. Squadron Leader P.B. Townsend: Typescript recollections. P.H.L. Archives.
15. For ferry pilot work see Air Vice Marshal H. Roach: Tape-recorded recollections and photograph album. P.H.L. Archives.
16. Brigadier A. Morton: Typescript recollections. P.H.L. Archives. Morton had sad reason to remember the Somme in 1916 as his father, a 54-year old Major in the Suffolk Regiment who had volunteered in 1914, was badly wounded in the battle and died when gangrene set in.
17. *Official History*. Vol. II, p. 135. Captain J. W. Woodhouse has written a fascinating account of his work. See *Cross and Cockade* Vol. II, No. 2, 1971.
18. B. Oliver: Typescript and tape-recorded recollections. P.H.L. Archives.
19. H. Bliss Hill: Typescript recollections. P.H.L. Archives.
20. E.L. Bishop: Tape-recorded recollections. P.H.L. Archives.
21. Air Vice Marshal Sir Geoffrey Bromet: 1916 Diary. P.H.L. Archives.
22. Squadron Leader A.B. Fanstone: Letter 11 July 1916. P.H.L. Archives.
23. E.W. Desbarats: Typescript recollections. P.H.L. Archives.
24. Lord Balfour: Tape-recorded recollections. P.H.L. Archives.
25. H.R. Skerratt: Typescript recollections. P.H.L. Archives.
26. P. Young: Typescript recollections. P.H.L. Archives.
27. W.J. Smyrk: Typescript recollections. P.H.L. Archives.
28. J.S. Castle: Typescript recollections. P.H.L. Archives.
29. Air Chief Marshal Sir John W. Baker: Letters October/December 1917. P.H.L. Archives.
30. A game combining leapfrog and piggy back with the front man of a lengthening line supporting himself (and the line) against a wall. Collapse and confusion was the natural and desired end result.
31. Squadron Leader A.B. Fanstone: Letter 10 August 1916. P.H.L. Archives.
32. Dr H.D. Chalke: Typescript recollections. P.H.L. Archives.
33. Rev. G. Worsop Hyde: Typescript recollections and letter 22 November 1917. P.H.L. Archives.
34. *Cinquante-Quatre*, France, 1917 Privately published by J. Palmer of Alexandra Street, Cambridge N.D. but in fact 1917. P.H.L. Archives.
35. Sir Royden Dash: Tape-recorded recollections. P.H.L. Archives.

Chapter 7

1. Professor A.C. Chibnall: Typescript recollections. P.H.L. Archives.
2. Baron Thomas of Remenham: Tape-recorded recollections. P.H.L. Archives.
3. Professor A.C. Chibnall: Typescript recollections. P.H.L. Archives.
4. C.A.L. Meredith: Manuscript recollections. P.H.L. Archives.
5. Squadron Leader G.W. Holderness: Typescript recollections: P.H.L. Archives.
6. Squadron Leader H.G. Penwarden: Contemporary account. P.H.L. Archives.
7. G. Thornton: Letters May–July 1916. (Per P. Thornton, Curator Sir John Soane's Museum.) P.H.L. Archives.
8. Marshal of the RAF Sir John Slessor: Tape-recorded recollections. P.H.L. Archives.
9. Air Vice Marshal F.N. Trinder: Manuscript recollections. P.H.L. Archives.
10. P.P. Eckersley: Diary 1915–16. P.H.L. Archives.
11. *Official History*, Vol. V, p. 300.
12. Corporal Candy: Typescript diary. Imperial War Museum, London.
13. N. Macmillan. *Tales of Two Air Wars*. G. Bell and Sons, London, 1963. pp. 122–123.
14. See *Cross and Cockade* Vol. 15, No. 2, 1984, p. 57: an article by Peter Wright on Lieutenant A.E. Skinner of No. 30 Squadron.
15. Air Vice Marshal R.S. Blucke: Letter, 25 June 1918. P.H.L. Archives.
16. See *Air Mail*, Autumn 1975, pp. 4–5.
17. A.A. Cullen: Typescript recollections. P.H.L. Archives.
18. *Chasing the Wind*. Major General K. van der Spuy. Books of Africa Ltd, Capetown, 1966.
19. F.E. Hale: Various Papers. P.H.L. Archives.
20. No. 31 Squadron History. Private publication N.D.
21. A. Perry: 1917–18 Diary. P.H.L. Archives.
22. P.P. Eckersley: 1916–17 Diary. P.H.L. Archives.
23. W.P. Watt: Log and memoir provided by his brother, Professor J.M. Watt. P.H.L. Archives.

24. Air Marshal Sir George Pirie: Log. P.H.L. Archives.
25. E.G. Chance: Letter in his papers. P.H.L. Archives.
26. Dr E.L. Roberts: Letters August–September 1918. P.H.L. Archives.
27. Air Commodore R.J. Brownell: Diary. P.H.L. Archives.
28. A.F. Wilson: Diary. Imperial War Museum, London.
29. F. Brook: Letters, October–November 1918. P.H.L. Archives.
30. See the Mitchell Report. 'The Report on the Enemy Defence of the Dardanelles Straits', the Dardanelles Committee 1921, p. 206 *et seq.*
31. W. Jefferies: Typescript recollections. P.H.L. Archives.
32. *The Naval Air Service*, Vol. 1, 1908–1918. Edit. Capt S.W. Roskill. Navy Records Society, Spottiswoode, Ballantyne and Co., London, 1969. p. 257.
33. C.R. Samson: *Fights and Flights*. Benn, London, 1930. p. 286.
34. See *The Naval Air Service, opus cit.* p. 259–62.
35. Air Vice Marshal Sir Geoffrey Bromet: Diary. P.H.L. Archives.
36. Squadron Leader H.A. Buss: Log. P.H.L. Archives.
37. F.D.S. Bremner: Letter, log and tape-recorded recollections P.H.L. Archives.
38. C. Smith: Manuscript recollections. P.H.L. Archives.
39. J.B. Sanders: Diary for August 1917. Royal Air Force Museum. According to Hauptmann Heydemarck in *War Flying in Macedonia* (John Hamilton, London N. D.) pp. 171–178, this raid was led by von Eschwege, the 'Eagle of the Aegean'.
40. Admiral Sir Reginald Portal: Contemporary account. P.H.L. Archives.
41. W.J. Kemp: Tape-recorded recollections. P.H.L. Archives.
42. Commander R.H.S. Rodger: Tape-recorded recollections. P.H.L. Archives.
43. *Official History*. Vol. III, pp. 2 *et seq.*
44. Commander B.T. Brewster: Typescript recollection. P.H.L. Archives.
45. Official Reports on the action of the Monitors v Königsberg 11 July 1915. P.H.L. Archives.
46. In an article in *Cross and Cockade*, Vol. 7, No. 4, 1976, it is maintained that one salvo was fired from guns salvaged from Königsberg [pp. 179]. This article, entitled 'The Origins of South African Military Aviation 1907–1919', was drawn from South African Air Force Archives by Dick Silberbaur.
47. *Official History*. Vol. III. p. 29.
48. *Chasing the Wind*. See Note 18. Ch. 6.
49. R.L. Lovemore: Manuscript recollections. P.H.L. Archives.

Chapter 8
1. 'Coastal Patrol Airships 1915–18', B.J. Turpin, *Cross and Cockade*, Vol. 15, No. 3, 1984. p. 126.
2. Air Chief Marshal Sir Ralph Cochrane: Manuscript recollections. P.H.L. Archives.
3. Air Marshal Sir Victor Goddard: Tape-recorded recollections. P.H.L. Archives.
4. Air Vice Marshal P.E. Maitland: Recollections and Log. P.H.L. Archives.
5. H.R.H. Ward: Log and diary. P.H.L. Archives.
6. Air Marshal Sir Alick Stevens: Tape-recorded recollections. P.H.L. Archives.
7. Wing Commander J. Bentham: Recollections. P.H.L. Archives. In that same month, Bentham had a further forced landing. He reached a cove, taxied the seaplane to the beach and got assistance in dragging it further up beyond the tide. An interested and helpful observer in these difficulties was the editor of *The Aeroplane*, C.G. Grey who was staying at a local hotel. He wrote about the incident in the magazine's January 1918 issue.
8. F. Thorp: Typescript recollections. P.H.L. Archives.
9. A.J. Price: Typescript recollections and log. P.H.L. Archives.
10. See *Official History*. Vol. IV, Appendix 11. p. 408. In the excellent volume, *The Story of a North Sea Air Station*, by C.F. Snowden Gamble, OUP, 1928, there are many detailed accounts of anti-U-boat encounters.
11. Air Commodore D. Iron: Typescript recollections. P.H.L. Archives.
12. Air Vice Marshal A.C. Kermode: Log. P.H.L. Archives.
13. Air Vice Marshal C.N. Bilney: Log. P.H.L. Archives.
14. D.P. Capper: Typescript recollections. P.H.L. Archives.
15. Rev. T. Crouther Gordon: Diary and log for 1918. P.H.L. Archives.
16. *Official History*. Vol. VI, p. 332–4.
17. D.R.B. Bentley: Typescript recollections. P.H.L. Archives.
18. See *The Sailor's War 1914–18*. Peter Liddle, Blandford Press, Poole, 1985. p. 54.
19. See *To the Ends of the Air*. G.E. Livock, HMSO, 1973. p. 23 *et seq.*
20. Air Marshal Sir Lawrence Pendred: Log. P.H.L. Archives.
21. *The Naval Air Service*, Vol. 1 1908–1918. The Navy Records Society, London, 1969. pp. 460/2.
22. G.N. Trace: Letters from August 1917. P.H.L. Archives.

23. See *Cross and Cockade* Vol. 15, No. 2 and No. 3, 1984, 'Coastal Patrol Airships, 1915–18', by B.J. Turpin.

24. The subject is particularly well covered in *Cross and Cockade* Vol. 13 No. 2, 1982, p. 70–73 in 'Hugh Williamson and the development of the aircraft carrier' (R.D. Layman). See also *Official History*. Vol. IV, p. 8 *et seq*.

25. Marshal of the RAF Sir William Dickson: Tape-recorded recollections. P.H.L. Archives. Sir William also described the Dunning landings on this tape-recording.

26. Commander G.F. Evans: Recollections. P.H.L. Archives.

27. Account taken from *The Story of a North Sea Air Station*. C.F. Snowden Gamble, OUP, 1928. p. 415 *et seq*. The precise quotation used by Snowden Gamble comes from pp. 238–9 of *The Spider Web* by 'Pix'.

28. Marshal of the RAF Sir William Dickson: Tape-recorded recollections. P.H.L. Archives.

Chapter 9

1. Published by William Kimber, London, 1973.

2. See Malcolm Smith's chapter in *Home Fires and Foreign Fields,* edit. P.H. Liddle, Brasseys, London, 1985.

3. There was a postponement of the closure in order to allow for an April raid on Freiburg im Briesgau as a reprisal for the torpedoing of two hospital ships while other night bombing in fact continued throughout April. The RNAS continued its day and night bombing but from the north at Dunkirk, the Handley Page O/100 and the DH 4 being used, but their targets were diverse and so the potential impact of the work was reduced.

4. *Official History*. Vol. V, p. 136.

5. A.S. Keep: Diary and log. P.H.L. Archives.

6. Air Marshal Sir Hugh Walmsley: Letters, diary, log and tape-recorded recollections. P.H.L. Archives.

7. *Cross and Cockade*, Vol. 10, No. 3, 1979. p. 118.

8. *Cross and Cockade*, Vol. 14, No. 1, 1983. p. 36.

9. S. Stevenson Jones: Manuscript recollections. P.H.L. Archives.

10. Air Vice Marshal A. Perry-Keene: Manuscript and tape-recorded recollections. P.H.L. Archives.

11. *History of No. 16 Naval Squadron (No. 216 Squadron RAF)*. Privately published, *c*.1923.

12. H.R.W. Ellison: Log. P.H.L. Archives.

13. *Cross and Cockade*, Vol. 10, No. 3, 1979. p. 117.

Chapter 10

1. Instructions issued by the Chief of the General Staff to all Armies and to the Royal Flying Corps, 16 February 1918. Quoted from *Official History of the War in the Air*. Vol. IV, p. 27.

2. Group Captain R.F. Barton: Contemporary volume of statistics. P.H.L. Archives.

3. The Watkins account was with the papers of Squadron Leader C.P.O. Bartlett. P.H.L. Archives. The British losses in this encounter amounted to eight aircraft. Twelve victories were claimed but this figure is not confirmed by German records.

4. W.C. Balmford: Typescript recollections. P.H.L. Archives.

5. R. Smart: Typescript recollections. P.H.L. Archives.

6. Air Chief Marshal Sir Hugh Saunders: Copy of his post-war Staff College essay. P.H.L. Archives.

7. *Official History*. Vol. IV, pp. 316, 320.

8. Major M. Le Blanc Smith: Typescript recollections. P.H.L. Archives.

9. The information proved inaccurate but the sad story is somewhat redeemed by the safe motorised evacuation of all the personnel and the re-equipment of the squadron at Serny within 48 hours. In the confusion of the retirement, B.U.S. Cripps, leading a flight of RE 8s from No. 9 Squadron, low-flying through mist to locate their new aerodrome, was perplexed at what he saw of Chris Draper's bonfire as he peered through the gloom at so unexpected a sight. Brigadier B.U.S. Cripps: Tape-recorded recollections. P.H.L. Archives.

10. Air Chief Marshal Sir John W. Baker: Log and personal papers. P.H.L. Archives.

11. Air Commodore H.G. Crowe: Typescript recollections. P.H.L. Archives.

12. H.R.W. Ellison: Log. P.H.L. Archives. In two nights, 740 bombs were dropped by 40 German machines on No. 214 Squadron's airfield at Coudekerque.

13. Air Chief Marshal Sir Keith Park: Staff College Essay, Ref. Air 10/973, Public Record Office, London, and tape-recorded recollections. P.H.L. Archives.

14. Group Captain A.B. Yuille: Log and Gotha report. P.H.L. Archives.

15. D.G. Lewis: Typescript recollections. P.H.L. Archives.

16. Sir Bryan Sharwood Smith: Typescript recollections, re 8 August 1918. P.H.L. Archives.

17. Squadron Leader H. Ibbotson. Tape-recorded recollections, re 15 September 1917. P.H.L. Archives. Ibbotson's burns were to his hands, face, thighs and back, yet he was to make three POW escape attempts.

18. Air Marshal Sir Victor Groom: Letter, 15 May 1918. P.H.L. Archives. Groom and his observer (No. 20 Squadron) had shot down two enemy

aircraft on the previous day. He has made the point that it was always the 'impersonal' German aircraft against which he was in combat, 'One quite forgot it was being flown by a human being until one was really close and saw the face.'

19. Squadron Leader H.E. Pryce: Log. P.H.L. Archives.

20. In October, the RAF assisted in low-level dropping of food rations in sacks to Belgian and French troops.

21. Air Commodore F.M.F. West: Tape-recorded recollections. P.H.L. Archives. West was to be awarded the Victoria Cross on 8 November 1918.

22. Group Captain J.A.G. Haslam: Tape-recorded recollections. P.H.L. Archives. Haslam was to be awarded the DFC. In his account, he makes no mention of the FK 8 being hit on 8 August 1918, but he does record seeing the wing folding back as it hit a corner of a hangar on the aerodrome.

23. See *Official History of the War in the Air.* Vol. VI, p. 507.

24. Air Chief Marshal Sir Donald Hardman: Manuscript recollections. P.H.L. Archives.

25. Air Vice Marshal T.C. Traill: Log and typescript recollections.

26. A.A. Partridge has given an account of another aerial collision at this time from which he himself suffered fearful injuries. It was the result of a pilot doing a celebration roll on return from a successful escort patrol in Camels on 19 September 1918. The pilot, who was killed, was Lt Nigel Bruce. A.A. Partridge: Manuscript recollections. P.H.L. Archives.

27. Air Chief Marshal Sir Trafford Leigh Mallory: Report dated 31 January 1919. P.H.L. Archives.

28. Major M. le Blanc Smith: Typescript recollections. P.H.L. Archives.

29. Source cited above. See Note 27.

30. S. Horscroft: Diary. P.H.L. Archives. Horscroft and his pilot, Lt Peffers, are credited in the Leigh Mallory report for their work on 13 October 1918.

31. Air Marshal Sir Lawrence Pendred: Log. P.H.L. Archives.

32. Source cited above. See Note 30.

33. Air Chief Marshal Sir Ronald Ivelaw Chapman: Log. P.H.L. Archives.

34. Sir Bryan Sharwood Smith: Typescript recollections. P.H.L. Archives.

Personal Experience Documention

In assembling the names of all the people from whose papers evidence has been drawn for this book, I have followed a policy of noting any rank held in retirement but not of cataloguing other distinctions or honours. By this means it is hoped to avoid giving cause for offence by error of omission or commission. Listed after the name is the year of the particular diary, letter or log-book record used in this book and the rank held at that time, the squadron, station, unit or ship in which the man was serving and the fighting front concerned.

For the Home Front, there is a further subdivision to indicate the nature of the service: training experience, Home Defence or coastal patrol work by airship, seaplane or flying boat. The RFC term Home Establishment has been used in a broad sense to include men from all ranks who were based in the UK as pupils, instructors or on experimental duties.

Some men are mentioned several times in the book and hence the listing given may seem to indicate complete wartime record but this could well be deceptive as no mention may have been made in the text of intermediate stages in a man's 1914–18 career. The present RAF ranks only came into effect in 1919. The ranks asterisked here together with those of air commodore, air vice marshal, air marshal and marshal of the RAF are listed as a rank held in retirement.

Unless specifically stated otherwise, all the material for the men and women here tabulated is held in my 1914–18 Personal Experience Archives presently based within Sunderland Polytechnic.

Abbreviations

A/M	air mechanic
Capt.	captain
C/P	coastal patrol
CFS	Central Flying School

Dard.	Dardanelles
Flt Sub-Lt	flight sublieutenant (RNAS)
Flt Lt	flight lieutenant (RNAS)
Flt Cdr	Flight Commander (RNAS)
Flt Sgt	flight sergeant
Gp Capt.*	group captain
Gall.	Gallipoli
Gib.	Gibraltar
H/E	Home Establishment
H/D	Home Defence
IF	Independent Force
HMS	His Majesty's Ship
Lt	lieutenant
Mac.	Macedonia
Med.	Mediterranean
Meso.	Mesopotamia
Pal.	Palestine
P/O	petty officer
POW	prisoner of war
R/S	reserve squadron (originally Reserve Aeroplane Squadrons and subsequently Training Squadron)
Sqn	squadron
Sqn Ldr	squadron leader
Sgt	sergeant
T/S	training squadron (retitled from Reserve Squadron on 31 May 1917)
W/F	Western Front
Wg Cdr	wing commander
W/Op.	Wireless Operator

Aldridge, Sqn Ldr J.A.: 1917, 2nd Lt, 2 R/S, RFC — H/E
1918, Lt, 19 Sqn, RAF — W/F

Allen, 2nd Lt J.M.: 1916, Civil Aviator's Certificate

Andrews, Sqn Ldr J.C.: 1914, Warrant Officer, RNAS 1916 Warrant Officer, RNAS — Gib.

Archdale, Lt Col F.A.: 1915, 2nd Lt, 130 Baluchis, Indian Army — E. Africa

Baker, Air Chief Marshal Sir John: 1917–18, 2nd Lt/Lt, 4 Sqn, RFC — W/F

Balfour, Lord Balfour of Inchrye: 1917, 2nd Lt, 43 Sqn, RFC — W/F

Balmford, W.C.: 1918, Lt, 6 Sqn, RFC — W/F

Bartlett, Sqn Ldr C.P.O.: 1918, Flt Cdr, 5 Sqn, RNAS — W/F

Barton, Gp Cpt R.F.: 1918, Major, HQ RAF — W/F

Beauman, Wg Cdr E.B.: 1914, Flt Sub-Lt, RNAS — H/D

Bell, R.N.: 1918, 2nd Lt, 217 Sqn, RAF — W/F

Bentham, Wg Cdr J.: 1917, Ft Sub-Lt, RNAS — C/P

Best, R.D.: 1917, Lt, 64 T/S, RFC — H/E

Bier, M.: 1917, Leutnant, III Reserve Infantry Regiment, German Army — W/F

Bilney, Air Vice Marshal C.N.: 1918, Ft Sub-Lt, RNAS — C/P

Bird, A.H.: 1918, Lt, 61 Sqn, RAF — H/D

Bishop, E.L.: 1915, Flt Sgt, 3 Sqn, RFC — W/F

Blackshaw, D.W.: 1917, 1st A/M W/Op., RFC — W/F

Bliss-Hill, H.: 1915–16, Flt Sgt, 12 Sqn, RFC — W/F

Blucke, Air Vice Marshal R.S.: 1918, Lt, 63 Sqn, RAF — Meso.

Bone, Gp Capt R.J.: 1912, Lt, RN Eastbourne School of Flying; 1914 CFS, RNAS Isle of Grain and RNAS Great Yarmouth

Bolton, E.F.: 1918, Lt, 1/5 Bn The Queen's Royal West Surrey Regt — Meso.

Boon, E.H.: 1917, 2nd A/M, HQ 9th Wing, RFC — W/F

Brand, W.H.: 1917, Sgt, 26 Kite Balloon Section — Mac.

Braybrooke, Lord (H.S. Neville): 1915, Flt Sub-Lt, Flt Cdr 1 Wing, RNAS; 1917 Isle of Grain, RNAS (Experimental) — H/E

Breffitt, G.D.: 1917–18, Cpl, Royal Engineers — Egypt

Bremner, F.D.S.: 1916, Flt Lt, 2 Wing, RNAS — Med.

Brewster, Commander B.T.: 1915, Midshipman, RN — E. Africa

Bristow, C.P.: 1918, 2nd Lt, RAF, Westgate on Sea — C/P

Bromet, Air Vice Marshal Sir Geoffrey: 1914, Lt, CFS and RNAS Westgate-on-Sea — H/E
1915, HMS Engadine — North Sea
HMS Ark Royal — Dard.
1916, Sqn Cdr, 8 Sqn RNAS — W/F

Brook, F.: 1915, 2nd A/M, Farnborough, RFC; 1917–8, Sgt, 28 Sqn, RFC — H/E / Italy

Brooks, T.S.: 1918, 2nd A/M, RAF Heliopolis — Egypt

Brown, Sir Vernon: 1917, Capt., RFC Experimental Station Orfordness — H/E

Brownell, Air Commodore R.J.: 1918, 2nd Lt, 45 Sqn RFC — Italy

Bulcraig, Mrs L.E. (née Cornish): 1918–19, WRAF — H/E

Burr, G.B.: 1917–18, Lt, 13 Sqn, RFC — W/F

Buss, Sqn Ldr H.A.: 1915, Flt Lt, 2 Wing RNAS — W/F & Dard.

Byron, A.G.: 1918, A/M RNAS Airship Station, Polegate — C/P

Candy:* 1916, Cpl, 30 Sqn, RFC — Meso.

Capel, Air Vice Marshal A.J.: 1915, 2nd Lt, 4 Sqn, RFC — W/F

Capel-Cure, Rev. R.: 1918, 2nd Lt, 15 Sqn, RAF — W/F

Capper, D.P.: 1917, Flt Sub-Lt, RNAS Felixstowe — C/P

Castle, J.S.: 1916, Lt, 11 Sqn, RFC — W/F–POW

Chalke, Dr H.D.: 1916–17, 1st A/M W/Op., RFC — W/F

Chance, E.G.: 1918, Lt, 28 Sqn, RFC — Italy

Chance, Sir Hugh: 1916, Lt, 27 Sqn, RFC — W/F–POW

Cheshire, Prof G.C.: 1916, Lt, RFC, attached RNAS Roehampton — H/E

Chibnall, Prof A.C.: 1917, Hon. Capt., 193
T/S, RFC — Egypt

Cochrane, Air Chief Marshal Sir Ralph:
1917, Flt Cdr, RNAS Airship Station
Scapa Flow — C/P

Coleman, E.: 1916, 2nd A/M, 11 Sqn, RFC — W/F–POW

Collins, R.F.:
1915, A/M, 3 Wing, RNAS — Dard./Gall.
1917, Flt Sub-Lt, 10 Sqn, RNAS — W/F

Corbett Wilson, D.:
1914, 2nd Lt, Reserve Aeroplane Sqn
Farnborough, RFC; — H/E
1914, Lt, 3 Sqn, RFC — W/F

Court, G.F.:
1916–17, 2nd Lt, 27 R/S, RFC — H/E
1917, 2nd Lt, 28 R/S, RFC — H/E
1917, 2nd Lt, CFS, RFC — H/E
1917, 2nd Lt, No. 1 School of Aerial
Gunnery, RFC — H/E
1917, 2nd Lt, 56 R/S, RFC — H/E
1917, Lt, 60 Sqn, RFC — W/F

Cripps, Brigadier B.U.S.:
1917, Lt, 9 Sqn, RFC — W/F
1918, Capt., 9 Sqn, RFC — W/F

Crowe, Air Commodore H.G.: 1918, 2nd
Lt, 20 Sqn, RAF — W/F

Cullen, A.A.: 1918, Lt, 72 Sqn, RAF — N. Persia

Dash, Sir Roydon E.A.: 1918, Major
Commanding 8 Sqn, RFC — W/F

Davidson, E.: 1917, Capt., 15 Sqn, RFC — W/F

Dean, Sir John N.: 1918, Lt, RAF — H/E

De Crespigny, Air Vice Marshal H.V.C.
1915, 2nd Lt, 3 Reserve Aeroplane
Squadron, RFC — H/E
1915, Lt, 11 Sqn, RFC — W/F
1916, Major, Commanding 16 RS, RFC — H/E

Dell, L.A.: 1915, P/O, RNAS Eastchurch — H/E

Desbarats, E.W.: 1917, Flt Sub-Lt, 1 Sqn,
RNAS — W/F

Dickson, Marshal of the Royal Air Force
Sir William: 1917, Flt Sub-Lt, RNAS,
and 1918, Capt., RAF, HMS Furious — Grand Fleet

Draper, Maj. C.:
1915, Flt Lt, RNAS Scarborough — C/P
1918, Major, Commanding 208 Sqn,
RAF — W/F

Duncan, Wing Cdr. J.: 1916, 2nd Lt, 13
R/S and 9 Sqn, RFC — H/E–W/F

Eckersley Capt. P.P.: 1915–17, Lt, 17 Sqn,
RFC — Egypt; Mac.

Ellison, H.R.W.: 1918, Flt Lt, 17 Sqn
RNAS: 1918, Capt., 217 Sqn, RAF — W/F

Elmhirst: Air Marshal Sir Thomas W.
1917, Flt Sub-Lt, RNAS Airships
Station Luce Bay — C/P

Evans, Commander G.F.: 1918,
Midshipman, RN, HMS Renown — Grand Fleet

Fanstone, Wing Cdr:
1916, 2nd Lt, 12 Sqn, RFC — W/F
1917, Lt, 12 Sqn, RFC — W/F
1918, Capt., 37 Sqn, RFC — H/D

Fletcher, Wing Cdr J.N.: 1912, 2nd Lt, Air
Bn, Royal Engineers

Foster-Hall, Capt. B.: 1918, Lt, 17 Sqn,
RFC — Mac.

Fullard, Air Commodore P.F.:
1916, 2nd Lt, School of Military
Aeronautics Oxford and 3 RS
Netheravon, RFC — H/E
1917, CFS and 2nd Lt-Capt., 1 Sqn,
RFC — H/E–W/F

Galley, Col E.G.: 1918, 2nd Lt, 56 Sqn,
RAF — W/F

Garner, W.M.: 1916, P/O, 2 Wing, RNAS — E. Med.

Gauntlett, Prof F.A.D.: 1918, Flt Lt,
Newlyn, RNAS — C/P

Goddard, Air Marshal Sir Victor: 1916, Flt
Sub-Lt, RNAS Roehampton — H/E

Gordon, Rev Dr T. Crouther: 1918,
Flt Sub-Lt, Great Yarmouth,
RNAS/RAF — C/P
Lt, Calshot, RAF — C/P
Lt, Lee-on-Solent, RAF — C/P
Lt, Houton Bay — C/P

Gray, W.E.: 1918, Lt, 213 Sqn, RAF — W/F

Green, E.G.: 1917, Lt, 25 Sqn, RFC — W/F

Groom, Air Marshal Sir Victor: 1918, Lt,
20 Sqn, RAF — W/F

Guttery, Wing Cdr T.E.:
1913, 2nd A/M, 3 Sqn, RFC
1914, 2nd A/M, 5 Sqn, RFC — W/F

Hale, F.E.: 1918–19, 2nd A/M, Elope Sqn,
RAF — N. Russia

Harding, Ella: 1918, Pte, WRAF — H/E

Hardman, Air Chief Marshal Sir Donald:
1918, Capt., 19 Sqn, RAF — W/F

Harris, Marshal of the Royal Air Force Sir
Arthur: 1917, Capt., 45 Sqn, RFC — W/F

Haslam, Gp. Capt. J.A.G.: 1918, Lt, 8
Sqn, RAF — W/F

Hawker, Major L.G., VC:
1914, Lt, CFS — H/E
1914–15, Lt-Capt., 6 Sqn, RFC — H/E–W/F
1916, Major, Commanding 24 Sqn,
RFC — H/E–W/F

Hemingway, A.H.: 1918, 1st A/M, 10 T/S,
RAF — H/E

Hill, Sir Austin Bradford: 1916, Flt
Sub-Lt, Chingford, RNAS — H/E
Cranwell, RNAS — H/E

Holderness, Sqn Ldr G.L.: 1917, Lt, 14
Sqn, RFC — Pal.

Horridge, J.L.:
1916, Lt, 7 Sqn, RFC — W/F
1916, Lt, 20 Sqn, RFC — W/F

Horscroft, S.: 1918, 2nd Lt, 8 Sqn, RAF — W/F

Ibbotson, Sqn Ldr H.D.: 1917, Lt, 70 Sqn,
RFC — W/F–POW

Illingworth, Sir Charles:
1917, 2nd Lt, Farnborough, RFC — H/E
1917, 2nd Lt, Oxford, RFC — H/E
1918, 2nd Lt, 65 T/S, RAF — H/E

Iron, Air Commodore D.: 1915, Flt Lt,
Dundee, RNAS — C/P

Isern Smith, F.W.: 1918, 2nd A/M,
Heliopolis, RAF — Egypt

Ivelaw Chapman, Air Chief Marshal Sir
Ronald: 1918, Capt., 10 Sqn, RAF — W/F

James, Wg. Cdr. Sir Archibald: 1917,
Major, Commanding 6 Sqn, RFC — W/F

Jameson, H.: 1914, Cpl, RFC Wireless
   Unit   W/F
Jefferies, Chief P/O W., 1915 P/O, 3 Wing,
   RNAS   E. Med.
Jeyes, Lt J.T.P.: 1917, 2nd Lt, 37 T/S,
   RFC   H/E
Keep, Capt A.S.: 1918, Lt, 55 Sqn, RAF   W/F
Kemp, W.J.: 1918, Flt Sub-Lt, RNAS
   Imbros   E. Med.
Kennedy, The Rev Dr J.: 1917–18, A/M,
   RFC Farnborough and Shawbury   H/E
Kermode, Air Vice Marshal A.C.: 1918,
   Lt, RAF Cattewater   H/E
King, C.: 1917, 2nd Lt, 17Sqn   Mac.
King-Smith, 2nd Lt S.: 1917–18, Warrant
   Officer, HMS *Riviera*   Home
                                 Waters;
                                 Med.
Lambert, Miss J.: 1918, WRAF   H/E
Le Blanc Smith, Major M.:
   1916, Lt, 18 Sqn, RFC   W/F
   1916, Capt, 20 Sqn, RFC   W/F
   1918, Capt/Major, Commanding 73
     Sqn, RFC/RAF   W/F
Leigh, Wing Cdr H.de Vere: 1917, Flt Lt,
   HMS *Empress*   E. Med.
Leigh Mallory, Air Chief Marshal Sir
   Thomas L.: 1918, Major, Commanding
   8 Sqn, RAF   W/F
Lewis, D.G.: 1918, Lt, 3 Sqn, RAF   W/F
Lovemore, R.B.: 1917, Lt, 26 Sqn, RFC E. Africa
Lywood, Air Vice Marshal O.G.W.G.:
   1914, 2nd Lt, Headquarters Staff RFC W/F
MacEwan, Col. M.: 1918, 2nd Lt, Royal
   Garrison Artillery   Mac.
Machin, G.D.: 1917, Capt., 39 Kite
   Balloon Section, RFC   W/F
MacLennan, The Rev Dr W.G.: 1918,
   Cadet, RAF Hastings   H/E
Maitland, Air Vice Marshal P.E.:
   1916, Flt Sub-Lt, RN Airship Station
     Capel   C/P
   1916, Flt Sub-Lt, RN Airship Station
     Kingsworth   C/P
   1916–18, Flt Sub-Lt/Flt Lt, RN Airship
     Station Longside   C/P
   1918, Capt., RAF Airship Station
     Longside   C/P
Marsh, F.H.: 1918, Lt, 149 Sqn, RAF   W/F
Marshall, B.S.: 1917, Lt, 20 Sqn, RFC   W/F
Meredith, C.A.L.: 1917, 2nd Lt, RFC,
   Heliopolis   Egypt
Methuen, C.I.: 1916, 1st A/M, 25 Sqn,
   RFC   W/F
Mooney, A.McL.: 1918, 2nd Lt, 11
   T/D/S, RAF   H/E
More, J.E.: 1915, 2nd A/M, RFC
   Farnborough   H/E
Morgan Davies, Mrs D. (*née* Howe): 1918,
   Cpl, WRAF, RAF Halton   H/E
Morris, Dr R.M.: 1917, Flt Sub-Lt,
   RNAS Calshot   H/E
Morton, Brigadier A.H.: 1916, Capt., 8
   Sqn, RFC   W/F

Mullens, Sir Harold: 1918, Probationary
   Flight Officer under training   H/E
Nicoll, Major R.E.: 1917, Flt Cdr, RNAS H/E
Oliver, B.: 1918, Sgt, 23 Kite Balloon
   Section, RAF   W/F
Park, Air Chief Marshal Sir Keith: 1918,
   Major Commanding 48 Sqn, RAF   W/F
Partridge, A.A.: 1918, Lt, 46 Sqn, RAF W/F
Pendred, Air Marshal Sir Lawrence: 1918,
   2nd Lt, 202 Sqn, RAF   W/F
Penwarden, Sqn Ldr H.G.: 1918, 2nd Lt,
   142 Sqn, RAF   Pal.-POW
Perry, A.: 1917–18, 2nd A/M, 26 Kite
   Balloon Section, RAF   Mac.
Perry-Keene, Air Vice Marshal A.:
   1918, Lt, 98 Sqn, RAF   W/F
   1918, Lt, 115 Sqn, RAF   IF
Pierce, E.: 1917, Flt Sub-Lt, 3 Sqn, RNAS W/F
Pigot, Brigadier General Sir Robert: 1913,
   Capt., 1 Sqn, RFC
Pirie, Air Marshal Sir George: 1918, 2nd
   Lt, 34 Sqn, RFC   Italy
Pitman, Capt C.R.S.: 1916, Lt, 27th
   Punjabis   Meso.
Portal, Admiral Sir Reginald: 1916, Sub-
   Lt, 2 Wing, RNAS   E. Med.
Price, A.J.:
   1917–18, Sub-Lt, Observer School
     Eastchurch, RNAS   H/E
   1918, Sub-Lt, Calshot, RNAS   H/E
Price, G.H.: 1917, A/M, Crystal Palace,
   RNAS   H/E
Pryce, Sqn Ldr H.E.: 1918, Lt, 9 Sqn,
   RAF   W/F
Ransford, Capt F.B.: 1917, Lt, 25 Sqn,
   RFC   W/F
Ransley, Capt F.C.: 1918, Capt., No. 3
   Fighting School, RAF   H/E
Roach, Air Vice Marshal H.: 1918, Capt.,
   Ferry Pilot, RAF   H/E
Roberts, C.L.:
   1916, 2nd Lt, R/S, RFC   H/E
   1916, 2nd Lt, 11 Sqn, RFC   W/F–POW
Roberts, Dr E.L.: 1918, 2nd Lt, 28 Sqn,
   RAF   Italy
Rodger, Commander RHS: 1918,
   Midshipman, RN, HMS *Agamemnon*   Aegean
Rowell, Sir Robin:
   1916, Lt, 12 Sqn, RFC   W/F
   1917, Capt., Experimental Station
     Orfordness   H/E
Russell, Sir Frederick:
   1917–18, Flt Sub-Lt, 2 Sqn, RNAS   W/F
   1918, Lt, 202 Sqn, RAF   W/F
Saint, Sir John: 1918, 2nd A/M, W/Op.,
   RFC   W/F
Sanders, J.B.,** A.B., AA Gunner, RNAS Mac.
Saunders, Air Chief Marshal Sir Hugh:
   1918, 2nd Lt, Capt., 84 Sqn. RFC/RAF W/F
Sellers, J.: 1918, Lt, 3 Sqn, RAF   W/F
Sharwood Smith, Sir Brian: 1918, Lt, 48
   Sqn, RAF   W/F
Shelton, C.H.: 1918, Lt, Royal Field
   Artillery   H/E

Sherbrooke Walker, Colonel R.D.: 1916,
Lt, 22 Sqn, RFC — W/F–POW

Skerratt, H.R.: 1915, 2nd A/M, 12 Sqn,
RFC — W/F

Slessor, Marshal of the Royal Air Force
Sir John:
1915, 2nd Lt, 17 Sqn, RFC — H/D
1916, 2nd Lt, 17 Sqn, RFC — Sudan

Smart, R.S.:
1915, 2nd A/M, Farnborough, RFC — H/E
1918, 1st A/M, 12 Sqn, RFC — W/F

Smith, C.E.: 1917, Cadet, St Leonards,
RFC — H/E

Smith, C.M.: 1916, 1st A/M, HMS *Ark
Royal*, RNAS — E. Med.

Smith, R.: 1917, Lt, 54 Sqn, RFC — W/F

Smyrk, W.J.:
1912, 2nd A/M, 3 Sqn, RFC
1917, Sgt Major, 60 Sqn, RFC — W/F

Smythe, Mrs I. née Maxstone Graham:
1918, VAD Nurse, No. 2 British Red
Cross Hospital — Rouen

Snelling, Major General A.H.J.: 1918, 2nd
Lt, 4th Rajputs — Meso.

Spurgeon, T.: 1915, A/M, HMS *Ark Royal*,
RNAS — Dard.

Stallibrass, Major T.L.W.:
1916, Lt, 3 Sqn, RFC — W/F
1917, Capt., 62 T/S, RFC — H/E

Stevenson Jones, S.: 1917–18, Lt, 55 Sqn,
RFC — IF

Stevens, Air Marshal Sir Alick: 1916, Sub-
Lt, Felixstowe, RNAS — C/P

Stoneham, Sqn. Ldr G.T.: 1917, Lt, 39
Sqn, RFC — H/D

Tait, V.H., Air Vice Marshal Sir Victor:
1918, Lt, RAF Wireless Experimental
Establishment — H/E

Thomas, W.M.W., Baron Thomas of
Remenham. 1917, 2nd Lt, RFC
Heliopolis — Egypt

Thorne, E.P.: 1918, Lt, 52 Sqn, RAF — W/F

Thornton, G.: 1916, 2nd Lt, 17 Sqn, RFC — Sudan

Thorp, F.: 1918, A/M, RNAS Cranwell
and RAF Calshot — H/E

Tisdall, W.B.: 1917, 2nd Lt, 8 Sqn, RFC — W/F

Townley, C.E.: 1917, Capt., Intelligence
Officer, RFC — W/F

Townsend, Sqn Ldr P.B.: 1918, 2nd Lt, 12
Sqn, RAF — W/F

Trace, G.N.:
1917, Flt Sub-Lt, RNAS Cranwell — H/E
1917, Flt Sub-Lt, HMS *Pegasus* — Grand Fleet

Traill, Air Vice Marshal T.C.: 1918, Capt.,
RAF, 20 Sqn, RAF — W/F

Trinder, Air Vice Marshal F.N.: 1917,
Hon Lt, 196 T/S, RFC — Egypt

Van der Spuy, Major General K.R.:
1913, Lt, South African Union Defence
Force
1915, Lt, South African Aviation Corps — German
S.W. Africa
1916, Capt., 26 Sqn, RFC — East Africa
1919, Lt Col, Elope Expedition, RAF — North Russia
and POW

Verry, F.W.: 1917, Flt Sub-Lt, RN
Airship Station Cranwell — H/E

Vincent, Air Vice Marshal S.F.: 1916, 2nd
Lt, 2 R/S, RFC — H/E
1918 Capt. S.E. Area Flying Instructor
School — H/E

Vousden, E.: 1917, Flt Sgt, 56 Sqn, RFC — H/E

Walker, T.W.: 1917, Sick Berth Attendant,
RN — E. Med.

Walmsley, Air Marshal Sir Hugh: 1918,
Lt, 55 Sqn, RAF — IF

Ward, H.R.H.: 1918, Lt, RAF Airship
Station Capel — C/P

Waring, F.E.: 1917, A/M — W/F

Watkins, C.R.: 1918, Flt Lt, 5 Sqn, RNAS — W/F

Watt, W.P.: 1918, Lt, 47 Sqn, RAF — Mac.

Welch, H.: 1917, Lt, 1 Sqn, RFC — W/F

West, Air Commodore F.M.F., VC: 1918,
Capt., 8 Sqn, RAF — W/F

White, G.J. 1918, Sgt, 217 Sqn, RAF — W/F

White, Air Vice Marshal H.G.: 1917,
Capt., 59 T/S, RFC — H/E

Whitehead, E.A.: 1917, 2nd Lt, No. 2
Auxiliary School of Aerial Gunnery,
RFC — H/E

Whitworth Jones, Air Chief Marshal Sir
John: 1918, Lt, 13 R/S, RAF — H/E

Wilkins, T.O.: 1918, A/M, 14 Sqn, RNAS — W/F

Wilkinson, Capt. F.: 1917, Lt, 23 Kite
Balloon Section, RFC — W/F

Wills, O.B.W.:
1916, 2nd Lt, 8 R/S, RFC — H/E
1916, 2nd Lt, 34 Sqn, RFC — W/F
1917/18, Lt, Orfordness Experimental
Station RFC/RAF — H/E
1918, Lt, Martlesham Heath
Experimental Station, RAF — H/E
1918, Lt, Butley Experimental Station,
RAF — H/E

Wilson, A.F.*: 1918, Lt, 34 Sqn, RAF — Italy

Wilson, P.: 1917, 2nd Lt, 1 Sqn, RFC — W/F

Worsop-Hyde, Rev G.: 1917, Lt, 54 Sqn,
RFC — W/F

York-Moore, Sqn Ldr T.P.: 1917, Flt Lt,
RN Airship Station Mullion — C/P

Young, P.: 1918, A/M, 58 Sqn, RAF — W/F

Yuille, Grp Capt. A.B.: 1918, Hon. Capt.,
151 Sqn, RAF — W/F

*Imperial War Museum Source.
**Royal Air Force Museum Source.

Bibliography

As this book relies above all on personal experience testimony from sources which, with few exceptions, have not previously appeared in published form, it has not been thought proper to provide here a comprehensive bibliography of the war in the air. Listed here, together with certain essential general works, are volumes from which either specific quotation has been made or valuable information gained or which conveyed so convincing a sense of atmosphere that the author of *The Airman's War* recognises that his feeling for the subject was advanced in reading them. To the authors and publishers of these works a debt of gratitude is herewith acknowledged and sincere appreciation is expressed. Squadron Histories and articles from the excellent journal *Cross and Cockade* (*G.B.*) are precisely listed in the end notes.

General Works and Official Histories

Raleigh, W. and Jones, H.A. *Official History of the War: The War in the Air* Vols I–VI and Volume of Appendices. The Clarendon Press. Oxford, 1922–1937.

Roskill, Capt. S.W. (Editor). *The Naval Air Service* Vol. 1 1908–1918. Navy Records Society (Spottiswoode Ballantyne and Co Ltd). London and Colchester, 1969.

Bruce, J.M. *The Aeroplanes of the Royal Flying Corps*. Putnam. London, 1982.

Monographs, Autobiographies and Biographies

Adkin, F. *From the Ground Up – A History of RAF Ground Crew*. Airlife. England, 1983.

Bartlett, C.P.O. *Bomber Pilot 1916–1918*. Ian Allan. London, 1974.

Boyle, A. *Trenchard, Man of Vision*. Collins. London, 1962.

Cole, C. and Cheeseman, E.F. *The Air Defence of Britain 1914–18*. Putnam. London, 1984.

Fry, Wing Commander W. *Air of Battle*. William Kimber. London, 1974.

Gibson, Mary *Warneford VC*. Fleet Air Arm Museum. Yeovilton, 1979.

Gould Lee, Air Vice Marshal A. *No Parachute*. Jarrolds. London, 1968.

Hawker, T.M. *Hawker VC*. The Mitre Press. London, 1965.

Hodges, G. *Memoirs of an Old Balloonatic*. William Kimber. London, 1977.

Jones, N. *The Origins of Strategic Bombing*. William Kimber. London, 1973.

Lambert, W. *Combat Report*. William Kimber. London, 1973.

Lewis, C.S. *Sagittarius Rising*. Peter Davies. London, 1936.

Lewis, Wing Commander G.H. *Wings over the Somme 1916–18*. William Kimber. London, 1976.

Livock, G.E. *To the Ends of the Air*. HMSO. London, 1973.

Liddle, P.H. *The Sailor's War 1914–18*. Blandford Press. Poole, 1985.

McCudden, James. *Five Years in the Royal Flying Corps*. The Aeroplane & General Publishing Co. London, 1918.

MacMillan, N. *Tales of Two Air Wars*. G. Ball and Son. London, 1963.

MacMillan, N. *Offensive Patrol*. Jarrolds. London, 1973.

Mead, Peter. *The Eye in the Air*. HMSO. London, 1983.

Revell, A. *British Fighter Units on the Western Front, 1914–16*. Osprey. London, 1978.

Rosher, H. *In the Royal Naval Air Service*. Chatto and Windus. London, 1916.

Samson, C.R. *Fights and Flights*. Benn. London, 1930.

Smith, Dr M. Chapter entitled 'The Tactical and Strategic Application of Air Power on the Western Front' in *Home Fires and Foreign Fields*. Liddle, P.H. (edit) Brassey's Defence Publishers. London, 1985.

Snowden Gamble, C.F. *The Story of a North Sea Air Station*. OUP. Oxford, 1928.

Spuy, Maj. Gen. K. van der. *Chasing the Wind*. Books of Africa Ltd. Capetown, Republic of South Africa, 1966.

Tennant, Lt Col. J.E. *In the Clouds above Baghdad*. Cecil Palmer. London, 1920.

Tredrey, F.D. *Pioneer Pilot*. Peter Davies. London, 1976.

Index

See also alphabetically listed Personal Experience Documentation